THE GRAVE ROBBER

THE GRAVE ROBBER

The Biggest Stolen Artifacts Case in FBI History and the Bureau's Quest to Set Things Right

TIM CARPENTER

The Grave Robber

Copyright © 2025 by Tim Carpenter

All rights reserved. No portion of this book may be reproduced, stored in a retrieval system, or transmitted in any form or by any means—electronic, mechanical, photocopy, recording, scanning, or other—except for brief quotations in critical reviews or articles, without the proper written permission of the publisher.

Published by Harper Horizon, an imprint of HarperCollins Focus LLC, 501 Nelson Place, Nashville, TN 37214, USA.

Any internet addresses, phone numbers, or company or product information printed in this book are offered as a resource and are not intended in any way to be or to imply an endorsement by Harper Horizon, nor does Harper Horizon vouch for the existence, content, or services of these sites, phone numbers, companies, or products beyond the life of this book.

The views and opinions expressed in this publication are solely those of the author and do not represent the official position, policy, or opinion of the Federal Bureau of Investigation (FBI).

ISBN 978-1-4002-4864-3 (eBook)
ISBN 978-1-4002-4863-6 (HC)

Without limiting the exclusive rights of any author, contributor or the publisher of this publication, any unauthorized use of this publication to train generative artificial intelligence (AI) technologies is expressly prohibited. HarperCollins also exercise their rights under Article 4(3) of the Digital Single Market Directive 2019/790 and expressly reserve this publication from the text and data mining exception.

HarperCollins Publishers, Macken House, 39/40 Mayor Street Upper, Dublin 1, D01 C9W8, Ireland (https://www.harpercollins.com)

Library of Congress Control Number: 9781400248636

Printed in the United States of America
25 26 27 28 29 LBC 5 4 3 2 1

To all those who work, often quietly and behind the scenes, to ensure that history is not lost to greed, indifference, or destruction. May your efforts counter the exploitation of cultures, the erasure of identities, and the disregard that for too long have allowed Indigenous peoples and their heritage to be treated as curiosities rather than as living communities deserving of dignity, respect, and justice.

Contents

Prologue: Summer Souvenirs ix

1. "He's Got Indian Bones" 1
2. Wearing Wires 22
3. Trips and Falls 47
4. Probable Cause 75
5. Six Days in April, Part 1 86
6. Six Days in April, Part 2 106
7. Handle with Care 122
8. Disturbed Spirits? 145
9. "Bury Me with My Indian": Measuring Bones and Consulting the Tribes 164
10. Charges to Bring, Changes to Make: From Miller to Malheur to Running the Art Crime Program 182
11. Adventures in Cultural Diplomacy: From the American Southwest to the People's Republic of China 207
12. Two Cops Drinking Beer and the Case of the Ceremonial Shield: What ARPA, NAGPRA, and the STOP Act Can't Stop 231
13. Getting Stoned in Haiti 255
14. Good Resting Places 273

Acknowledgments 295

About the Author 299

Prologue

Summer Souvenirs

CHAMBERLAIN AND OACOMA, SOUTH DAKOTA; SUNDAY, JULY 23, 1961

The bright morning sun was already warm on their tanned necks as Don and Sue Miller and Phil and Betty Mitchell discussed where to dig first.

Excited to be out of the car, the Mitchells' three little children—the girls with pageboy haircuts and their buzz-cut kid brother, all under nine—ran through the mixed prairie grass toward a big sandbar just above where the White River flowed out of the west into the Missouri River. They'd been cooped up in the back of their parents' dark blue 1948 Ford Tudor sedan for a couple of hours. First thing that morning, their parents had hustled them out of bed and, after a quick breakfast of oatmeal, into the car to go and meet the Millers at eight o'clock sharp.

They'd reached the appointed place, the intersection of US 16 and Dougan Avenue, five minutes late, and Dad was relieved that the Millers weren't there waiting. Only then they'd had to wait themselves. Dad drummed his fingers on the steering wheel. Mom started a game of I-spy-with-my-little-eye, but there wasn't anything interesting that they hadn't seen countless times. Just to the south was the little town of Oacoma, and due east, across the river, was Chamberlain, the bigger town where everybody got groceries and gas.

The Millers had finally pulled up alongside in their pickup truck at 8:30, and they'd all smiled and said good morning to each other through the open car windows. Then Phil put the Ford in gear and headed west on US 16. With the Millers following, they'd bounced and jounced over

PROLOGUE

rough and pitted dirt roads for another forty minutes until they came to where the rivers met. They'd been to this spot a few days before, when Mom and Dad were making sure it was still a good a place to take the Millers, but they hadn't been able to explore the big sandbar then like they wanted to.

The short and tall bunchgrasses and many companion shrubs were blooming purple, blue, pink, yellow, and red, attracting hummingbirds, bees, and the short-lived butterflies that spent their larval and caterpillar stages inside the same grasses. Running through the grass, the children slowed, trying in vain to catch a few butterflies with their bare hands, and then carried on down the last slight slope to the sandbar.

They knew the rules. They had to stay in eyesight and earshot of their parents, and they couldn't go in the water. Otherwise, they were free to play and explore until they got hungry or thirsty for something in the picnic cooler.

They were country kids, and the older girl was old enough to have charge of the younger ones, make sure no one got hurt, and mind they all came when they were called. The most important thing was to be patient and not bother the adults while they dug up the graves.

———

Don and Sue Miller liked to think of themselves as crackerjack amateur archaeologists, and they were always looking for Indigenous archaeological sites where they could dig up something interesting. Back home in rural Rush County, Indiana, Don and Sue volunteered on local university archaeology digs, picking up valuable pointers on reading terrain to locate old habitation and burial sites. Don was becoming a mainstay of the Indiana Archaeological Society, and in time he'd come to serve as its publications editor, vice president, and president.

Don had caught the archaeology bug in his childhood. As a US Army Signal Corps technician assigned to the Manhattan Project in New Mexico during World War II, he spent his free time combing the surrounding area for arrowheads and pottery shards. For the rest of his life, he loved to recount his undocumented, impossible-to-confirm-or-refute

PROLOGUE

interactions with "Oppie," Manhattan Project scientific director J. Robert Oppenheimer. Don claimed to be the one who sent the radio signal that detonated the historic atom bomb explosion at the Trinity Site in Alamogordo. Ironically, it was an anonymous complaint from someone who heard these tales, and saw Don's Manhattan Project memorabilia, that in 2008 first brought the Millers' artifacts to the attention of the FBI. The agents who visited the Millers at the time—investigating claims that Don possessed a nuclear trigger (he didn't)—made only a passing mention of the artifacts they saw in their report.

Tall tales about Oppie aside, Don's prosperous engineering career allowed him and Sue to spend weeks each year traveling to Indigenous archaeological sites across North America and dozens of other countries, including Sweden, Mexico, Peru, Papua New Guinea, and China. Class of 1941 high school sweethearts (Sue was eleven months older, but Don skipped a grade because he was so bright), they had to postpone their wedding until 1946, following Don's discharge from the service. In the first years of their marriage, Don embarked on bachelor's, master's, and doctoral degrees in engineering at The Ohio State University, the University of Illinois, and Purdue University, respectively. Sue soon caught the archaeology bug too. They were vigorous people who didn't mind arduous travel or hours of digging if it meant the chance of a good find, especially when it involved the artifacts of Native Americans—and even more so, their buried remains.

Sue prepared detailed itineraries before their trips, kept journals during them, and compiled scrapbooks afterward. Together Don and Sue took thousands of photographs over the years—the prints often bore Sue's notations on the back—and shot travel and dig footage on a succession of media, from 8mm film to videocassettes to digital hard drives. All this material later became crucial evidence when the FBI eventually did investigate their collection and had to distinguish between their lawful and unlawful possessions.

Don's income as a defense and space industry engineer, including valuable patent royalties, also underwrote their charitable efforts. They were well known and highly regarded in Rush County for supporting their church and for helping to fund the reconstruction of one of the local

PROLOGUE

landmarks, a covered bridge. Through their church, they organized and led twenty missions to Haiti. On those occasions they combined openly digging foundations for churches and schools with secretly collecting Taino artifacts in Haiti and the Dominican Republic. Those trips alone yielded hundreds of museum-quality artifacts—and a skull taken from the altar of a Vodou temple.

Over their long marriage, Don and Sue's collection—acquired through both purchases and illicit digs—grew to tens of thousands of items, surpassing the holdings of some major museums. The collection not only filled the big house they built on Don's family farm but was haphazardly crammed in nooks, crannies, attics, and basements of the original farmhouse, barns, sheds, and other buildings on the property. They sometimes hosted local Boy Scout and Girl Scout troops, along with area school and church groups, to view portions of their collection. Notably, though, special holdings were in locked rooms, accessible only to a close circle of family and trusted confidants.

Of all their travels and digs from 1946 until Sue's passing in 2000, late July 1961 stood out the most. That dig yielded their most prized—and most carefully hidden—trophy.

They'd left home on Sunday, July 2, in their blue-gray 1950 Studebaker pickup truck with "Miller Radio Service" on the doors. Tucked in Sue's travel journal was their typed itinerary for the next four weeks. The previous summer, they had embarked on an even longer—and equally memorable—journey to the Yukon and Alaska in their 1958 Chevrolet Yeoman station wagon, often camping along the way. They'd returned with a huge haul of material, including two mammoth tusks they'd unearthed, crossing back and forth into Canada and the United States with never a question from either country's border officials.

This trip, they hoped, would yield even better results, and the pickup was preferable because they'd be rattling down a lot of dirt roads and even going off-road from time to time. Much of the interstate highway system was still under construction, so they drove the old US highways and state roads north through Illinois, Wisconsin, and Minnesota to

PROLOGUE

Manitoba, where they headed west on Canada 1 through Saskatchewan to Alberta. Undoubtedly thanks to the local tips they cultivated, they stopped and dug in buffalo jumps around Calgary. Then they turned south across the border—again without a question from border officials about the things they'd collected along the way so far—to see Montana's Glacier National Park and Custer Battlefield National Monument (as it was called at the time) and Wyoming's Devils Tower. The last stage of their trip, in South Dakota, was where the pickup's high clearance and cargo capacity were really going to come in handy, if all went as hoped and planned. To prepare for the chance they'd hit the jackpot at one of their digs, Don had built an insert of wooden slats for the pickup bed, so they could pile finds higher than the roof of the cab.

Late on Saturday evening, July 22, they reached the Dinehart Ranch in Reliance, South Dakota, fifteen miles west of Oacoma and Chamberlain, where they were paying guests of Mrs. O. C. "Ocie" Dinehart. They'd stayed there on previous visits over the past several years, always finding the Dinehart family congenial hosts and good guides to nearby paleontological and archaeological sites.

Don and Sue's previous visits had brought them together with the Mitchells, who lived in the area. During their travels, Don and Sue were always keen to meet well-informed locals who shared their appetite for pot-hunting. That sometimes happened through intermediaries they got to know in different places or, more often, through Don's use of ham radio communications in advance of a first visit to an unfamiliar location.

On Sunday morning, they overslept and woke just five minutes before their scheduled rendezvous with the Mitchells at eight. Sue recorded in her journal, "Don didn't shave, I didn't wash my face. We dashed into our clothes, gulped our coffee and got there at 8:30 AM." Whether the Mitchells were exasperated at their friends' lateness or not went unmentioned. Sue noted only, "They were waiting."

Then, "We followed them south from main highway at Chamberlain golf course—turning (keeping to left each choice) until even with a railroad station house. There through a lamb gate and out to where the White river and the Missouri meet was a graveyard of Indian burials (about 10 miles off highway)." Just visible to the north were the lattice

PROLOGUE

trusses of the Chamberlain Bridge. Decades later these were all clues for the FBI in identifying the site.

The Millers and Mitchells were exactly where they wanted to be, but they had yet to find precisely what they were searching for. They knew the confluence of the White and Missouri Rivers was a favored habitation for a succession of Native American tribes. They knew it had been part of the Lakota Sioux heartland, until most of the Lakota people were forced to move to reservation lands in the late 1870s and 1880s as part of the US government's reaction to Custer's defeat at the Battle of the Little Bighorn, the Battle of the Greasy Grass in Native American memory.

This particular crook of land between the rivers was part of a prairie ecosystem that had long supported herds of bison, pronghorn, and white-tailed deer, along with hosts of other wildlife: insects including pollinating bees and butterflies; birds such as hummingbirds (also great pollinators), warblers, grouse, birds of prey, and migrating sandhill and whooping cranes and other waterfowl; coyotes and wolves; and colonies of prairie dogs, among other animals. The rivers teemed with fish: walleye, pike, trout, salmon, catfish, and sturgeon.

The Missouri River was now closer than it had been historically. The US Army Corps of Engineers was constructing a series of dams and reservoir lakes on the Upper Missouri, displacing Native American communities like the village of White Swan. The stretch of river where the Mitchell children played and picked wildflowers—plants Native Americans valued for their nutritional, medicinal, and aesthetic qualities—was officially part of Lake Francis Case, named after a South Dakota US senator who served from 1951 to 1962. Completion of the Fort Randall Dam to the south in 1954 had flooded over 100,000 acres of prairie, submerging many historic and prehistoric sites.

Standing on the little rise where they'd parked their vehicles, Phil Mitchell said, "Look at all those prairie dog holes. There's hundreds of them."

"Thousands," Don replied. "But none of them is the kind of hole we want." He pointed down below them. "Those little depressions are more like it."

They knew that small, narrow depressions in the ground could signal

PROLOGUE

a burial site, where the soil had settled over time. Using those depressions as markers, they began probing the earth with lengths of concrete rebar. As Sue's journal entry for the day put it, "We saw sunken holes—probed with rods and hit casket tops." The caskets suggested mid- to late nineteenth-century graves, a period when some Native American burial practices in the area began incorporating elements of white-settler traditions. The wood of the casket tops had deteriorated to the point where they "were soft, but one could feel it [the rebar rod] go through."

Over the course of the day's digging, they found "dishes and cans right on top of caskets . . . lots of wampum and beads . . . scissors, spoons, knives, pans, ladles, mirrors . . . horse bridles," and what they thought was "red, yellow, blue and white war paint," along with a "war club" and "whet stones." In addition, there were "rings on fingers and bracelets on arms."

If any of the grave goods struck Sue as poignant, her journal entry gave no hint of that. Summing up the day's finds, Sue wrote matter-of-factly, "We dug three graves and found 4 skulls," and in one grave there were "3 baby bottles." To which she added, apparently without irony, "When we got back to Mrs. Dinehart's, we were filthy. Her daughter and son-in-law were there for supper."

The temperature had reached 88 degrees that Sunday, but by the time they woke up the next morning, they could already feel it was going to be even hotter. By noon on Monday, July 24, the temperature had climbed to 89 degrees, reaching a high of 95 that afternoon. Despite the oppressive heat, they stayed the course and were glad they did. Sue's journal entry for the day begins, "We met the Mitchells again—went to same place, dug all morning and didn't find anything of significance. Then in [the] afternoon (in sunken holes again) we started finding bones, beads, hatchets, and possessions—Phil and Don dug out 4 heads in one hole. Some of these were fragmentary."

Sue's journal entries and later notes on the backs of photographs often reflected ignorant, racist assumptions—or deliberate misrepresentations—about their findings. "Note the scalp," she penciled on the back of a photo that depicted a selection of grave goods, including a lock of hair. It wasn't a scalp, just a lock of hair—but that didn't align

PROLOGUE

with their assumptions or the stories they later enjoyed telling about "our Indians."

Likewise, in her July 24 journal entry, Sue claimed that the leather belts they unearthed from graves that day "usually had a sheath with a scalping knife right in it"—though in reality, they were simply utilitarian knives for everyday use. Despite their pretensions to archaeological expertise, the Millers seemed blind to the fact that the items they were unearthing, whether ceremonial objects or ordinary personal possessions, were buried with the people they belonged to because they were indelibly touched by the spirits of those unique individuals, and they were meant to stay buried.

Finished digging for the day, the Millers and Mitchells agreed to meet later at the Mitchells' trailer. Recording the event in her journal, Sue wrote, "That evening we were at Mitchells' and divided up our finds. We ended up with all the [whet]stones. Betty served watermelon."

Don and Sue had planned to begin the nearly thousand-mile drive back to Indiana the next morning, but their discoveries on Sunday and Monday changed their plans.

They decided to stay and dig for another day.

———

Tuesday, July 25, was brutally hot. By noon, the temperature had reached 95 degrees, peaking at 101 that afternoon. But Don and Sue didn't mind.

Sue's entry for the day begins, "We all returned again to the same place." They dug two holes and found graves that had already been "dug out" by other pothunters. In a third hole were "small leather shoes and toys—china dolls, little bottles, a spare pair of shoes, and game sticks," clear signs they had disturbed children's graves. In a fourth hole, however, they struck a "casket down about 2 ½ feet." As they dug deeper, they began to uncover a skull that "pointed approximately north" and was "turned slightly to the left." They began to work more slowly. As Don used a brush to remove dirt from around the top of the skull, he joked that he was "polishing his pate," words Sue later penciled on the back of one of the many photographs they took to document the excavation of this grave. From the first glimpse of the skull they felt sure it was a major find.

The skeletal remains in this grave were better preserved, and the grave goods more abundant, than in any they had excavated that morning or the previous two days. Both the Millers and the Mitchells were convinced it was a chief's grave. Giving him a depersonalizing nickname, they called him "Chief Kick-in-the-Face" because of his "head turned slightly to the left."

Sue recorded in her journal, "The skeleton had a beautiful heart plate [breastplate] made of old type shell wampum with [a] three-foot string of copper beads with mirror medallions. He had rings on his fingers, bracelets on his arms, dressed with purple chest cloth. He had ear rings. On his right side was a pipestone ceremonial pipe. . . . On his left side was a pipestone 'T' shaped pipe. . . . Near the 'T' shaped pipe was yellow, red, and blue war paint."

As they uncovered the skeletal remains from skull to foot, the adults posed for photographs inside and beside the grave. They even called the Mitchell children to come sit beside the skeleton and gaze innocently up at the camera, too young to have any sense of the occasion except that both their parents and the Millers were excited.

Still photographs weren't enough to commemorate such a find. Sue grabbed their well-used Kodak 8mm camera to capture the moment on reel-to-reel film. Mugging for the camera, Don held the skull and detached lower jaw next to his head and clacked the upper and lower jaws together while he opened and closed his own grinning mouth. Then Don took the camera, and with a grin of her own Sue mimed gnawing a femur and licking it clean.

Back home in Indiana, Don mounted the remains from this burial, commingled with bones from another Native American grave, inside a display case labeled "Sioux Warrior, 19th Cent." To the select few granted access to the locked room, Don liked to boast that the bones belonged to Crazy Horse, the Oglala Sioux war leader who, alongside Chief Gall of the Lakota, was chiefly responsible for defeating Custer and his regiment.

For the next four decades, Don and Sue continued looting Native

PROLOGUE

American graves, collecting skeletal remains and burial goods as trophies and souvenirs. With the same obsessive fervor, they invested considerable time and money in exploring—and looting—archaeological sites around the world. After Sue's passing at seventy-eight, Don continued digging, eventually joined by his second wife. When his collection came under FBI scrutiny in his ninety-first year, supporters insisted he had never done anything illegal or immoral. A few months before he died, Don received the Indiana Archaeological Society Lifetime Achievement Award for having "given unselfishly . . . to the advancement of not only the Indiana Archaeological Society, but amateur archaeology in general." To the end, he could never understand why anyone would want to deprive him of "my Indians."

One

"He's Got Indian Bones"

It was 1:30 p.m. on a chilly, overcast Indiana afternoon—Friday, November 1, 2013. I was riding shotgun in fellow FBI agent Bruce Guider's late-model, navy blue Ford Expedition, as we headed straight east through fallow brown corn and soy fields on State Road 244 in rural Rush County, about forty minutes southeast of Indianapolis.

Bruce and I both worked at the FBI's Indianapolis field office. He served as the coordinator for all matters related to weapons of mass destruction (WMD), while I was the bomb tech coordinator. In those roles, we frequently collaborated as part of the domestic terrorism (DT) squad.

Today, however, was not typical. While my FBI day job was defined by explosive ordnance disposal expertise and my role as bomb tech coordinator, my true passion was art crime. I was one of about a dozen FBI art crime team members scattered here and there among the bureau's fifty-six field offices. It was because of my art crime role that Bruce and I were going to visit a ninety-year-old man named Don Carlin Miller, on suspicion of his looting Native American burial grounds and other archaeological sites.

Two tipsters—they must remain anonymous under FBI protocols—had reported that over his long life Miller had repeatedly looted Native American graves, stealing human remains and burial objects, while also amassing a vast collection of other artifacts from around the globe. According to these tipsters, Miller kept his collection in his house and other buildings on the farm where he was born and raised.

Just a few days earlier, on the evening of Tuesday, October 29, my supervisor on the DT squad, Leslie Lahr, had called me at home and said, "Hey, Tim. I've just gotten a lead that references Native American artifacts and human remains. Is it something you're interested in on the art crime side, or should I push it out to Fish and Wildlife or the Bureau of Indian Affairs?"

Thousands of tips a day flow into the FBI via dedicated 800 lines, field offices' local telephone numbers, the internet, and snail mail. People report potential crimes or suspicious behavior involving business associates, rivals, family members (estranged or not), friends, acquaintances, public figures, and even strangers. Some tipsters are misinformed or unstable, while others are driven by personal grudges or revenge. But the motivation behind a tip doesn't necessarily mean it's not true.

Regardless of how tips arrive, they all funnel into the FBI's information hubs in West Virginia, such as the National Crime Information Center (NCIC) in Clarksburg and the Internet Crime Complaint Center (IC3) in Fairmont. FBI professional support staff follow a detailed protocol to weed out tips that come from people who are known to be unreliable for one reason or another or who are merely ranting and raving. They also filter out tips that don't involve an alleged federal crime, often referring them to state agencies. The support staff then initiate leads on the remaining tips after determining the field offices best suited to assess and investigate them.

When a lead reaches a field office, the appropriate management determines which squad—or, in some cases, which agent—should handle it. A tip on the looting of Native American remains and artifacts, a cultural patrimony-related crime, was bound for the art crime program. Everyone at the Indianapolis field office knew I was the region's only art crime team member. So when the tip arrived at the office, it was up to Leslie, as my supervisor, to decide whether to pass it on to me.

Aside from referring it to another agency, an FBI supervisor considering a lead has three options. If a lead appears insufficient or lacking merit on its face, the supervisor can "zero file" it, meaning the FBI retains a record but takes no further action. Or maybe a lead has only general information about crimes or other intelligence issues the FBI might be interested in—information that is not specific to a singular investigation or doesn't warrant immediate investigation. In those instances, a supervisor can place the information in a "control file" of background information and intelligence on the topic. Or a supervisor can assign the lead to an agent to assess it or move straight to a preliminary or full investigation.

Leslie knew about my passion for art crime cases and supported my involvement, as long as it didn't interfere with my bomb tech and DT duties. She gave me the choice of handling the lead or referring it to another agency, trusting my judgment and recognizing that my full-time FBI responsibilities already demanded more than enough of my time.

The Indianapolis field office, or division, is responsible for all of Indiana. At the time there should have been three special agent bomb technicians (SABTs) in Indianapolis, but due to transfers and retirements I was then the only SABT assigned to the office.

Indiana had twelve local law enforcement agencies and two national military units with bomb-disposal squads. Although each squad operated independently within its own jurisdiction, I worked closely with all of them on bomb threats and explosives incidents, bomb sweeps at special events, and federal investigations related to terrorism or other explosives-related crimes. I was also responsible for helping the squads maintain their accreditation from the FBI's Hazardous Devices School in Huntsville, Alabama.

Most other SABT coordinators were responsible for working with five or six squads, and a few had as many as fourteen. The Indianapolis Metropolitan Police Department's bomb squad alone handled an average of a hundred or more call-outs per year for suspicious packages and both hoax and real explosive devices. Most of those calls didn't require any response from me, but some always did.

An incident involving a suspected or actual explosive device could take me anywhere in the state at any time, and sometimes I needed to go out of state to support other SABTs. Major sporting events (the Indianapolis 500, NCAA basketball playoffs, Notre Dame football, and every Indianapolis Colts home game), occasional political gatherings, and other special events required bomb sweeps by both local squads and the FBI. That might sound great, if you're a sports fan. But if I never have to attend another crowded, rowdy sports arena, I'll be glad of it.

In 2013, I was particularly busy. On top of everything else I was also unexpectedly building one of the FBI's first Level 3 Stabilization teams in the field. These teams were intended to stabilize a WMD situation until national-level resources could be deployed. FBI headquarters in Washington, DC, had mandated that every field office establish such a team but, in typical bureaucratic fashion, had provided no real guidance on how to do so.

The lack of specific guidance struck me as an opportunity to do something innovative and create a team that would fit Indiana's needs and perhaps be a model for other field offices. The concept of the Level 3 Stabilization team was pretty straightforward. The FBI didn't have the manpower to do the mission alone, so we had to get buy-in from our state and local bomb squads and bring them in as partners. With that concept in mind, it seemed natural then to just build it as a quasi task force and deputize each officer I brought onto the team as a federal agent, a process long used already in joint terrorism task forces, violent crime task forces, and others around the country. The plan was simple, and things went reasonably well. But making the Level 3 team fully operational required a lot of additional work and training beyond what I was already doing or overseeing.

Leslie knew I had my hands full. But she also knew two other things: I was on top of my day job, and I was eager for a good art crime case.

In my immediately previous assignment at the Miami field office, I was one of a handful of SABTs sharing bomb tech duties. That left me time to focus on investigative priorities as part of the major theft squad, including many cargo theft cases.

Because Miami is one of the world's major art trade hubs, I was quite busy with art crime matters. Some of those early cases included recovering a stolen painting by Juan Gris, a leading figure in the cubism movement along with his better-known fellow artists, Pablo Picasso and Georges Braque; the heist of a painting by another cubist artist, Albert

Gleizes, where all the people involved were scamming each other; and the repatriation of a few hundred pre-Columbian artifacts discovered in a house after the owner died. I also had the chance to save several valuable stolen prints that the Miami Beach Police Department had in its evidence locker and was going to destroy, thinking they were worthless. There were plenty more, but those are stories for another book.

I asked Leslie what else she could tell me about the lead. She said that the day before, on Monday, October 28, a man had called an FBI tip line and said that Don Miller, born May 25, 1923, had told him about traveling all over the United States to dig up Native American remains and objects buried with the remains. The man alleged that Miller had a vast collection of artifacts that included human skulls, entire skeletons, and burial goods such as breastplates. The tipster didn't give his name, but he left his cell phone number and expressed a willingness to provide more information.

After sharing these details with me, Leslie probably wasn't surprised when I responded, "Don't push this out to another agency just yet. Let me take a look at it."

When I got to my desk early the next morning, Wednesday, October 30, Leslie had forwarded the documented lead to me. There was nothing in it besides what Leslie had told me. Was it worth the time and effort to call the tipster? Before considering doing that, my first step was to run a quick background check on Don Miller on our internal systems. With luck, that would indicate whether the lead had any credibility. Oftentimes a lead has been looked into three or four times already and found to be without real merit. Just like every other law enforcement agency on the planet, the FBI suffers the occasional serial tipsters—whether they be crackpots, misinformed, or just plain malicious—who bombard the agency with nonsense or baseless claims.

On my desktop computer, I opened the FBI's Sentinel case management system and ran Don Miller's name. At the most basic level, an agent can enter a person's name into Sentinel and it will reveal whether the FBI has ever opened a case on them or referenced them in an investigation. This could range from a criminal inquiry to routine background checks, such as interviews with neighbors of someone nominated for a federal judgeship.

To my surprise, Sentinel showed me a February 2008 case report from Bruce Guider. An anonymous lead called into the Boston field office had been cut to Indianapolis and assigned to Bruce as case agent. Amazingly, the tipster was worried that Don Miller had a nuclear trigger from the Manhattan Project.

The first detail in Bruce's report that caught my eye as potentially relevant to my lead about Native American artifacts and remains was that both the 2008 tipster and Miller were members of the American Society for Amateur Archaeology. More importantly, Bruce had documented seeing a large number of Native American artifacts in the basement of Miller's house himself while investigating the 2008 tip. An FBI agent's prior eyewitness account agreeing with an anonymous tipster's complaint—you can't get much better than that.

With regard to the nuclear trigger, the report documented that Miller had served as a US Army technician in the Manhattan Project. The triggers on the first nuclear bombs were exploding bridgewire (EBW) detonators that fired when they received a radiowave pulse. When Bruce and his fellow WMD team agents visited Miller, along with some Department of Energy (DOE) personnel, they didn't find an EBW detonator or any other kind of "nuclear trigger." But they did find a small amount of depleted uranium, which Miller had picked up somewhere, perhaps before strict regulatory limits came into effect in the 1960s. Although his possession of the depleted uranium wasn't considered a crime, it wasn't exactly safe to have in his house. At the request and safety recommendation of DOE personnel, Miller voluntarily turned over the depleted uranium. Mission accomplished, they all left Miller to carry on with his life, his massive collection of artifacts relegated to a passing note in an FBI case file.

As surprising as these revelations were, the good news was that in ten short minutes I had partially corroborated this new anonymous tip about Miller. Bruce's observation that Miller did, in fact, have a collection of Native American artifacts lent credibility to the allegation that he had obtained many of them illegally.

Bruce sat a few cubicles away from me. I went and tapped on his cube's frame.

"Do you remember a guy named Don Miller that was supposed to maybe have a nuclear trigger?"

"Sure," Bruce said, "but if you read my report, which I assume is how you know that, you know he only had a little bit of depleted uranium. He voluntarily gave it up, and that was that."

"Yeah, I saw the report. What I'm interested in is the artifacts your report mentions. Do you remember seeing his collection?"

"Oh, yeah. That guy had artifacts everywhere. And he wanted to talk my ear off about them too."

"Was it mostly Native American stuff?"

"That was a lot of it, yeah. But he had World War II stuff and all kinds of other things too. Not that I could tell you what they were."

"You didn't see any skeletons or skulls or other human bones by any chance, did you?"

"What? Hell, no! And I sure wouldn't have left it out of my report if I did. What's going on?"

"Somebody called in a tip that Miller's been robbing Native American graves."

"Huh. What are you going to do about that?"

"Based on your report and what you've just told me, I'm going to call the tipster and see what else they have to say. Maybe there's something to it, maybe not."

As much as I wanted to jump right into this potential new case, my bomb tech duties took me away from my desk and kept me busy most of the rest of the day. But shortly before 4 p.m., I got back to my desk and called the tipster's cell phone. When a man answered, I introduced myself as an FBI agent and verified that he was the source of the lead on Miller. The man was willing to talk, and we spent about an hour on the phone together.

The man (I'll call him "Richard" for the purposes of this story) had a tone of voice and manner of speaking that gave me the impression he was a reluctant tipster. Still, he had plenty to say.

Richard told me that Miller had countless skulls and at least two complete skeletons from Native American graves; that he had been part of the Manhattan Project; that he lived in a modern, 9,500-square-foot house on a 720-acre farm with his second wife, Sandra; that his collection was huge and was scattered throughout the house and other buildings on the farm, including the old white farmhouse he'd grown up in; that a bomb shelter in the basement of one building was used to store human remains; that many of the pieces came from Native American gravesites in St. Johns, Arizona; that he had robbed cemetery crypts in New Orleans; that he had traveled and dug extensively in Mexico, Central America, and South America, and even been arrested for looting artifacts in Mexico; that he had a particular love for Haitian artifacts; and that he had openly talked about acquiring things illegally and personally digging them up at gravesites.

It was a lot to take in on a first call, but one thing Richard kept saying stuck with me. Throughout the call, he kept repeating that Miller's collection was enormous. After maybe the tenth time he'd used that language, I finally had to ask, "Just how big is the collection?"

"It's huge, man. Huge."

"How huge? How many objects do you think he has?"

"I don't know. I'd say there's at least a hundred thousand, maybe two hundred thousand objects. I mean, he's got thousands of arrowheads, and that's just a small part of everything."

I snorted in disbelief—I couldn't help it. Still, I didn't challenge the number. The Philadelphia Museum of Art (the one Rocky ran up the steps of) is one of the world's foremost museums. It has over 240,000 objects (only a fraction of them on display at any time) in a massive building with almost 634,000 square feet of floor space. The Indianapolis Museum of Art, a major regional museum with many world-class holdings, has about 50,000 objects displayed and stored in at least 120,000 square feet of floor space.

A private collection with just a few thousand objects would be an outlier. Ten thousand objects would be among the largest private collections in the world. My colleagues and I on the art crime team had seen large private collections that held several hundred to a thousand objects. Something like that would not be a surprise. But one hundred to two hundred thousand objects sounded preposterous. For an individual collector to have anything approaching fifty thousand objects was unheard of.

In the course of the interview, Richard told me his real name and gave me the name and cell phone number of a woman who also knew about Don Miller's collection. They had both been acquainted with Miller over the past several years, and they had each visited his house many times. But their friendships with Miller had gone sour after he married his second wife, Sandra.

As soon as the call ended, I documented it using the FBI's 302 form for interviews, relying on the notes I had been jotting down. I didn't record the call, because at the time the FBI still followed a Hoover-era rule that agents should not record interviews without special authorization. J. Edgar Hoover firmly believed that an FBI agent's written summary of an interview—memorialized in a 302 report—was all the proof anyone should need. This policy, rooted in his distrust of electronic recordings and his insistence on agent control over the record, remained bureau doctrine for decades, despite criticism from legal experts and courts.

The rule had the benefit of forcing an agent to focus closely on what someone was saying and take good mental and physical notes. The FBI has finally abandoned that rule, and agents now routinely record interviews. While this change enhances accuracy, it has also, in my opinion, fostered a degree of counterproductive laziness. Many agents now rely on transcripts rather than promptly summarizing key details, often delaying 302 reports for days or even weeks—losing the immediacy and clarity of fresh recollection. In the interim you can easily forget relevant details about the circumstances of an interview that a transcript won't capture.

Before heading home for dinner with my wife, Risa, and our three children, I did some open-source hunting for mentions of Don Miller on the internet. The hits that came up included a book on Native American artifacts in Indiana that Miller and his first wife, Sue, had written and self-published. There were also local media stories about Miller's contributions to his church and small-town community. He had played a leading role in funding the rebuilding of a historic covered bridge in nearby Moscow, Indiana. A tornado had destroyed the bridge in June 2008, and the reconstructed bridge had opened in September 2010. Whenever you're investigating someone, it's good to learn about their standing in their community and how the community might react to your investigation, so you can keep it from being derailed for the wrong reasons. But that's getting a little ahead of the story.

Midmorning on Thursday, October 31, I phoned the woman Richard had told me about (I'll call her "Joan" for the purposes of this story) and spoke to her for about half an hour. Joan told me the same things Richard had, but she added some intriguing details. She said that Miller had recently moved many items in his collection from the white farmhouse that was his childhood home into another building, the Wyman Research Building (Wyman being his first wife's maiden name), where he'd operated an electronics business until he retired. "That includes a bunch of the Indian bones he's got," she elaborated. "I took pictures of some of those bones."

"I need to see those pictures," I responded. "Can you send them to me?"

She said she would have to email them to me, and I gave her my email address.

We hung up, and I documented the call with a 302 form. Late that afternoon, I received an email from her with two color photographs of six skulls sitting haphazardly on shelves, five in one picture and one in the other.

The pictures added a grisly touch of reality to Halloween. Unfortunately, they were consistent with past cases involving illegal pothunters who kept a few skulls or other human remains. Seeing them only reinforced my suspicion that Miller's collection could be far more troubling—and that it warranted a full investigation.

First thing the next morning, Friday, November 1, I went to Leslie's office to show her the pictures and tell her about the two tipsters' information and Bruce's recollections of his 2008 visit to Miller's house. I wanted to open a preliminary investigation, but I had to have Leslie's approval to do so. The pictures clinched it for her too.

"This is amazing," she said. "Follow it up."

I found Bruce at his desk and asked him to call Miller and say he had a colleague who was nuts about archaeology, had just heard about his amazing collection, and was eager to see it. Bruce dialed Miller and asked if he could bring me out for a look that afternoon. Miller replied, "Sure. Come on out." Bruce said we'd be there around 2 p.m.

We quickly ran over how we'd handle things. Bruce would introduce me to Miller and then fade into the background, unless circumstances dictated otherwise. I was going to have to use my knowledge of art and archaeology to draw out Miller and hopefully elicit something useful.

The beauty of this ruse was that we were identifying ourselves as FBI agents, while disguising the true nature of our interest. So, if Miller told us anything incriminating, it would be in full knowledge of our law enforcement jobs.

Back at my own desk, I started the paperwork to authorize a preliminary investigation. It would take a few days to complete the process, including notifying the local US Attorney's Office. But that morning I wrote in proper FBI fashion, "Based on the information provided by [the two complainants], Special Agent Carpenter believes sufficient predication exists to warrant the opening of a preliminary investigation and will be opening appropriate case files."

I also called FBI headquarters to give a heads-up to Jeff Croake, the FBI supervisory special agent who was then the art crime program manager, and Bonnie Magness-Gardiner, the staff professional who was the art crime team's management and program analyst (MAPA). Technically, Leslie's approval was all I needed to move forward, but I wanted to let Jeff and Bonnie know that something was brewing.

Jeff wasn't actually an art crime agent, despite the fact that he was supervising the program. His career had focused on major theft cases, eventually resulting in his leading the FBI's major theft program. Because art crime was a subprogram of major theft at the time, Jeff was also responsible for the art crime team. Although he didn't have specific art crime expertise, Jeff was nevertheless quite capable and an experienced agent. He didn't miss a beat and was supportive right out of the gate.

Bonnie, who had a PhD in archaeology and whose contributions to the art crime team were far greater than was usual in a MAPA role, recognized that I could be on the verge of something big. She suggested that I reach out to another agent who had handled a similar case some years prior. After I got off the phone with Jeff and Bonnie, I called that agent.

Operation Cerberus Action, which had unfolded from 2006 to 2009, concerned illegal trafficking in Native American artifacts in the Four Corners region of Utah, Colorado, New Mexico, and Arizona. In a joint operation, the Bureau of Indian Affairs (BIA), the National Parks Service (NPS), and the FBI had run a sting operation to buy artifacts from people who had taken them from public and tribal lands in violation of the Archaeological Resources Protection Act of 1979 (ARPA) and the Native American Graves Protection and Repatriation Act of 1990 (NAGPRA).

The cooperating personnel from those three federal agencies named the case Cerberus Action for the three-headed dog that guarded hell in Greek and Roman mythology. In keeping with US government traditions of producing large celebratory or "challenge" coins for various initiatives, the case task force had coins made with "Cerberus Action" and a picture of the mythological dog on them. When the joint task force made an arrest sweep, Secretary of the Interior Ken Salazar and Deputy Attorney General David Ogden held a press conference in Salt Lake City on the United States' "largest investigation of archaeological and cultural artifact thefts."

The case turned into a public relations disaster for the BIA, NPS, and FBI when two of the twenty-four people indicted—one of them a sixty-year-old Utah physician—committed suicide. To make matters worse, one of the dealers who had cooperated with federal authorities to implicate the defendants charged in the case also committed suicide less than a year after the arrests.

Many of the people indicted in the case were well known and respected in their local communities. People in those communities, particularly the very tight-knit Mormon communities in Utah, were outraged over the government's treatment of their friends and neighbors, including making arrests with a SWAT team. They focused most of their ire on the FBI, which they felt had entrapped upstanding people in small transgressions and then magnified them into big ones. Echoing their constituents, Utah's United States senators threatened a congressional investigation of the FBI's tactics.

When I got the Cerberus Action case agent on the phone, I said, "I think I've got a case with a lot of similarities. Have you got any advice for me?"

"Don't do it," he replied.

The problems with the Cerberus Action case were a warning sign. But I also saw them as a road map for what to do differently if I pursued a case involving Native American artifacts, especially if human remains were involved.

The negative perception of the Cerberus Action case wasn't the only challenge I had to consider. Two additional complications loomed: the long time span of Miller's alleged activities and the fact that his archaeological looting extended beyond the United States into other countries. If my complainants' information was accurate, much of Miller's collecting predated 1979 and 1990, before ARPA and NAGPRA, respectively, took effect. This was neither a small problem nor a new one.

The US Constitution prohibits ex post facto laws, meaning laws cannot be applied retroactively to criminalize actions that were legal at the time they were committed. Establishing probable cause that Miller had committed crimes before ARPA and NAGPRA would depend on whether he had violated earlier laws by robbing graves on public, private, or tribal lands and transporting the remains or artifacts across state lines to Indiana. Any looting he had done in other countries was going to require sorting out how international laws and treaties, a particular country's cultural patrimony law, or the status of its relationship with the United States might implicate potential criminal activities.

These issues were going to be big headaches to resolve in the best of circumstances. Even before opening the file, I knew this case would demand significant resources and the expertise of many people. It was easy to see a mountain range of challenges looming ahead, and I had no intention of embarking on such a daunting expedition recklessly.

But there were those two color photographs of skulls on Miller's shelves. I couldn't unsee those skulls. I couldn't get them out of my mind's eye.

If the photos were any indication and the tipsters' information was accurate, Don Miller had repeatedly committed serious crimes against Native Americans, the history and culture of the United States, and the heritage of an unknown number of other countries. Exposing such injustice and seeking to redress it—however possible—were exactly the kind of work the FBI was meant to do.

I had to see what else might be on Don Miller's shelves and what he might tell me about them.

"Hey, look over there," Bruce said, pointing to the right and slightly ahead of us. "That's Miller's ham radio tower."

I looked south-southeast across the flat landscape and saw the tower, about a hundred feet tall, rising above the sparse trees and the local electrical utility's power lines. In a few minutes the tower was directly south of us, and Bruce turned right onto South County Road 850 West. A quarter mile down the road and a hundred or so yards to the right was a large house that I guessed dated to the late 1970s or early 1980s, with other buildings south of it sheltered by a line of oak trees.

A sparsely graveled drive ran straight to the two-story house and then circled around it, with a parking area big enough for five cars directly in front of the house. The outside temperature gauge on the Ford's dashboard read 57 degrees Fahrenheit, but fifteen-to-twenty-mile-an-hour winds made it feel a lot chillier as soon as I opened my passenger side door.

The walkway from the parking area to the front door was flanked with metates, roughly circular stone slabs that Native peoples of the American Southwest, Mexico, and Central America used to grind corn into flour from pre-Columbian times onward. Metates are the Western Hemisphere's version of querns, a technology that preindustrial cultures around the world have used for grinding grains into flour. I counted six on each side of the walkway—all authentic, all museum quality. Miller was exposing them to the elements like cheap garden gnomes. They were probably hardy enough to withstand any number of thaw-and-freeze cycles in Indiana winters, assuming nobody damaged them heedlessly. But if Miller could casually display twelve superb metates like this, it suggested both that he had lots of excellent things in his collection and that he could be cavalier about how he treated them.

The house was a rectangle with longer sides on the east and west and shorter ones on the north and south. The north end pointed due north, following the rigid grid pattern of the surrounding fields and roads. From a distance the house looked like it was made of stone. Up close I could see that it was an ordinary stick house, but a solidly built one. The north and south facades had some kind of stone or fake-stone cladding from bottom to top. The east and west facades had cladding only on the ground floor, with tan walls on the second story. A hefty wooden balcony ran the length of the second story on the east (front) side of the house.

The complainants had told me the house was 9,500 square feet. It was a big house, sure, bigger than any we'd passed since we left I-74 for state and county roads, but I guessed it was more like 6,500 to 7,500 square feet. It had to have been the most impressive dwelling in the area when it was built. It was still impressive but showing signs of neglect. The tan walls needed cleaning and painting. Brown wooden window shutters and red roof tiles had visible minor damage from wind and weather. The shrubs in front of the house needed pruning.

To the right of the front door stood a five-foot-tall Chinese terracotta warrior, a replica of one of the terracotta figures from the third century BCE that Chinese farmers famously unearthed in Xi'an in 1974. The contrast of the genuine metates and the terracotta replica was a striking mix of fact and fantasy, an indication that Don Miller had an approach to collecting I'd never encountered before.

We rang the bell, and a few minutes later it opened to reveal a thin, frail old man about five feet ten, with greasy, thinning gray hair swept back on the sides and top of his head and pleasant, regular features. Thinking of all the digging he was supposed to have done in his lifetime, and allowing for the height people lose with age as vertebrae settle and compress, I could envision a vigorous, perhaps handsome younger man around six feet tall.

"Mr. Miller, it's good to see you well," Bruce said.

"And you too," Miller answered in a weak, reedy voice that forced me to lean in to hear better. "No Geiger counter today?" Miller added, showing he still had a spark to him.

"No, sir, no. Not this time," Bruce said with a smile. He turned sideways and extended his left arm toward me. "Mr. Miller, this is Agent Carpenter. He's the archaeology enthusiast I mentioned."

"You're interested in antiquities?" Miller asked me.

"Yes, sir," I said. "I'm fascinated by them." We smiled at each other and shook hands.

"Please come in," Miller said, standing aside.

We stood in a spacious fifteen-by-fifteen-foot foyer, its wooden floor adorned with a handsome inlaid design. The nine-foot-high ceiling left plenty of clearance beneath a small chandelier. Directly opposite the front door was an opening to the dining room, with two replica suits of Renaissance-era European armor flanking the entryway. Were all the fake warriors guarding genuine treasures? I hoped I was soon going to find out.

The dining room table was cluttered with mail, magazines, a McDonald's bag, and a paper cup filled with pens and pencils. To the right through the dining room was a double-height living room, where I could see a medium grand piano, three electronic keyboards, a pipe organ keyboard, and a fireplace. I glimpsed organ pipes rising along a wall and shelves crammed with pottery, stone figurines, family photos, framed arrowheads, a stuffed animal, and assorted glassware. Without a closer look, it was all likely inventory for a yard sale, except maybe the arrowheads.

Miller slowly led us left down a hallway, past stairs to the second floor and an entry to the kitchen on the right. Glancing into the kitchen, I saw unwashed dishes and pots filling the sink. A musty smell pervaded the whole house, but there was another odor in the kitchen. An old black Labrador stood there looking at me, a few feet away from the pile of feces and puddle of urine he'd recently deposited. He was either incontinent or simply hadn't been taken outside for too long a time.

The hallway ended at a passage to the attached garage, where the vehicles included classic Harley-Davidson and Indian motorcycles. Bruce and I followed Miller through the garage and out into the wind-chilled day. Despite his slow pace, he seemed to be doing fairly well for ninety. I wondered if my mental image of him as a strapping younger man was accurate.

About seventy yards south of the house, several trees lined the drive to the old farmhouse. Painted white as I'd been told, it looked like it dated to around 1900. Another ten or fifteen yards to the right stood a much newer, Old West–style building, its front facade topped with a sign that read, "Wyman Research Building."

"Bruce told me you were an engineer," I said. "Was this your workspace?"

"Yes. I ran a business out of here for quite some time," Miller said, confirming what the complainants had told me.

Inside the front door of the Wyman Research Building was an anteroom, with openings to other rooms beyond and on either side of it. A big area off to the right had spools of wire on holders along with other various electrical and electronic equipment. The space and the equipment were dirty and dusty but organized. I asked what sort of work he'd done here, aiming to build rapport and get him talking comfortably.

"Everything from radio and television repair to the space race," Miller said proudly. "Video transmission from satellites was my specialty up at Raytheon's Naval Avionics operation," he added, mentioning one of Indiana's premier companies and its Indianapolis facility. "I built some equipment for that here. But that's not what you've come to see, is it?"

"No, sir. But it's very interesting just the same. Thanks for telling me about it."

Miller gave me a pleased look and then took us down a staircase to the basement. There were a couple of hundred artifacts on shelves and tables, mostly pots and arrowheads. It was impressive as far as it went, but nothing shocking for a hobbyist collector to have.

Some pieces looked questionable because they were in such fine condition. Seeing intact Anasazi pots likely from New Mexico or Arizona, I thought, *This stuff has to be funerary. It looks too good to be anything else.* Pots buried ceremonially with a person's remains weren't typically used in daily life, save perhaps special occasions and religious ceremonies, and they had a decent chance of remaining intact until they were excavated.

At one end of the room there was a massive antique saloon bar holding pots in various stages of repair.

"Are you doing conservation work on those pots?" I asked.

"Yes. A girl down the road comes and helps me with them from time to time. I can't do it all by myself anymore, like I used to."

"Well, you have some amazing things here, that's for sure," I said.

As I hoped, Miller began to open up with stories about different pieces I remarked on. In every story, he described personally acquiring the artifact—digging it up himself or alongside others—never mentioning purchases from dealers or artifact shows. He mentioned digging in Kentucky, Indiana, Arizona, New Mexico, South Dakota, and North Dakota. He also said he sometimes used backhoes to excavate dig sites. That was very interesting to hear because some states, including New Mexico, forbid the use of heavy equipment for archaeological excavation without a permit, even on private land.

With my cell phone in hand, I discreetly snapped a few photos of objects whenever Miller's back was turned. Then, on a shelf in the middle of the room, I spotted what appeared to be a human femur among deer antlers and other obvious animal bones. Miller was standing next to me, but when he turned his head I caught Bruce's eye and flicked my own eyes toward the shelf.

"This is a beautiful pot over here, Mr. Miller," Bruce said, drawing his attention. I quickly took a photo of the bone, although I wasn't certain it was human. It takes an expert to tell whether a femur comes from a human being or an animal, but it looked human to me.

We spent about twenty minutes in the small room, and if that had been all I saw, I might have left Miller's place thinking there wasn't much of a case. I was having little dialogues in my head about the possible human femur and the intact Anasazi pots, but nothing stood out as definitively illegal. Problematic? Maybe. Requiring FBI attention? Maybe, maybe not. There was certainly no sign of tens of thousands of burial objects—let alone human skulls on shelves or complete skeletons. There had to be more.

As if in answer to my thought, Miller said, "I have some better things back up in the house, if you're interested."

"Yes, sir, I am. I'd love to see them."

Leading us back into the main house, Miller said, "Sandra is out. But when she returns, perhaps you'd like some tea."

"No, no, thank you," Bruce said.

"Kind of you, sir, but no, thank you. That's not necessary," I chimed in.

Just inside the door from the garage, a staircase led down to the basement. The walls on either side were lined with photographs—snapshots of Don's world travels and excavations he had participated in. They showed an unmistakable Don Miller at various stages of his life, aging slowly from his thirties and forties, looking as vigorous as I'd imagined, to his present state. The woman in the pictures had to be his first wife, Sue. They were a perfect match—smiling, pleasant faces, their clothes often streaked with dirt from digging.

As I neared the bottom of the staircase, I was overwhelmed by red. It was everywhere: red carpet on the floor; red felt backing in display cases; red cloth covering tables and shelves groaning with pots, arrowheads, stone tools, weaponry dating from the Bronze Age to the Revolutionary War, the Civil War, and World War II, along with countless other artifacts. The number of objects was staggering. After a few minutes of trying to comprehend what I was seeing, my rough guess was maybe ten thousand artifacts. *Holy shit*, I thought.

The stairs led to the center of the basement. When I turned around, I saw that the other half was just as packed with artifacts. The entire room spanned roughly fifty by thirty-five feet, and I quickly revised my estimate. There had to be at least twenty thousand artifacts. I had never seen anything like it. A good general rule of thumb is that collectors typically display only about half of their total holdings, with the rest tucked away for storage, cleaning, or repair. If that held true here, Miller's collection could easily number forty thousand artifacts, maybe even more.

The variety of the objects was as astonishing as their number: dinosaur eggs; pre-Columbian weapons from throughout the Americas; Danish celt stone axes; ancient Chinese ceramics; so many display cases of arrowheads placed edge-to-edge that they looked like wallpaper; cabinets labeled with the names of tribal nations and different cultural groups (Arikara, Caddo) or present-day locations (Costa Rica, Arizona, South Dakota); a green-white marbled stone axe-head with "Neolithic China, 7000–5000 BC" written directly on it with a Sharpie; a South American dugout canoe filled with paddles, stone figurines, and other loot.

Most staggering of all was the uniformly high quality of the artifacts. I wasn't an expert in any of the specific areas Miller had collected in, but I knew enough to recognize that museum-worthy objects surrounded me.

As I was taking it all in, Miller began to talk, telling stories about individual pieces and his different expeditions and collecting practices. Much as he had done while we were in the Wyman Research Building basement, when I asked about particular pieces, Miller often said something that suggested probable cause for a thorough investigation: "I dug this," "I found that," and even "I found those on a reservation."

In the course of his recitations, Miller told me that he'd begun collecting artifacts when he was eight years old and that he'd conducted digs in more than 220 countries. That was a bit comical because there aren't that many independent countries in the world, but I got his point—he'd traveled the entire world to satisfy his obsession for digging and collecting.

Showing Bruce and me a display case he said held his most valuable arrowheads, meticulously arranged in groups, Miller pointed at one group in particular. He said that he and Sue were digging them up with friends on a riverbank in South Dakota when some other people, presumably the landowners or their employees, came along and ran them off. For me that was an interesting comment. If Miller was digging on people's land without their permission and fled when they showed up, he had to know he was acting illegally.

The same was true for a collection of Chinese artifacts from the Ming dynasty (1368–1644 CE). Miller proudly told us that he and Sue had personally dug them up in China. That was a significant admission, given that China has some of the world's strongest cultural patrimony laws. Broadly speaking, anything excavated in China within the past 150 years or so is likely the legal property of the Chinese government.

As for Native American human remains, where were the skulls jumbled together on shelves in the photographs the tipsters had emailed me? Where were the complete skeletons they'd told me about? By now I was convinced that they must be somewhere in the house or elsewhere on Miller's property and that he was too cagey to reveal them to anyone he didn't fully trust. He might look frail, but he still had his faculties and wasn't going to let a couple of FBI agents see everything he had, even if they were visiting simply out of personal interest.

Even if I didn't see the human skulls I had been told about, there was one definite piece of human bone in the basement of the main house. On a shelf lay a four-and-a-half-inch fragment of a human frontal bone, the section of the skull that curves over the forehead, extending from just above the eye sockets to where it meets the parietal bones at the top. Embedded in the skull fragment was a Minié ball, a mid-nineteenth-century bullet. Once again, I discreetly snapped a photo with my phone while Bruce kept Miller occupied.

Bruce and I had now been with Miller for about an hour. Worried that we might stay too long and arouse his suspicions, I said, "Mr. Miller, I can't thank you enough for this opportunity. Your collection is truly amazing. But we'd better get going now."

Bruce added his thanks, and Miller told us we were very welcome and he'd enjoyed our visit.

Driving west on State Road 244 back to I-74, Bruce was the first to speak: "Well, what do you think?"

"Holy shit!" I said. "What I think is, What the hell am I going to do now?"

The tally of things I couldn't unsee had grown beyond my immediate comprehension.

Two

Wearing Wires

Over the weekend, I kept trying to make sense of Don Miller's collection. Was it a mostly legitimate collection with a few problematic pieces, or was Miller a serial grave robber? Generally speaking, the larger a collection is, the more likely that some pieces will have a dubious history. Even the most reputable museums have material that can make an objective visitor wonder, *Under what possible legal scenario did this come to be here?*

Museums around the world are wrestling with what to do about such holdings, many of them acquired in past eras and via circumstances that no one questioned until recently. That doesn't mean museums should be disbanded. They still have an important role to play in safeguarding, maintaining, and displaying precious cultural material in the public interest. But they also have a duty to repatriate ill-gotten items to their rightful owners and descendants, and doing this appropriately is an increasingly urgent part of a responsible museum's mission.

To my astonishment, Miller's collection, although seemingly not as large as the tipsters had reported, was indeed museum size and museum quality. The number of intact pottery pieces and other artifacts indicated that many of Miller's best pieces were likely funerary items. His own stories strongly suggested that he had frequently looted graves to acquire artifacts. But I wasn't an expert in Native American artifacts—or in any other category of Miller's collection. Aside from a single skull fragment and a possible human femur, I hadn't yet seen the extensive human remains the tipsters had described. And weighing heavily on my mind was the real possibility that these tipsters had a personal grudge against Miller and just wanted to see him jammed up.

The legality of specific items in Miller's collection hinged on when, where, and how he acquired them and transported them home—entangled, so to speak, in a web of local, federal, foreign, and international laws and treaties that varied over time. The one thing I felt sure of was that the Department of Justice (DOJ) would have zero interest in indicting and prosecuting a ninety-year-old man who was a pillar of his local community and that Don Miller would never see the inside of a courtroom or cell because of his collection. The suicides and the broader public relations debacle of Operation Cerberus Action made that a near certainty in my mind.

Bringing the law to bear would have to begin with establishing sufficient probable cause that Miller had committed crimes in assembling his collection. A compelling probable cause affidavit could then secure a warrant to search his premises and seize problematic material, including both artifacts and human remains, so they could eventually be restored to their rightful owners and custodians.

Given the breadth of Miller's collection—spanning numerous Native American tribal cultures and artifacts from civilizations around the world—a search and seizure operation would require a large cast of personnel from across the FBI, along with a diverse team of subject matter experts from outside the agency. How was I going to organize that while staying on top of my bomb tech duties?

These thoughts filled my mind over the weekend and kept pointing in one direction: I had to go back to visit Miller with an expert, someone who could render a professional opinion on his holdings and help me gather more specific information to develop probable cause. We had to probe for specific information about specific objects to establish if there was, in fact, a significant criminal case to make.

No one could be an expert in every category of material Miller had accumulated, but given the volume of Native American artifacts, securing a specialist in that area was especially critical. Fortunately, I knew someone who fit the bill, if she was interested.

Holly Cusack-McVeigh was an assistant professor of Native American and museum studies at Indiana University–Purdue University Indianapolis (IUPUI). We had met the summer of 2011, my first year at the FBI's Indianapolis field office. Not long after transferring in from Miami, I had gone to the Indianapolis Museum of Art, the Eiteljorg Museum of American Indians and Western Art, and other museums in Indianapolis and the rest of Indiana to introduce myself as a member of the FBI's art crime team. Those efforts led to an invitation to give a presentation on the art crime team at a summer conference of Indiana museum curators and others in the cultural heritage industry. Holly attended the conference, and after my presentation she asked if I would speak to her graduate museum studies class at IUPUI. I was delighted to say yes and began visiting her classes each semester.

Holly was super smart. She'd done the field work for her PhD in anthropology among the Yup'ik people of Alaska, so she was well versed in Native American cultural issues. She'd also been involved in a number of successful repatriations to Native American tribes by museum and university collections. If anyone could help me get a handle on how problematic Miller's collection really was, I figured it was Holly. Before reaching out to her about that, however, I needed to brief Leslie Lahr—along with others at the field office and headquarters in Washington, DC—on what I had seen at Miller's house.

———

As soon as I arrived at the office early that Monday morning, I spoke to Leslie, who agreed that my initial visit to Miller provided a basis for upgrading my preliminary investigation into a full field investigation. After a full day handling my usual bomb tech matters, I called Bonnie Magness-Gardiner at headquarters to bring her up to speed.

At the time, the art crime program was in its ninth year, but in many ways it was still flying under the radar across the organization. Without Bonnie's many contributions, I doubt the program would have survived the rigors of the FBI bureaucracy that long.

The FBI had long handled art crime cases, and it had had a National

Stolen Art File (NSAF) since 1979. Yet few in the bureau had even considered the need for a dedicated art crime team like long-established specialty programs and teams for bomb tech, evidence recovery, polygraph, SWAT, child abduction, or behavioral analysis. That changed with the April 2003 looting of the National Museum of Iraq in Baghdad, which happened more or less under the noses of occupying American troops.

Not surprisingly, the US Congress reacted with outrage to the looting, condemning the failure to protect Iraq's cultural heritage and pressing military and government agencies, including the FBI, for answers on how such a historic loss had occurred. Despite the tragedy of the looting, this pressure was the catalyst that those in the bureau who had long been advocating for a dedicated art crime team needed.

To answer the call, the FBI's Criminal Investigative Division turned to the major theft program, which had long overseen traditional art theft matters, treating them largely like any other major theft. In turn, the major theft program looked to a small cadre of agents and professional support staff who had backgrounds or experience in art and art-related investigations. At the head of that list were two highly seasoned agents, Bob Wittman and Eric Ives, who along with a handful of others at headquarters set about building the FBI's first art crime team.

The initial team comprised only half a dozen or so agents with some prior experience and interest in art crime cases, spread across the entirety of the FBI. The idea was that this small team could provide a rapid response to major art crime cases or to situations where the US government was responsible for safeguarding or recovering imperiled cultural property, like the looting in Baghdad.

Most specialty programs in the bureau are typically managed by a supervisory special agent serving as program manager. Although art crime team agents—and, to some extent, others within the FBI—naturally began referring to the art theft program, this new formalized effort wasn't actually an official program within the bureau's organizational structure. Rather, it began as, and for more than ten years formally remained, merely an initiative within the major theft program. Accordingly, during these years the art crime team was managed by supervisory special agents assigned to the major theft program—most with little or no art crime experience—who oversaw the team as a collateral duty.

The average tenure for a program manager in the FBI tends to be about eighteen to twenty-four months. The career trajectory for FBI agents ambitious to join the bureau's executive ranks mirrors the corporate world, where managers rotate through roles in finance, manufacturing, and sales to gain diverse experience and demonstrate success across multiple sectors on their path to the C-suite. If you wanted to become an FBI executive, you needed to demonstrate a broad base of experience across multiple programs, whether related to criminal investigations or national security programs.

Rapid leadership turnover wasn't usually a problem for long-standing FBI specialty programs. They all had established systems for training in best practices, and they knew how to drive the stats on successful cases and other measures that kept them looking good with the top brass. Most programs also had one or more non-agent support professionals to provide continuity as a management and program analyst (MAPA). However, for the art crime team and its hopes of transforming from merely an initiative into a proper specialty program, the rapid turnover of program managers was a problem.

The bureau recognized that, even if the art crime team was not a full specialty program in its own right, it needed someone with good knowledge of art and the art world as its own management and program analyst. Lynn Richardson, who was managing the NSAF at the time, became the art crime program's de facto first analyst, but she was retiring soon. So in 2005 Eric Ives, the major theft program manager overseeing the creation of the art crime team, hired Bonnie from the Department of State, where she was a cultural property analyst, to handle the NSAF and replace Lynn as the art crime team's program analyst.

Of the supervisors who succeeded Eric Ives (all highly capable agents with experience investigating major theft or, because of a subsequent reorganization of headquarters supervisors, La Cosa Nostra), some embraced the art theft program and saw its great potential value. Others never took it seriously. Regardless of their view of the program, none of these supervisors remained in the role long enough to professionalize it to the same level, or win it the same official status, as other programs.

The art theft program desperately needed someone to diplomatically exercise tacit leadership and, in effect, become the de facto program manager. Bonnie did that brilliantly, leveraging her intelligence, her expertise as a PhD archaeologist, her network of relationships with cultural property experts inside and outside the government, and most of all her organizational political savvy. Her impressive poise and speaking skills made her the credible and compelling public face of the art crime program, including on a number of FBI web pages.

People who join the FBI after serving in other government agencies—especially without prior law enforcement experience—often struggle and fail. The transition from the Department of State to the FBI is particularly challenging due to stark cultural differences. Bonnie is the only person I've seen navigate that shift successfully.

During the fall of 2013, my fellow art crime team agents and I all relied on Bonnie, as we would until the day she retired from the FBI. We counted on her valuable advice about art matters and ability to connect us with outside subject matter experts (SMEs) and other figures in the art and cultural property world. Bonnie also connected us with each other. The dozen agents on the team at that point had never actually worked together as a cohesive unit, despite the stated goal of being a "rapid deployment art crime team." Scattered across the country in our respective field offices, we typically saw each other only once a year for a three-day training session.

One reason I was eager to speak to Bonnie after my first view of Miller's collection was that, if the case went forward as I thought it might, we were going to have to mount a massive search and seizure operation, one that was wholly unique and unlike anything the bureau had done before. We wouldn't be seizing illegal guns, contraband drugs, or records of financial fraud. We would be seizing potentially priceless artifacts, burial goods, and human remains, some of which could be thousands of years old and most of which would require very special handling and packaging before we could even move them. Seizing even a portion of Miller's collection, if justified, would require the full involvement of the art crime team, additional FBI personnel, and numerous subject matter experts to assess problematic objects and determine their likely cultural or national origins.

During my call with Bonnie, I outlined these concerns and the many legal hurdles in establishing probable cause for a search warrant. I also emphasized my immediate need for an SME to accompany me to Miller's house to get a better understanding of the authenticity, potential illegality, and condition of the collection. And I knew I needed help identifying other issues I hadn't even begun to consider. Having already seen a couple of the photos supplied by the tipsters and having processed what I had told her, Bonnie was on top of things and immediately began tossing out suggestions.

"On the legal issues, you should talk to Patty, of course," she said, referring to Patty Gerstenblith, a professor of law at DePaul University College of Law in Chicago and the founding director of the college's Center for Art, Museum and Cultural Heritage Law. Patty was the author of an important casebook in cultural property law, and she was an early fixture in the art crime team's annual training sessions.

"I'll call Patty soon," I said. "Do you have any ideas on an SME to take to Miller's? There is somebody here I can ask," I continued, giving her a thumbnail description of Holly's expertise, "but I'll need someone else if she's not interested or not available."

"Nobody comes to mind in the Indianapolis area," Bonnie replied. "But your friend at IUPUI sounds like an excellent candidate. Let me know if that doesn't work out."

"I'll keep you posted."

The next day, Tuesday, November 5, 2013, I put through the paperwork to make my preliminary investigation of Miller's collection a full field investigation. Leslie had verbally approved it the day before, but her approval wasn't the only one I needed. As supervisor of the Indianapolis field office's domestic terrorism squad, Leslie was my day-to-day boss, as I've mentioned. But since art crime at the time was housed under the major theft program, responsibility for those cases in Indianapolis fell to the violent crime squad. To open a full field investigation for an art crime case, I also needed the approval of Greg Massa, that squad's supervisor.

Greg was one of those FBI agents who saw little value in fighting art crime. A native New Yorker, he had spent his entire FBI career working violent crime, organized crime, and the like, and my guess was that he saw my art crime cases as nothing more than an unnecessary distraction. When I went to see him about the Miller case, his response was, "Artifacts? Really?"

"Yes."

Greg shook his head but he signed off on the paperwork, warning me, "So long as you don't ask me for any resources or personnel for this, I don't care what you do. Knock yourself out."

From this point forward, as long as the Miller case remained active and didn't fizzle out, I had to report up two chains of command. On the domestic terrorism and national security side, I needed Leslie Lahr's clearance to continue working the case alongside my bomb tech duties. On the criminal investigation side, I reported to Greg Massa, meaning all official case paperwork for Miller would go to him rather than Leslie.

When I got home that afternoon, I hadn't yet had a chance to call Patty Gerstenblith. Risa was home from her teaching job at a local technical college, and our kids were home from school. I left them chatting about their day, making a few mental notes on things I needed to pick up on with them over dinner, and went outside to call Patty as the afternoon light slowly began to fade. Leaning over the hood of my beat-up 2003 Chevy Silverado, I laid it all out: Miller's massive collection, my certainty that the DOJ would never want to prosecute him, and the challenges of establishing probable cause for a search warrant, which by my estimation would likely revolve around his commingling of illicit goods with legal ones.

Patty confirmed that I would have to navigate a labyrinth of potentially applicable laws. But she was adamant that this was the right thing to do: "There is no way Miller could have legal possession of the material you've described."

As usual, bomb tech duties consumed most of my time throughout November. On November 13, I carved out enough time to interview

Tipster 1 ("Richard") in person at his workplace. This discussion was far more in-depth and wide-ranging than our initial phone call on October 30.

Richard told me the following:

- He and Tipster 2 ("Joan") had known Miller for over a decade, and throughout that time Miller had been adding to his collection of fossils and Native American and foreign cultural artifacts.
- They had extensive knowledge of the Miller property and had seen all the places where the collection was stored.
- Miller kept a large amount of Native American artifacts in a room off the bottom landing of the staircase to the basement in the Wyman Research Building.
- An approximately sixteen-square-foot room on the basement level of the Wyman Research Building had recently held many human remains.
- The basement of the main house contained Miller's most prized pieces.
- A locked room off the central basement area had a full Native American skeleton in a display case.
- Miller spoke about conducting digs all across the United States and around the globe, uncovering human remains and artifacts for his collection.
- St. Johns, Arizona, was Miller's base for digs in the American Southwest.
- Miller owned two backhoes he used on digs in the Southwest.
- Miller often talked about personally digging up material and told anecdotes indicating he knew possession of much of this material was illegal.
- Miller frequently referred to collecting as an addiction, as strong as any drug.
- Miller spoke about digging up artifacts in South America and how many things were there for the taking.
- Miller had a particular passion for Haitian artifacts, which he dug up on missionary trips.

- Because so much of his collection was illegal and could not be safely sold, Miller had told family and friends that, after his death, they should dig a large pit on his farm and bury the entire collection—especially the human remains.
- Miller had a skull with several gold teeth still in its mouth.
- Miller had been arrested once for archaeological looting in Mexico but had escaped any consequences, presumably by paying a bribe.
- A small office in the basement of the main house had records of Miller's digs and purchases.
- Miller kept audio and video recordings discussing his collection in the old white farmhouse.

Richard's assertions, if true, provided ample probable cause to suspect that Miller had knowingly committed crimes in assembling his collection. Particularly telling was Miller's alleged statement that after his death, the artifacts and human remains should be disposed of—because they could never be legally sold.

One morning the next week, Holly Cusack-McVeigh and I met in a boutique coffee shop near the IUPUI campus. After the normal pleasantries about how we and our families were doing, I said, "Holly, there's an FBI matter I'd like to tell you about. But it has to be in total confidence."

"Sure, Tim," Holly said, her brow wrinkling slightly with both concern and interest. She leaned forward and asked, "What is it?"

"Tell me what you think of these," I said, sliding a few of the photos of artifacts I'd surreptitiously taken at Miller's house out of an envelope. I couldn't lead Holly to a conclusion in any way, and her first reaction to the photos was crucial.

Holly bent over the photos and studied them closely. After a couple of minutes she looked up and said, "There's an amazing collection here, and I would guess much of it has to be illegal."

"Why do you say that?"

She speared one photo with her finger and pushed it into the center of the table. "Well, these are funerary pots in absolutely pristine condition. They were meant to stay interred with the dead forever. If this is a private collection, they were likely obtained in clandestine digs of grave sites. If I saw them in a museum or university department collection, I'd be marching into the director's or chairperson's office to ask why they weren't being repatriated."

Holly's eyes were wide with curiosity. I said nothing and instead took two more photos out of the envelope, the ones Joan had sent showing human skulls on shelves.

Holly examined the photos. When she looked back up, her eyes blazed with anger as well as curiosity.

"Are these skulls from the same place as the artifacts?" she asked in a calm but steely voice.

"At the moment, that's only a matter of suspicion," I said. "If the FBI is going to take any action, I need to strengthen that suspicion, and I need the help of an expert like you to do that."

I quickly filled Holly in on the tip about Miller and my visit to his house, then went on. "I wasn't there long enough, and I just don't know enough yet to assess the legality of what Miller has. But this is a man who soaks up attention like a sponge and enjoys talking about his collection. If you're willing, I'd like to take you with me to see his collection again and help draw him out about specific objects that you judge to be questionable. We'll tell Miller that you're an anthropologist friend of mine, that I described his amazing collection to you, and that you begged me to get you a tour of it."

"You got it," Holly said without a moment's hesitation. "I'd be very glad to help."

Holly's reaction was exactly what I'd hoped and expected it would be. Before the meeting, I'd been thinking that a curator at the Eiteljorg Museum of American Indians and Western Art might be my fallback option. But I was glad that wasn't necessary. I couldn't have asked for a better, more knowledgeable, or more steadfast ally than Holly.

Later that day, I met with the field office's tech agents—Q from the James Bond movies—to explore options for concealed microphones and video cameras I could take to my second meeting with Miller. I had gotten some fairly incriminating statements from Don during my first visit, but I was expecting more with Holly in tow. This time, I wanted to get them on tape.

In most states, including Indiana, only one party's consent is required to record a conversation—meaning my own consent would be enough for any recordings made with a device I was wearing. My primary concern was securing concealed microphones—always wearing more than one to ensure redundancy in case of failure—that could clearly capture Miller's whispery voice without being drowned out by incidental noises, like fabric rustling, that might obscure his statements. Don was so soft-spoken that I needed to ensure the microphones could pick up his voice clearly.

As I thought it through, I realized that if I were the only one wearing mics and video cameras, I'd have to stay glued to Holly and Miller the entire time—especially since I expected Holly to do most of the talking. That would hardly look natural, and it could easily arouse Miller's suspicions and make him clam up.

For the recordings to be effective, Holly would have to carry her own recorder as well—if she was willing. That way we could move about separately and each interact and converse with Miller as circumstances dictated. In the scenario I was envisioning, Holly would handle most of the conversation with Miller, using her expertise to draw him out on particular objects in his basement display, while I wandered around the room looking for other evidence.

I called Holly and told her all this. She was apprehensive but after a moment's thought said she was in.

"Okay, good," I said. "But you can't get carried away. This isn't like getting deputized in the old westerns. You won't be a temporary FBI agent or gain any kind of law enforcement authority. You're just coming along to talk to Miller about his collection. If he says things that are useful for us, great. If he doesn't, I'll figure out a plan B."

"Understood," Holly said. "And reassured."

This type of operation wasn't terribly unusual in the FBI, and there was a process to get it approved. The process was tedious but routine.

In the meantime, on Friday, November 22, I interviewed Joan in person at her home. For the most part, Joan echoed Richard. But there were a few intriguing variations and additions. Joan said:

- Miller never stopped looking at the ground to see what he could pick up everywhere he went.
- Miller had so many arrowheads, he used them for landscaping instead of pea gravel.
- Miller had gone to Arizona for digs there and in New Mexico at least twice a year until he grew too frail to do so.
- Joan had seen boxes of human bones at Miller's home, along with many loose human bones and skulls on shelves.
- Joan didn't know where all the human remains came from, but Miller said he and Sue had dug up many of them along the Ohio River near Cincinnati.
- Instead of burying the human remains in a pit after his own death, Miller said that all the remains should be put through a woodchipper to eliminate any evidence that he'd ever had them, with one exception—the complete Native American skeleton in a display case in a locked room in the basement.
- About that skeleton Miller said, "Bury me with my Indian."

It was up to the FBI, with Holly's help, to make sure that never happened. Thanksgiving was the next week, and Holly and I agreed that we'd drop in on Miller, unannounced, soon after the holiday.

Midmorning on Thursday, December 5, 2013, I picked Holly up in the FBI-supplied, late-model Chevy Suburban I used daily as a bomb tech. Despite what television and movies might suggest, most FBI agents don't drive around in big black SUVs. Thanks to the Obama administration's federal "green" fleet initiative, many were issued modest compact cars instead. But because my bomb tech duties required me to carry a vast amount of specialized equipment at all times, I actually did drive a Suburban. The day before had been mild, with a high of 61, but the temperature was dropping steadily toward the 30-degree mark, and the afternoon forecast called for rain.

We chatted for a while about the nasty turn in the weather and other small talk before settling into a comfortable silence as we drove. Ten minutes out from Miller's farm, I asked, "How are you feeling, Holly?"

"I haven't been this nervous since I got called into the room for my oral exams for my PhD. The anticipation was the worst part. Once the professors started asking questions and we began batting around different topics, I was fine."

"There you go," I said. "This is the same kind of thing. Like we've discussed, just respond to what you see and what Miller says. Let the conversation take its own course, and it's all going to be fine."

Parked in front of Miller's house, I looked at Holly and said, "Deep breaths," before taking a few myself. Although this was nothing new for me, I couldn't help being a little keyed up myself, as you might imagine. We put on our concealed mics and cameras and switched them on. Following standard procedure, I began recording with my usual preamble—my name, who else I expected to be on the recording, and the location, date, and time. After ensuring everything was working as expected and was properly concealed, we stepped out into the cold morning.

At the front door we could hear Miller playing the piano inside. When he answered our knock, I introduced myself as the fellow who "was over here a couple of weeks ago" with a colleague and said, "You were nice enough to show us around your collection downstairs."

Miller recognized me and answered, "Yeah."

Apologizing for not calling ahead and claiming I didn't have his phone number, I continued, "This is my friend Holly. I've been raving to her about how awesome your collection is. We were just driving back from Cincinnati on our way to Indy, and I was hoping we could come in so she could have a look, if that's not an inconvenience."

"Sure. Yeah."

"Would that be okay?" I asked, to confirm that we were being invited in.

"Yeah, I'll take you through," Miller said.

We thanked him, and Holly said, "It's nice to meet you." Gesturing to the Millers' old Labrador retriever, she added, "Your dog's out. Is that okay?"

Miller called the dog and ushered us inside, then led us straight to the stairs to the basement.

"I apologize for interrupting your piano session," I said.

"Oh, I practice a lot," he said, flicking on the basement lights. "Come on down."

The old Lab trailed us down the stairs. At the bottom Holly said, "I can't believe it. This is amazing."

Miller asked, "Are you an archaeologist or something?"

"I studied anthropology," Holly answered. "I love these kinds of collections."

Miller perked up, pleased to have someone knowledgeable admire his collection. "Let's start over here," he said, pointing to the left. "Ask me any questions."

"Mr. Miller, this is unbelievable," Holly said. We went around the basement displays counterclockwise, stopping first at cases with American Revolutionary War and Civil War memorabilia.

Holly read aloud an identifying label in the Civil War case: "Union Minié balls." Claude-Étienne Minié was a French engineer who invented these conical bullets with a hollow base, which inflicted far more devastating injuries than the round musket balls they replaced, often necessitating amputations.

"You find those with a metal detector and dig 'em up," Miller said—his first admission during the visit that he excavated artifacts himself.

Resting in a wooden cradle on the floor, directly in front of the cases, was a small cannon.

"We found that in the Gulf of Mexico," Miller stated. "It's what they call a swivel gun, and it was probably mounted on the rail of an old Spanish galleon."

I stepped to the side and petted the dog while Miller talked about how heavy the iron cannon was.

Prodding a bit, Holly asked, "Was that with a shipwreck?"

"Well, we don't know."

Without further prompting, Miller explained that he had hired someone to free dive the wreck, tie a rope around the cannon, and haul it up.

A free dive—conducted without scuba gear—suggested the cannon was likely recovered from shallow territorial waters. If so, its removal could be subject to the legal jurisdiction of the United States or another nation bordering the gulf. As I had expected, we'd been looking at the collection for only a few minutes, and Miller was already making possibly incriminating statements to Holly. It was not exactly the crime of the century yet. But we were just getting started.

As we moved on from the cannon, Don talked about the Civil War–era weapons in a nearby display case. With obvious pride, Don said the rifle hanging above the case had been used at the first Battle of Bull Run.

"Unbelievable," Holly gushed.

"If you want to take a picture, go ahead."

"Tim, you had my camera. Did you bring it in?" Holly asked.

I held up the cheap point-and-shoot camera I'd bought at Walmart and began openly taking still photos in addition to the video our concealed cameras were already capturing. Meanwhile, Miller was telling Holly he'd traveled to two hundred countries, repeating what he had told me during my first visit.

Referring to a New Zealand travel poster at the top of the stairs, Holly mentioned her own visit to that country. She said that she was fascinated with the stone tools and weapons that the Māori and other Pacific Islanders made, and that as an anthropology student she'd worked with people who made stone tools and weapons in the traditional way, by flint knapping, the process of using a hammerstone to chip away at another stone to create an edge or point.

"Do you have stone weapons, Mr. Miller?"

Miller directed her attention to a display nearby. "I've got all these here."

"Oh, there's just too much to see. I can't believe it. Are you an archaeologist?"

Miller beamed and said no, he was a PhD electrical engineer who had graduated from Purdue with high honors.

"How did you learn to excavate?" Holly asked.

"Somebody gave me a spade once," Miller wisecracked.

Innocuous as it might sound, Miller's admission was helpful. It confirmed that he was not a trained archaeologist, and it reinforced my growing belief that he did not follow accepted archaeological protocols and likely did not secure proper authorization for his excavations. It wasn't a wholly damning statement, but it provided a glimpse into his knowledge and understanding of the material he had collected. I tucked it away in my mind for later.

We continued moving through the basement, though I wasn't always at Holly and Miller's side. Their conversation was unfolding just as I had hoped, keeping them both occupied and giving me the chance to examine other displays and snap additional photos.

Standing in front of the case displaying Miller's World War II memorabilia—including a vintage US Army radio and a photo of himself with the same model—Holly said, "This is so amazing. Tim told me it was, but I had no idea. This is a museum."

Pointing to the picture of himself with the radio, Miller boasted, "I blew up three atomic bombs." He then recounted the story I had already heard—claiming he sent the radio signal to ignite the Trinity Gadget at Alamogordo, New Mexico—and added that he had also been involved in two nuclear test explosions at Bikini Atoll in the Marshall Islands in 1946.

"Wow," Holly said. "You should write a book."

It was a nice segue to engaging Miller in conversation about his Papua New Guinea artifacts, which he claimed he'd collected in 1946, when going to and from the Marshall Islands, and on later visits with his first wife, Sue. Amid his fantastical tales of New Guinea cannibals, Miller spoke about traveling with cartons of cigarettes, despite not being a smoker, to trade for artifacts, including the exquisite wooden animal figures and mask adornments displayed in his collection.

Holly asked, "Did you get to do any excavations in New Guinea?"

"Yeah, a little bit." Miller paused and then went on about how the local people "will guide you to good sites" for digging, in exchange for cigarettes. Like his other statements so far, this one wasn't exactly a smoking gun, but it did provide a potential foothold for establishing probable cause to suspect that Miller had imported illegally obtained

New Guinea artifacts into the United States. However, I would need to corroborate it with additional relevant evidence.

Miller led Holly to display cases filled with pottery and other artifacts from Arizona and New Mexico. Casually, he mentioned that he leased land from ranchers in the region for excavations, a common enough practice for pothunters but also a well-practiced statement by many to disguise illegal digs on government or tribal lands. On the wall above the cases hung a photo of Sue, beaming as she held a freshly unearthed Anasazi effigy pot. The pot itself, however, was nowhere in sight.

Holly, playing her part perfectly, widened her eyes in admiration. "I can't believe something like that could be found intact!" she said.

Miller, seeming to be fully at ease and enjoying the attention, waved off her amazement. "Oh, that piece was six feet down," he said, as if it were no big deal. "We used a backhoe to get started that day—like we often did in the Southwest."

I kept my expression neutral, but that was another useful admission. New Mexico strictly prohibits the use of heavy machinery for archaeological digs without a permit, even on private land. If that piece had come from New Mexico, as both his statements and the signage on the case suggested, then Miller had just handed me another potential piece of the probable cause puzzle.

Beyond the countless artifacts neatly arranged in labeled display cases, Miller had pottery stacked on top of nearly every case. Other artifacts sat on the floor, on lined rows of neatly arranged folding tables, or leaned against display cases and walls. He had filled every available space in the room from floor to ceiling. The collection spanned cultures and continents: woodland pots from eastern North America, Aztec stone figurines and obsidian blades, and a dugout canoe from South America overflowing with stone tools, weapons, and other Indigenous artifacts from across the Americas. Mixed in were fossils and a vast array of artifacts from around the world, creating a breathtaking, somewhat chaotic, display of history.

Even though I'd seen it once before, it was hard to take in the diversity and volume of the collection. Holly's discussion with Miller ranged through it all, and he kept incriminating himself.

After mentioning that he kept a number of replicas upstairs—"I don't like copies down here"—Miller directed our attention to a collection of Minié balls and metal arrowheads. "I used a metal detector at Custer's Last Stand to find those. I dug a hole in the middle of a dirt road, and that's the stuff I got."

That made me look up at Miller. He had just stated, for the benefit of our concealed recording devices, that he had looted material from the Little Bighorn Battlefield National Monument in Montana, about sixty miles southeast of Billings.

The same display case contained tribal police badges from the Rosebud Reservation in South Dakota. Miller spoke of visiting both Rosebud and what he called the "1890 Battle of Wounded Knee" on the nearby Pine Ridge Reservation—though the more common term is the Wounded Knee Massacre, where US Army soldiers killed nearly three hundred Lakota men, women, and children.

A little farther along, a shelf held the same skull fragment with a Minié ball embedded in it that I had noticed during my first visit.

Holly stopped and said, "Where'd you get that?"

"Found it in the battlefield."

"Wow. That's Rosebud also?"

"Yeah."

If taken at face value, as all of Miller's statements had to be, this meant he had stolen the skull fragment from tribal land. "The battlefield" was presumably the Wounded Knee site on the Pine Ridge Reservation, not Rosebud.

Discussing more artifacts from Arizona and New Mexico, Miller remarked, "We used to dig on reservations, but now we rent ranchland where we're allowed to dig." His casual acknowledgment of excavating on tribal land suggested both awareness of wrongdoing and a past willingness to engage in it.

While we were all examining several Native American pottery pieces, we heard the door at the top of the stairs open. A woman called, "Don?"

"Down here," Miller called back. "Got guests."

Miller explained that his second wife, Sandra, was home from shopping. Sandra came down the stairs, and I said, "How are you, ma'am? I'm Tim Carpenter. I was over here a couple of weeks ago."

"Oh, okay."

"I was raving about the collection to my friend Holly here, and I had to come show her. Don's so nice to take us around and tell us about things."

"Well, it's something to rave about," Sandra said.

Holly chimed in, "It's an amazing collection. Tim described how amazing it is, but I was like, no way. Now that I'm seeing it, I can't get over it."

Sandra smiled and said, "It's kind of a shock to find something like this out here in the middle of a cornfield."

"Yes, exactly," Holly said.

Sandra excused herself to continue bringing in the groceries.

Although I mostly let Holly take the lead in asking questions, I chimed in occasionally. Noticing the label on a fossilized animal skull, I remarked, "Two hundred million years old, huh?"

Miller said, "I dug this up in Morocco. It's from an extinct alligator species. It's a real job digging something like that out of the rock."

Gesturing toward the fossil, Miller added, "I had three or four guys helping me."

I seriously doubted that Morocco had ever granted Miller permission to dig up that fossil and take it out of the country. He had an impressive number of fossils in his collection, but only a few had labels indicating where they came from. Without that key detail, proving whether a particular fossil had been obtained or exported illegally would be nearly impossible.

But every now and then, Miller made things easy. The ancient alligator skull was one such case. Its label, and his own statements about the piece, might offer a path to investigate its origins. The same went for the woolly mammoth tusks he had tagged as coming from Alberta, Canada. His documenting of the tusks' provenance might be enough to start pulling at a righteous legal thread.

A small shadowbox leaned against the wall, displaying a few bronze spear tips labeled as ancient Roman. Curious, I asked Miller about them. With a casual shrug, he said, "I dug a grave or two over in Rome," as if he were reminiscing about a routine vacation. I made a mental note—offhand remarks like that had a way of becoming very useful later.

Holly saw some bone thimbles in another shadow box and said, "I'm going to guess that came out of an Indian site."

"An Indian grave," Miller said.

"Oh, a woman's grave?"

Miller said no, it was from a man's grave.

Holly pressed a little more. "I see. Where's that man now? Did you just take these things or did—?"

Realizing he'd said too much, Miller backpedaled. "No, well, see, these were from a soldier's grave."

When Holly admired a knife, Miller described it as "an original Bowie knife and probably a white man's too." Then he shifted gears. "The best artifacts I own are Danish," he declared.

He gestured toward a collection of stone axe heads and other implements. He said he had obtained them in Denmark, where they were remnants of Viking trading networks. Casually, he added that together they were now worth around $700,000.

I tucked that detail away in my mind along with the others, but Miller was already moving on, showing Holly another section of his collection, this time artifacts from Peru.

Gesturing to a woven basket sewing kit, Miller remarked, "I dug this up." Holly's admiration kept him talking, and he revealed that he had excavated it from a woman's grave near Lima. He also mentioned another find: cloth that had once wrapped mummified human remains in Peru.

I let the conversation flow, but internally I was a bit surprised. Don was being much more forthcoming about the origins of these objects than he had been during my first visit. No doubt this was due to Holly's genuine interest and knowledge, and I was glad to have it.

One of the biggest questions lingering in my mind was whether Miller was merely a collector or if he was also trafficking artifacts—selling to other collectors or dealers in addition to digging and buying for himself. As the discussion about the Peruvian material wrapped up, I circled back to something he had mentioned earlier. "That celt collection you said is worth $700,000," I said, feigning curiosity. "I imagine it's pretty lucrative to sell some of this stuff, huh?"

Miller fixed me with a long, searching look. "Are you interested in archaeology?" he asked.

It was a noticeable shift—his tone sharpened, his usual air of ease and eagerness to talk momentarily replaced by something more guarded. For the first time since I'd met him, I wondered if he was piecing things together, if some flicker of realization was telling him that I was more than just a curious visitor. He knew I was an FBI agent—I had been clear about that. But maybe my question was making him reconsider that fact.

Keeping my tone light, I shrugged and said, "I'm fairly well traveled. I always keep an eye out for interesting artifacts for sale when I'm in different countries."

Sensing the change in Miller's demeanor, Holly jumped in before the silence could stretch too long. "What culture is this?" she asked, pointing to a bracelet in a display case.

Her perfectly timed distraction pulled Miller's attention away, giving me a moment to reset.

Miller said, "That came out of China." Then he added, "There's a bone in there."

Indeed, a dirt-compacted section of arm and wrist bone was still inside the bracelet. It had clearly been looted from a grave.

Also among the artifacts from China were miniature models of houses. As I studied them, I knew I needed some confirmation that Miller had obtained them illegally. Feigning forgetfulness, I said, "You told me about these things when I was here before. But I don't recall what you said."

Miller had completely forgotten about my $700,000 question, and without hesitation he gave me exactly what I was looking for. "Well, those are from China," he said. "They make models of their homes to go into the grave with them."

It was invaluable to have this statement on record, along with his comments about the bracelet. Even then, I knew Chinese cultural patrimony laws were among the strictest in the world, and there was little chance these could be possessed legally, particularly if he had excavated them.

The house models in his collection spanned centuries—some from the Han dynasty (206 BCE–220 CE), others from the much later Ming dynasty (1368–1644 CE)—and all were in remarkable condition. These would have been welcome additions at any museum, and Miller had nearly a dozen. I mentally added the models and the bracelet to my growing list of artifacts Miller could not have obtained legally.

As I studied the Chinese artifacts, my eyes landed on a photograph hanging near the display case—Don and Sue, posing at the Great Wall of China. Seizing the moment to reingratiate myself, I smiled and said, "A trip to the Great Wall is on my bucket list."

Miller responded, "China's a pretty good place to go. But let me ask you, what's the worst country in the world, in your opinion?"

"Well, you're probably not going to like this, because of all the wonderful things you have from there, but the worst place I've visited, the most troubled and scary, is Haiti."

Miller agreed about Haiti but said, "No, what I really meant is how you get treated when you're an American traveling somewhere. I went to Vietnam, and I got treated fine. The worst place for an American is France. That's the worst damn place I've seen in my life."

"I've not been to France, sir," I said.

"Don't spend your money," Miller scoffed, before launching into a tirade about how anti-American the French were.

Reading him perfectly, Holly nodded in agreement. "Yeah, I didn't feel very welcome in France either," she said, playing along. With Miller now fully engaged, she smoothly steered the conversation back to the mummy cloth from Peru. As he talked, he once again admitted that he had taken the cloth from graves.

After more than an hour and a half, we had completed a full circuit of the central basement displays, and the collections in the Wyman Research Building, discussing far more artifacts than I could recount here. Though we hadn't seen the human remains the tipsters had described—like the full Native American skeleton supposedly locked in an adjacent room—I hadn't expected Miller to show us that.

What we had gained, however, was just as valuable. Our recordings now held a satisfying number of incriminating statements, and I had a better sense of his potentially illegal collecting activities, all adding weight to the growing case against him.

"Well, Mr. Miller, thanks so much," I said. "I'm sorry we just showed up, but I didn't have any way to call and ask permission. So I didn't know what else to do but knock on your door. I really appreciate your taking time to show these wonderful things to us."

Miller was clearly enjoying our visit and wasn't quite ready to see us out just yet. He began to tell us stories about working with J. Robert Oppenheimer at Los Alamos, saying that Oppenheimer had personally arranged for him to operate the radio that sent the pulse to trigger the Trinity Gadget. Miller went on to claim that he had performed so well at the Bikini Atoll nuclear tests in 1946 that "Oppenheimer owed me something." According to him, this debt resulted in an early discharge and a hefty bonus payment to kick-start his pursuit of electrical engineering degrees.

Back upstairs, we kept trying to say our goodbyes. But Miller eagerly took us to his ham radio room, then out to the garage to show off his prized Indian and Harley-Davidson motorcycles. Miller then led Holly into the living room, excited to show off its contents. Among them were his massive pipe organ and Steinway piano, an exact replica of the derringer John Wilkes Booth used to assassinate Abraham Lincoln, and a section of an ancient Roman mosaic hanging over the fireplace. He said he bought the mosaic from another soldier for $100 while in Italy at the end of World War II. He also gestured to what he insisted was a piece of a wall from Hitler's bunker.

While Miller and Holly talked, I glanced through the doorway at the kitchen table, where several Native American pots sat in various stages of repair. Sandra walked in, and I seized the moment.

"Are you prepping some of these to sell?" I asked casually. It was worth one last attempt to see if Miller was trafficking in Native American artifacts.

Walking toward me, Sandra said, "There's a lady that comes here and helps put these together."

"To sell them?" I asked.

"He doesn't sell," Sandra said flatly.

She was at least ten years younger than her ninety-year-old husband. Not caught up in the thrill of showing off the collection, she seemed a bit more measured. I couldn't help but wonder what she might say to him once we were gone.

A few minutes later, Holly and I had finally said our goodbyes and were back in the Chevy Suburban. I switched off our recording devices and slipped them into my jacket pocket.

As I turned the ignition, I said, "You were a rock star in there, Holly."

Embarrassed, she asked, "Did it go okay? I couldn't tell."

"Nobody could have done a better job of getting him to open up about his stuff."

She paused and said, "He can't be allowed to keep those things. Are you going to be able to take them away from him and repatriate them the way they need to be?"

"I sure hope so."

"And what about the human remains? We don't know about those yet, do we?"

"No, we don't. But thanks to you, we're a lot farther along on both counts."

Three

Trips and Falls

After my visit to Miller's home with Holly in early December, I briefed Leslie Lahr, Greg Massa, and Drew Northern on what we had seen and recorded. Everyone agreed that Miller's collection was troubling, but everyone also saw that doing something about it would be complicated and expensive. Searching Miller's property and seizing objects that were likely unlawful, along with any human remains, would be as large an operation as any ever conducted by the FBI for this type of material. It was going to require a lot of resources to do it right.

In addition to professional support staff, the Indianapolis field office had only about seventy agents at any given time, forty or so in Indianapolis and another thirty or so in satellite offices across Indiana. We were already spread thin handling our national security and criminal case priorities, and Greg Massa was justifiably concerned about any drain on personnel resources in the violent crimes squad.

I shared those concerns. To my mind, at least with regard to the Indianapolis office, this wasn't about launching a long-term criminal enterprise investigation that would drain resources for months or even years. Instead, it was fundamentally a recovery operation that would demand an intense but short-lived commitment of resources. Once the search and seizure were complete, the burden would shift squarely to the art crime team.

Hell, I didn't think the DOJ would have much interest in prosecuting Miller, even if we proved his illicit activities. While charging decisions rested solely with the DOJ, not the FBI, you didn't have to be a US attorney to see that there would be little appetite for prosecuting a ninety-year-old man for what would essentially amount to a property crime. Still, I firmly believed that federal crimes had been committed, and it was our responsibility to act. With the specter of Operation Cerberus Action looming over the bureau, I saw this as a rare chance for the FBI to protect and preserve cultural heritage and offer some form of justice to the communities victimized by Don's looting. The case was an opportunity to turn a page in the FBI's relationship with tribal communities and to send a clear message that this kind of criminal behavior would not go unanswered.

Unless we were going to let this opportunity slip away, we had to search Miller's house and the other buildings on his farm, seizing any material we had good reason to suspect was unlawfully obtained. That obviously pointed straight to a search and seizure warrant.

However, I told the meeting, "I don't think we're really going to need a warrant. I think we can do it all with Miller's consent."

Eyebrows went up around the room, and I laid out my reasoning. At ninety years old and in frail health, Miller knew he didn't have much time left. He also knew he had broken the law in assembling his collection. His statements to Holly and me frequently reflected guilty knowledge, as did his keeping parts of his collection locked away. According to the tipsters, he had admitted to being arrested in foreign countries and having looted objects seized by foreign customs officials.

The last thing he would want was to have his misdeeds exposed in open court. More than that, he would want to protect his second wife, Sandra, from any legal fallout. His local philanthropy and his missionary work suggested that he saw himself as a good person, an upstanding member of his community. And in my experience, people like that usually cooperate with law enforcement.

I finished by saying, "All things considered, Don Miller strikes me as a person who will listen to reason and who will want to do the right thing in other people's eyes. I believe he will consent to let us search his collection and return the things he's looted to where they belong."

Everyone in the meeting understood that obtaining consent was always the better route, if possible. Executing a search warrant came with procedural constraints that could limit our flexibility and tie our hands in ways that cooperation wouldn't.

Drew weighed in thoughtfully. "Assuming we pursue this case, I agree that prosecution of Miller is very unlikely. But that doesn't mean it's off the table. Things could still take that turn if he refuses consent—or if he grants it and later revokes it.

"We also have to think about what happens to the evidence if he refuses consent and you don't have a search and seizure warrant in your back pocket. One of your informants said Miller told them to put the human remains through a wood chipper when he died. If he was willing to say that, he might just try to do it himself or have someone else take care of it for him."

Pausing just a moment to consider his words, Drew continued. "If we have the facts to secure a warrant, tactically we should get it—then try to do things by consent."

There was no arguing with that. But before I could start drafting an affidavit for a search warrant, the field office's leadership had to decide whether to pursue the case. Besides Drew as chief division counsel, an important voice in favor was Kevin Lyons, the assistant special agent in charge (ASAC, pronounced "A-SACK") of the field office's criminal branch. But not everyone agreed with Drew and Kevin. Ultimately the decision was up to Bob Jones, the field office's special agent in charge (SAC, pronounced "S-A-C").

Bob had become the Indianapolis SAC in 2012 and was proving to be a solid leader for the office. I thought he would recognize the value in the case, but I couldn't be entirely confident about that.

Drew later told me, "There were different opinions within the leadership group about whether the office could support the case. There was doubt about straining resources for a case that would probably never result in arrest and prosecution. But there was also concern for the cultural heritage perspective, the FBI's relationship with Native Americans, and the public impact and legacy of the FBI. Kevin thought the Miller case could be very positive in that regard. We gradually reached a consensus that the search would be an all-hands effort for the field office, but the rest of the case would be the art crime team's responsibility. And then Bob decided that we should go ahead, pending budgetary approval and support from headquarters."

Following this decision, with Drew at my side, I briefed Bob in greater detail. The meeting went well, and at the close of it I learned that Bob had a long-standing interest in Native American history and culture. In fact, it had been part of his graduate studies at Syracuse University's Maxwell School of Public Affairs. When I discussed this with Drew, he said he had found it out during his first meeting with Bob. That's when I learned that Drew had a deep personal interest in Native American history and culture too.

In addition, Drew had firsthand experience with repatriating cultural artifacts. During a temporary duty deployment to Iraq from September 2007 to January 2008, he supervised a major crimes task force in Baghdad composed of personnel from US agencies and the Iraqi Ministry of Interior. Among their cases was an investigation into the trafficking of Iraqi antiquities.

Drew and his team helped recover over six hundred artifacts, including a four-thousand-year-old cuneiform tablet linked to the lost city of Irisaĝrig. But what stayed with him the most wasn't the thrill of the recovery. It was the deep, unwavering importance that the Iraqi members of the task force placed on their cultural heritage and their sense of urgency about its repatriation.

The universe has a way of aligning events in strange and unpredictable ways. Had I not been in Indianapolis as an art crime agent when the tip about Miller came in, the field office likely never would have even considered the case and it would have gotten lost in the cracks between federal agencies. Even if another agent in the field office had picked it up, without Bob and the others in their leadership roles at that exact moment, the case almost certainly wouldn't have been approved. Many things had to fall into place for the investigation to move forward, but having Bob Jones and his leadership team in position when it mattered most was one of the luckiest breaks of all.

Despite his many other responsibilities, Drew waded hip-deep into the Miller case and quickly became an indispensable ally. I relied on him constantly as a sounding board, and he never failed to offer something valuable—whether it was a key piece of information, a sharp insight, or a question that cut straight to the heart of an issue. And he always did it with a twinkle in his eye.

At the same time, Drew kept us grounded in our duty. He never let us lose sight of the need to ensure that every step we took would hold up under scrutiny, both in protecting Miller's constitutional rights and in recognizing the very real harms that archaeological looting inflicted on Native American tribes and other cultural communities.

Bob Jones's decision meant the Miller case could move forward. But given its scope and sensitivities, I knew it would be an operation under a microscope. Because of Operation Cerberus Action, because it was an art crime case tied to Native American heritage and Indigenous cultures worldwide, and most of all because it involved human remains, the case would draw many eyes—from inside and outside the bureau.

With the personnel and resources required and the nature of Miller's collection, any full-scale search and seizure operation would attract national and global media coverage. It had the potential to become a culture war flashpoint, igniting protests from Native American activists and counter-protests from Miller's supporters in the local community—not to mention others drawn to the scene for their own reasons. This wouldn't be a normal investigation. It would be an event.

I couldn't screw this up. First and foremost, this was about delivering a measure of justice to the tribes and other cultural groups victimized by Miller's crimes. Given the attention the case was bound to attract, it was also going to be pivotal for the future of the art crime team, either by proving our value or exposing our limitations.

The art crime team was about to enter its tenth year, but in many ways, it remained a team in name only. We were just a dozen agents scattered across the country, coming together only once a year for a three-day training—far less than well-established teams like SWAT or the evidence response team (ERT).

Other specialized teams regularly functioned as *actual teams*. Within the bomb tech program, for instance, SABTs from around the bureau regularly deployed together for major events like the Super Bowl or large post-blast investigations. The art crime team, by contrast, had never been tested in that way.

The initial paperwork for the art crime program bore the ambitious title, "The Rapid Deployment Art Crime Team." The FBI envisioned it as a unit that could swiftly respond to major cases involving art and cultural patrimony, like the 2003 looting of the National Museum of Iraq. But that vision had never been realized. The Miller case would be the team's first full-scale deployment, and I knew in my gut that it would either make or break the team in the FBI's eyes.

Before dawn on Monday, January 6, 2014, I set out on the 575-mile drive east on I-70 to Washington, DC, heading for FBI headquarters, the Hoover Building. Bob Jones had signed off on the Miller case as Indianapolis's SAC, but I wasn't done yet. Not with the amount of resources and funding I was going to need.

Special agents in charge and the most senior headquarters executives are in the top tier of the bureau's nearly fourteen thousand agents and thirty-eight thousand total employees. The typical career path for SACs involves serving in senior positions at FBI headquarters before being assigned to lead a field office, then often returning to another high-level headquarters role before commanding another field office. Because SACs and senior headquarters executives frequently rotate as each other's predecessors and successors, they have both a collegial relationship and a constantly shifting pecking order.

At any given time, SACs belong to an exclusive club—they have the authority to green-light cases in their field offices and report directly to the deputy director. For the most part, however, control of the funding to move cases forward lies with individual programs that ultimately report to senior headquarters executives.

First I needed approval from the assistant director and executive assistant director of the bureau's Criminal Investigative Division (CID).

But securing their approval was just the beginning, because funding for the search and seizure operation had to come from multiple budget pools, each controlled by different divisions and units. For example, funding to deploy evidence response team members stationed outside the Indianapolis division would come from the evidence response team unit (ERTU) at Quantico. Funding to deploy photographers to the scene would come from the operational photography unit (OPU), and so on.

It was up to me to negotiate successfully with all of them. I not only had to plead for financial resources from each of these programs but also had to begin coordinating logistical planning with all the units that would participate in the operation, ensuring everything came together seamlessly.

After a lengthy meeting about funding with Jeff Croake, Bonnie Magness-Gardiner, and the CID executives, I spent a day and a half going around headquarters and introducing myself to the unit chiefs whose cooperation would be crucial to the operation. I also had multiple discussions—both together and separately—with Jeff and Bonnie, covering the many complexities of the operation. Although I had told Jeff and Bonnie over the phone in December, "I'm going to need the whole art crime team in Indy," my thinking had evolved.

For the search itself, I wanted select members of the team, those best suited for the operation on the ground. But once we moved into the next phase—processing evidence and working to establish the cultural affiliation of artifacts and human remains—I expected nearly every member of the team to play a role.

The current art crime team roster had one major expertise gap when it came to the search and seizure. I told Bonnie, "I need someone with collection management experience—someone who understands both evidence collection and the museum storage environment."

Bonnie chuckled. "I've got just the guy for you," she said. "I recently brought an agent onto the team as an adjunct—Jake Archer, out of the Philadelphia field office. And trust me, he keeps reminding me that he joined the FBI specifically to become an art crime team agent. He's a member of the evidence response team, and he's working on a master's in museum studies at Rutgers. I think you should talk to him."

Bonnie's use of the term *adjunct* spoke volumes about the art crime program's status within the bureau. It was an academic term—fitting, given her PhD in archaeology. But no well-established FBI specialty team would ever call prospective members "adjuncts." It was the kind of label that marked the art crime program as a quirky, niche initiative—the smallest specialty team in the bureau, one that many didn't take seriously.

Then again, we hadn't exactly forced them to. The team had yet to do anything that truly turned heads inside the FBI. And most of us knew that until we did, we were on borrowed time.

That afternoon, I called Jake twice and left messages. He got back to me the next morning while I was driving west on I-70, winding through the Appalachian Mountains in southwestern Pennsylvania. The terrain made for a frustrating connection—the call dropped out now and then—but most of the time, Jake's rapid-fire energy and intense enthusiasm for the Miller case came through loud and clear. Bonnie had already given him a brief rundown, but he was eager to hear more—and just as eager to tell me how he thought he could help.

Jake talks a mile a minute—a fist-pumping, high-octane dynamo straight out of Jersey. My Tennessee drawl comes out slower, but I'm a talker too, and our conversation never missed a beat.

Beneath our surface differences, I quickly realized we had a lot in common. We were born more or less in the same generation, although Jake is a few years younger. We had both started out as local cops—Jake in New Jersey, me in South Carolina. And we'd both developed a strong interest in art growing up.

From the time I was a little kid, I liked to draw. I started out drawing comic book characters and Dungeons & Dragons scenes, then progressed to sketching portraits of family members and friends and even painting some. That side of me—my hands-on approach and problem-solving mindset—got an early boost from learning carpentry and woodworking from my maternal grandfather. It also found another outlet in drumming, much to the disdain of everyone around me. For a while, I thought I might become an artist, until military and law enforcement service took me on another path.

My first field office assignment after graduating from the FBI

Academy in Quantico, Virginia, in June 2004 was Louisville, Kentucky. The next summer, I was among the agents who answered a call for volunteers to help search the home of a man suspected of stealing Revolutionary War and Civil War–era documents from Louisville's Filson Historical Society. The search confirmed his guilt. It was also my first inkling that the FBI even handled art crime cases. It wasn't until later that I learned the bureau had an art crime program. And as soon as I knew, I wanted in.

In Louisville I was also part of the Joint Terrorism Task Force, which made sense based on my background as a bomb technician. As my luck would have it, one of my earliest cases developed into a high-stakes operation handling a deep-cover asset who infiltrated a terrorist organization. For obvious reasons, that's about all I can say on the matter.

As a bomb technician, I was accustomed to handling high-stress situations. But it was much harder to cope with the relentless stress of running an operation of this kind, lying awake at night worrying what would happen if we lost control of things. Still, that was a great, if challenging, experience and one that I'm proud to have been part of.

Thanks to former FBI director Bob Mueller's infamous mandatory transfer policy, I was unexpectedly reassigned from Louisville to the Miami field office after nearly four years in Kentucky. Honestly, I didn't mind the move. After years in the military, I was used to relocating at the government's whim. And after grinding away on that counterterrorism case for so long, I needed a break. The only thing I asked for with the transfer was to go back to working criminal cases—just like I had as a cop.

So in the summer of 2007, freshly married, Risa and I headed to Miami. Unfortunately for me, the powers that be weren't too interested in honoring their promise to move me to a criminal program. Instead, I landed right back on the Joint Terrorism Task Force. Frustrated but not deterred, I dug in and got back to work on counterterrorism cases.

After about a year, I finally managed to shift to the criminal side of the field office, working cargo theft cases. I let the head of the major theft squad know I was eager for any art crime cases that came along, and before long, I got my shot. With Bonnie's blessing, I officially joined the art crime team.

In his own boyhood, Jake loved to watch one of his grandfathers doing pen-and-ink drawings and other artwork. He'd begun collecting art as a teenager when a local gallery let him help out during events, and he was fascinated by the art world. Leaving his police work behind, Jake had gone to law school and worked for a law firm in Trenton, New Jersey. But he still had the law enforcement bug. One day, he ran across a description of the art crime program on the bureau's website. That inspired him to apply to the FBI and leave lawyering behind.

Jake had been an agent for almost five years, primarily working drug and gang cases, with a collateral duty assignment on the evidence response team. Since 2012, he'd been pitching in on art crime cases in the Philly field office, working alongside another art crime team agent, Donny Asper. At the time of our call, Jake was writing his master's thesis in Rutgers University's cultural heritage and preservation studies program. His topic was the care and handling of art in a law enforcement context. As part of that, he was interning at the Princeton University Art Museum.

"You're tailor-made for the Miller case," I told him. "What do you say to coming out to Indy to get the lay of the land and help me plan this search and seizure operation?"

"Hell, yes!" Jake shot back. "That's what I say."

In the Indy field office the next day, SAC Bob Jones, Drew Northern, Greg Massa, Leslie Lahr, Administrative Officer Diana Ryll (head of the professional support staff), and I attended a coordination meeting led by ASAC Kevin Lyons. With budgetary approval in place, we targeted mid-February for the search and seizure operation, with all field office hands on deck.

The first of many questions I had to answer was how much material we needed to seize. Following the age-old adage of planning for the worst, I had to start with the presumption that we would seize everything—however unlikely that scenario might actually be. The last thing we could afford was to grossly underestimate the number of artifacts and find ourselves without enough packaging materials or personnel to handle the job.

Remember, my rough estimate was that Miller's collection contained around forty thousand objects. Considering that the FBI had never attempted a seizure on this scale before, it was no surprise when I was asked how long it would take to properly document, photograph, condition report, package, and transport forty thousand artifacts.

I had no idea. But knowing we needed an answer, I ran some quick mental calculations and estimated that it would take thirty days. On its face, that was an absurd number. No federal magistrate in the country would sign off on a search warrant that displaced someone from their home for that long—especially not for these types of offenses. And even if they did, the FBI wasn't about to dedicate resources for a full month on an art crime case, no matter how significant.

Taking a more realistic approach, I adjusted my estimate. Assuming we would seize, at most, roughly half of Miller's collection—and that we would work in shifts around the clock—I revised the timeline to a more manageable ten days. Manageable, but far from ideal.

It didn't take long to realize that targeting February for the operation wasn't going to cut it. Coordinating the logistics and personnel alone would take time, and there were other obstacles that made moving that fast impossible.

Before long, we had to push our target search date back to sometime in March, possibly even early April. One major roadblock? To take a search warrant application to a federal magistrate, I needed approval from the US Attorney's Office for the Southern District of Indiana. And there I hit a bit of a stone wall. But I'll get to that later.

Combined with the demands of our respective day jobs, the delay also forced Jake and me to postpone his planned visit to Indianapolis. In the meantime, we did as much planning as possible over the phone, working through contingencies and trying to keep momentum going.

Even before I took Holly to visit Miller in early December, I told Drew, "If we wind up with a viable case, we're going to need a good understanding of Native American perspectives. I'm going to want to consult members of the tribes on how we should treat their cultural heritage—and even more so any ancestral human remains. I'm hoping Holly will help with that. But I don't want to leave any stone unturned."

Drew said, "There's a graduate of our FBI Citizens Academy we should talk to. Her name is Charmayne Champion-Shaw, although she goes by Charli. Charli's a member of the Southern Cheyenne, part of the Cheyenne and Arapaho Tribes in Oklahoma. She's the director of the Native American Studies Program at IUPUI, so Holly must know her. Charli is really a wonderful person. I'm sure she'd at least be willing to talk to us and give us some pointers."

The FBI Citizens Academy was a headquarters-mandated, field office–led initiative conducted in every field office across the bureau. When Drew joined the Indianapolis field office in 1997, he significantly expanded the Citizens Academy program while managing media and community affairs—on top of his role as chief division counsel.

Over the course of a two-month period, the Citizens Academy met for four hours once a week, offering participants an inside look at how the FBI operates. The highlight for most? A culminating trip to the firing range to fire a wide array of current and historical firearms used by FBI agents.

In addition to giving classroom presentations on the special agent bomb technician program, I usually took part in the range visits, putting on explosives demonstrations and blowing up a car or two. That, unsurprisingly, was always a crowd-pleaser.

Another fan favorite of the Citizens Academy was the Firearms Training System (FATS), a state-of-the-art virtual reality simulator designed to test decision-making under pressure. Using realistic scenarios projected onto a large screen, FATS placed participants in tense, split-second situations that law enforcement officers often face in the field. Armed with laser-modified firearms that mimicked the weight and recoil of real weapons, they had to decide—immediately—whether to fire, hold their ground, or take cover.

Most were unprepared for just how difficult those decisions were. The results were telling—90 percent of participants fired inappropriately, shooting an unarmed person who posed no threat. Others hesitated when they shouldn't have, failing to react to an actual threat and getting themselves "killed" in the simulation. It was an eye-opening experience, leaving many with a deeper appreciation for the complexity of use-of-force decisions in real-world law enforcement.

Charli had gone through the Citizens Academy before I transferred to the Indianapolis field office, and the fact that she'd graduated with positive views of today's FBI was a great benefit. Beyond that, Drew told me he had learned a great deal from his candid discussions with her—particularly about the American Indian Movement (AIM) and the government's past use of the FBI to infiltrate AIM and counter its activism. They had talked about the deadly clashes on both sides during AIM's protests and occupations at Wounded Knee and elsewhere on the Pine Ridge Reservation in the mid-1970s—events that remained painful memories for both Native American communities and the FBI.

In its early engagement with the tribal community, there were actions the FBI could not be proud of, just as there were in the government's deployment of the bureau during the civil rights movement. Like American soldiers in the Vietnam War, FBI agents in the field were oftentimes caught in the pincers of history along with their counterparts on the other side. Sadly, the same may hold true today.

The FBI wasn't the root cause of what happened with AIM. The events of the 1970s reflected a broader national struggle to reckon with the often brutal legacy of Manifest Destiny and the government's long history of unjust policies toward Native Americans. Still, when I talked with Drew and other agents about the need to turn the page in the FBI's relationship with Native communities, those AIM-era incidents were among the things I had in mind.

With approval and funding for the Miller case secured, we invited Charli and Holly to a meeting at the field office. We laid out our plans for the search and seizure operation and asked if they'd be willing to reach out to contacts in the Native American community on our behalf. We wanted the community to know that we were investigating a major collection of Native American cultural property and that we welcomed their input and guidance on how to proceed. I dare say that bringing the tribal community in to consult at the beginning of an investigation was unprecedented, and it helped to set the stage for a shift in our relationships with the various nations.

Despite Charli's packed schedule—completing her PhD in social work and social justice at Indiana University's flagship campus in Bloomington while working full-time at IUPUI—and Holly's own demanding commitments, both graciously agreed to help. They also suggested bringing in their senior colleague, Larry Zimmerman, an IUPUI professor of anthropology and museum studies who had strong relationships with Native American tribal elders in Indiana and the Upper Midwest.

Over the winter, Charli, Holly, and Larry laid a strong foundation for my direct engagement with the Native American community. They let us know what they were hearing in their conversations and also provided insights drawn from their own experience and research. For example, Charli was the first to advise us on Native American sensitivities about photographing the dead or their remains. For a law enforcement operation and evidence recovery effort, thorough documentation and photography of any Native American remains recovered from Miller's collection was necessary. At the same time, we were committed to handling the process with the utmost respect, ensuring it was done in a culturally appropriate and sensitive manner. These were people, not merely evidence, and I was determined that we would treat them with dignity.

This case was full of daunting challenges, but I will always be grateful for the extraordinary allies who stepped up to help—Drew, Charli, Holly, Larry, and, not least of all, Jake Archer. And they were just the beginning. Countless others, both inside and outside the bureau, played critical roles in making this case possible.

Early in the morning on Monday, February 10, 2014, Jake arrived at the Indianapolis field office. A buff, fist-bumping, Bruce Springsteen–loving, wisecracking guy, he stood about five feet ten with every hair on his head perfectly in place. He'd rarely visited the Midwest, and it showed.

As rapid-fire in person as he was on the phone, he said, "Great to finally meet in person, Tim. You said I gotta be ready for those brutal winds coming down from Lake Michigan, but it's not much colder here than in Philly. And there's no wind to speak of. I'm breaking a sweat in this heavy coat."

"Did you look at the forecast for the rest of the week?" I asked, smiling. "Maybe you should hold that thought."

In a few minutes, we were in my Chevy Suburban headed for a discreet drive-by of the Miller farm. On the way, our conversation bounced between the many elements of the operation we needed to plan—everything from ensuring the safety of our team and the Millers to protecting the artifacts and human remains we'd be seizing.

"Tim, it just hit me," Jake said, nearly bursting with enthusiasm. "The Indianapolis Museum of Art has one of the absolute masters of art packing and crating. His name is Jesse Speight. I learned about him in my Rutgers program. This guy is amazing. He builds these crates with double-butt joints that can float for hours without a drop of water getting in. We gotta meet him and pick his brains."

"We'll look him up at the museum tomorrow. Maybe we can hire him to work on the op."

"That'd be awesome." Jake was like a little kid who was going to meet his favorite superhero.

Heading west on State Road 244, we turned south on South County Road 850 West and slowly drove past the Miller compound on the right. Jake swiveled his head around to keep the compound in sight as long as possible. When South 850 West T-boned into West County Road 900 South, I made a U-turn.

Jake peered up at the intersection road sign, shaking his head slightly. "These road designations out here are something, man."

"It all goes with the farmland grid, Jake."

"Yeah, yeah, yeah. I get it," he said. "Miller's is the only house on his side of the road, and there are just those two other houses farther south on the other side of the road, right?"

"Right."

"So, if we shut this road down with checkpoints north and south, and only let the people from the two other houses through, we won't have to worry about anybody disturbing the integrity of the search."

"Sure," I said. "Assuming we can get the personnel. We can't waste agents on checkpoint duty, and I doubt the county sheriff or the state police can lend us enough officers to secure the site for ten days, 24/7."

As we cruised by the Miller compound again, Jake craned his head to fix the layout in his mind's eye.

Back at the field office, I introduced Jake to some of the agents and support professionals we'd be working with closely. For a streetwise New Yorker like Greg Massa, Jake's high-energy style was nothing out of the ordinary, and Drew took it in stride.

But for some of my more laid-back Midwestern colleagues, his natural intensity was a bit unexpected. Jake was nothing but friendly and engaging, but his fast-talking, high-octane approach was different from what they were used to. I wondered if I might need to help bridge the gap as everyone adjusted to each other's styles.

For the next couple of hours, Jake and I brainstormed operational logistics, hashing out details and troubleshooting potential challenges. The day only reinforced what I had sensed during our phone calls. Despite our surface differences, we were kindred spirits when it came to this kind of work.

First thing the next morning, we began making the rounds of the major area museums—the Indianapolis Museum of Art (IMA), the Eiteljorg Museum of American Indians and Western Art, and the Children's Museum of Indianapolis—with two goals. One was to line up subject matter experts to assist with the search; the other was to ask if any of the museums could provide storage space for whatever we seized.

When we asked about storage space, every museum person we spoke to immediately put their guard up. And when they heard we needed space for thousands of objects, the answer was always an immediate and unequivocal no. I wasn't surprised.

At the IMA, we had a good talk with Jesse Speight, whose expertise and wry sense of humor impressed us both. He not only had a number of crates he could give us (rather than breaking them down for disposal) but was also genuinely intrigued by our operation and eager to be involved.

In the following days I signed him to a consulting contract to oversee and lead the packing of artifacts and human remains during the search. Working under him would be a team of Holly's museum studies students, participating as volunteers.

As luck would have it, while we were at the IMA meeting with Jesse and the rest of the team there, I received an unexpected phone call from the Indianapolis Metro Police Department (IMPD) bomb squad commander. They were en route to investigate an apparent improvised explosive device (IED) left behind at the scene of a bank robbery.

"We have to roll, Jake," I said.

"What's up?"

"Bomb tech call."

"Really?"

Jake was almost as excited as he'd been about meeting Jesse Speight. He wisecracked, "Tell you what. I'll stay in the car, and if you get blown up, I'll help process the scene."

"You do that."

These situations aren't like what you see in movies and on TV, where the FBI storms in and takes over. That's kind of nonsense. This was the IMPD bomb squad's operation. I was there to advise unless circumstances dictated otherwise.

Traditionally, bank robberies have been a staple of FBI jurisdiction, dating back to the days of J. Edgar Hoover. However, local law enforcement often handles them unless there's a federal nexus. In this case, the presence of a suspected IED raised the stakes and increased the likelihood that the case would be handled federally—which is why I was there.

The essence of explosive ordnance disposal is to operate safely, taking no unnecessary risks. The squad commander briefed me: The bank robber had shown the device to a teller before leaving it behind as he fled. The bank had been evacuated, and now the question was whether the device was real or, more likely, a hoax.

After a brief discussion, a bomb-suited squad member carried a remote-controlled water cannon into the bank, aiming it at the suspected bomb—a section of PVC pipe. Once he exited, the device was triggered, and a high-pressure jet of water blasted the pipe apart, rendering it harmless.

Once the device was rendered safe, we went inside to process the scene—yes, Jake insisted on coming along, pointing to his role as an evidence response team member. He wasn't about to miss the action.

The suspected bomb turned out to be a fairly convincing hoax, nothing more. With the scene processed and the immediate threat neutralized, we left the crime scene behind and shifted gears, back to the long list of challenges in the Miller case.

The day had started out cold and became steadily colder. It was now in the low teens, with twenty-mile-an-hour winds. Jake was blowing into his hands and holding them in front of the heating vent on the passenger side of the dashboard.

"Would you rather be in Philadelphia?" I asked.

"Hell, no. But at least back there we've got some trees to block the wind a little."

"I warned you, brother. I warned you."

It might seem odd that Jake and I were deep into planning the Miller search when we weren't even sure we could secure a warrant, but across the whole of law enforcement, that's fairly standard practice. For large-scale takedowns, it's common to plan logistics well in advance while securing arrest and search warrants at the last minute—sometimes just a day before or even the day of.

I was used to that kind of stress. It came with the job.

In fact, my life had given me plenty of preparation for planning and executing complex operations under pressure. I've already mentioned how my maternal grandfather, Paul, taught me carpentry and woodworking. But even before I was old enough to use tools under his direction, I loved helping him solve the big jigsaw puzzles he always had in progress. That problem-solving mindset stuck with me.

Throughout my childhood and teenage years, I was the kid who took things apart—toys, radios, televisions, engines, computers, electronic game consoles—and then put them back together, always making sure they still worked. I didn't just want to see how things functioned; I wanted to understand how all the pieces fit together.

My grandfather and uncles were rough-and-ready pranksters—not malicious, just the kind who believed in teaching lessons the hard way. When I was eight, they tossed me into a pigpen with a baseball bat and told me to clobber the pig for that weekend's cookout. I was covered in mud by the time they stopped laughing long enough to pull me out. Of course, they had a different method of dealing with the pig.

At thirteen, they taught me another lesson—this time about electricity. I learned firsthand why you should never touch a spark plug while pushing the starter button on a motorbike. More important, I learned not to take everything someone tells me at face value. Things like that were good life lessons if you were resilient enough to take them the right way.

After graduating high school in June 1990, I had ambitious plans to pursue my fledgling art career. I intended to go to Memphis College of Art on a scholarship alongside one of my closest friends. But the start of the Gulf War that August changed everything—not just for me but for many young men and women across the country.

Inspired by *Top Gun*, I initially set my sights on a US Navy program for prospective aviators. That plan didn't last long. Once I realized they were going to make me a regular swab instead of sending me straight to flight school, I reconsidered. The US Air Force recruiter, on the other hand, was more straightforward.

My high scores on the enlistment aptitude and intelligence tests gave me my pick of (nonflight) specialty programs. Sitting in the recruiting office, flipping through a massive binder of options, I came across Explosive Ordnance Disposal (EOD) School. I stopped, pointed, and asked, "What's EOD?"

The recruiter chuckled and said, "Oh, those guys? You don't want to do that. They disarm bombs and play with explosives for a living. Those guys are all crazy."

I smiled and said, "That's it. I'll take that one."

The recruiter couldn't believe my choice, but I knew it was the right one for me.

At the time, EOD training had one of the highest attrition rates of any military specialty. Its unofficial motto was, and still is, "Initial Success or Total Failure." The program demanded technical precision, intense mental and physical resilience, and the ability to perform under extreme pressure.

The training lasted a full year, covering an expansive curriculum, from the most rudimentary explosives to sophisticated nuclear weapons. EOD wasn't just about technical expertise; it required adaptability. An EOD tech had to be prepared to neutralize threats in any environment: on a battlefield, at sea, in the desert, deep in the jungle, or even in urban settings crowded with civilians. Success meant lives were saved. Failure wasn't an option.

And that was exactly the challenge I wanted.

After completing EOD school, I was stationed in southern Georgia, where my work primarily involved training and occasional callouts for pipe bombs and deteriorated dynamite. But my role wasn't confined to stateside operations—I also deployed to Saudi Arabia and Kuwait in support of Desert Shield and Desert Storm.

When my initial tour of active duty ended, I transitioned to the US Air Force Reserve, balancing military service while attending college and eventually becoming a police officer in South Carolina. For a time, I thought my path was set, building a career in law enforcement while keeping one foot in the military.

Then came 9/11.

Like for so many others, my world shifted that day. I was recalled to active duty and began preparations for deployment to Afghanistan, answering a call that would profoundly change the course of my life. That, however, is a story for another time.

Above all, my EOD training and experience honed my ability to plan and execute complex operations under intense pressure. As an EOD technician, I wasn't just responsible for disarming explosive devices. I also planned and led major field exercises, coordinated range clearances, and managed large-scale operations where meticulous preparation and adaptability were critical. Every mission required assessing risks, deploying resources effectively, and executing plans with precision, often in high-stakes environments where failure wasn't an option.

That skill set carried over seamlessly into my FBI career. In addition to responding to real-world threats, I regularly deployed to major events as part of the bureau's bomb tech team. For Super Bowl XLVI in February 2012, held in Indianapolis, I helped with the planning and coordination of the counterexplosives program, ensuring seamless integration with other FBI assets and law enforcement partners. The same was true for the Indianapolis 500, which required extensive planning every year I worked in the Indy field office.

Whether securing a major event, coordinating large-scale searches, or executing complex field operations, the principles were the same: anticipate problems, allocate resources efficiently, and get the job done under pressure. Those lessons, forged in EOD school and reinforced in every mission I took on, were what I drew on while planning the Miller case.

Of the thousand things that Jake and I had to worry about, we were seriously stressing out about trip-and-fall hazards in the Miller residence and the rest of the property. It was all too easy to envision someone carrying a five-thousand-year-old artifact and then tripping on the carpeted stairs from the basement of the residence, or colliding with someone going around a corner. To reduce the risk of accidents, we had to limit the number of people in the house at any given time. But with only ten days to complete the search, we had to seize more material each day than the last. We were going to need a solid plan.

On Thursday, February 10, we wrapped up a long day's work with a late dinner at a downtown steakhouse and sports bar. Sipping our beers, we discussed how to prevent trips and falls without falling behind on our schedule. Jake grabbed a cocktail napkin and began sketching an operational plan, while I gave input on what I thought was needed. Seeing it take shape, we realized we had the foundation we needed: a carefully choreographed system to coordinate FBI agents, support staff, subject matter experts, and student volunteers as they moved seized materials through registration, photography, and packing stations. That rough schematic on a napkin became the blueprint for our plan.

Jake had met Holly earlier in the week, and the three of us had already put our heads together a few times. I felt good about our core team—Jake, Holly, Drew, and me—but I had some concerns about how Jake's Jersey Shore style would affect the rest of the search team, most of them laid-back Midwesterners who took things a bit more slowly.

Jake and I were already hitting it off well and developing a good-natured rapport. As we wrapped up dinner, I razzed him a bit. "Jake, your fist-bumping, Bruce Springsteen-worshipping approach might work great with your squad mates in Philly, but this is the Midwest. Things are more low-key here. For the sake of everyone's sanity, you'll need to dial it back when you return for the search. No Springsteen solos."

"Yeah, yeah, yeah. I get it," Jake said, an ear-to-ear grin spreading across his face. After the briefest of pauses he added a bit more seriously, "Don't worry. I got it."

His rapid-fire response told me this would be a challenge, but I suspected he'd do his best to meet it. So far I was impressed with Jake Archer, and Bonnie's suggestion to bring him on as a co–case agent seemed spot-on. We were going to get along just fine.

We spent most of Friday before Jake's flight home refining our cocktail napkin plan. There were plenty of issues to resolve, but it was coming together. After Jake left, we stayed in touch by phone, ticking off items on our punch list while juggling our regular bureau duties.

We also checked in regularly with Holly, relying on her expert input as we planned the search. That covered everything from estimating the number of archival boxes we'd need to coordinating how her grad students could help collect and package artifacts to identifying and engaging other subject matter experts from the tribal, academic, and museum communities.

One area of concern was the potential contamination of some organic artifacts with arsenic. In the first half of the twentieth century, collectors had treated textiles, leather, and items containing human hair with arsenic to preserve them and prevent pests. Holly knew an archaeologist at the University of Georgia who specialized in detecting such contamination using a portable X-ray fluorescence device, which could analyze the elemental composition of materials without damaging them. It was an easy decision to arrange for him to be one of the search contingent's subject matter experts.

Among the biggest items on my growing punch list was ensuring the integrity of the search site. I still hoped and expected that Miller would consent to the search and the seizure of problematic material. But regardless of his cooperation, the site would remain a crime scene and had to be treated as such, with a secure chain of custody for everything.

We couldn't divert agents from search and oversight tasks to securing the site. Although the Indiana State Police and the small Rush County Sheriff's Office planned to assign a few troopers and deputies to assist us, we still needed more personnel to staff checkpoints and maintain 24/7 security.

During my time in Miami, I'd gotten to know Noel Gil, an agent on the major theft squad. As I was busy building out my case on Don Miller, Noel was returning to the Miami field office after an eighteen-month stint at headquarters as a supervisory special agent, serving as assistant chief of the FBI police. Unlike FBI special agents, FBI police officers are uniformed federal law enforcement officers responsible for securing FBI facilities, protecting personnel, and responding to threats at key bureau locations, including headquarters, the FBI Academy and Lab in Quantico, the bureau's information hubs in West Virginia, and the Washington, DC, and New York City field offices. (All other field offices use private security.) They also deploy to major events like presidential inaugurations and the Super Bowl. But I had never heard of them being involved in a standard FBI case.

I was on a brief catch-up call with Noel one weekend when I mentioned my personnel problem. "Why don't you use the FBI police?" Noel asked.

"Is that possible?"

"If you've got the funding, they'll send you some officers," Noel said. "The uniformed cops get bored just checking doors and such."

None of us had ever heard of using the FBI police in this way, but it was a welcome insight that helped solve our perimeter security challenge. I took Noel's suggestion, and soon we had a few FBI police officers lined up to handle site security, working alongside a few state troopers and sheriff's deputies.

My unexpected issues didn't stop with perimeter security. Feeding a search team wasn't something we typically had to worry about, but this case was different. The length of time we'd be at Miller's house, the pace of work, and the site's remote location made it a real concern. Local restaurants or other food sources were too far away to be a convenient option, and even with three shifts running around the clock for ten days, there wouldn't be time to send people off-site for meals. We also couldn't expect everyone, including student volunteers, to brown-bag it or work eight-hour shifts without a proper meal break. Since we were already planning to set up latrines and a medical tent, adding a chow tent and supplying the food just made sense.

When I told the Indy admin staff I wanted to provide food in the middle of every shift, they said it was impossible.

"Why?"

"Congress passed a law against spending appropriated funds on food or services for government employees."

That made sense to prevent abuse. On the other hand, plenty of government employees attended formal dinners at the White House or the State Department that the government paid for.

"There's got to be some leeway," I said. "Ask around and find out."

A few days later they said, "You have to get special approval from Congress and the Government Accountability Office."

They thought that would be the end of it. Instead I said, "Fine, what Congress member do we have to call?"

The admin people looked at each other uncertainly.

"We just need to bring in sandwiches and burritos twice a day," I said. "That shouldn't be impossible."

It wasn't. With the help of FBI headquarters staff, our admins got the right forms to the right staffer at the Government Accountability Office, and we were able to budget a few thousand dollars for mid-shift meals. The proviso was that all FBI personnel from outside the Indy field office had to deduct the lunch portion of their daily expense allowance, so taxpayers weren't paying double for anybody's meal.

Miller's fragile health was a major concern. His collection had been the focus of his life's work for decades, and the stress of our arrival to remove a significant portion of it could take a serious toll on him. The last thing any of us wanted was to cause Miller to have a heart attack or stroke. To ensure his well-being, we arranged to have an ambulance on-site when the search began and on standby for the duration of the operation.

Food, bathrooms, security, and medical support were just the beginning of our planning challenges. While all of these were essential for a successful operation, the real test lay in the collection itself. Its sheer size, scope, and condition presented significant obstacles we would have to navigate carefully.

From my second visit to Miller's, I knew we would need to handle human remains and artifacts separately. Figuring out how to do that determined many of the steps in the ballet that Holly, Jake, and I were choreographing.

As planning progressed, we realized that seizing most of Miller's collection was both impractical and unnecessary. For example, arrowheads collected from the surface of public land are generally legal, and with thousands in his collection, there was no way to determine which were surface finds and which were not. Given these complexities, we adjusted our expectations for the scope of the seizure and mapped out a triage procedure to quickly identify unlawful and potentially unlawful objects. We settled on a red/yellow/green classification system: red for items clearly unlawful to possess, yellow for those that were probably unlawful, and green for those that could be presumed lawful. Marking individual pieces appropriately would allow us to move more efficiently, leaving anything labeled green alone and focusing our efforts on the red and yellow items.

The sheer size of Miller's collection was our biggest challenge. While not completely unheard of, it is highly unusual to seize ten to twenty thousand of anything—let alone priceless artifacts, some thousands of years old. Handling such a vast quantity of evidence required a level of organization, efficiency, and recordkeeping beyond that of a typical FBI case.

The FBI uses several forms to document the seizure of evidence, but the two primary ones are the FD-192 and the FD-1004, both of which track chain of custody. Bureau personnel commonly refer to these as "green sheets," a holdover from when they were printed on green paper.

If we ended up seizing thousands of objects, that meant completing thousands of green sheets, signing each one multiple times, and entering all of them into Sentinel, the FBI's new case management system. I didn't have time to scrawl tens of thousands of signatures, and even with a dedicated team, inputting that many forms into Sentinel would take weeks. Adding to the challenge, Sentinel, the centerpiece of a $500 million IT overhaul, was still relatively new—and not yet as robust as it needed to be for an operation of this scale.

On a conference call, Jake and I found ourselves caught between three different FBI units, each with a different perspective on how to handle the sheer volume of evidence we expected to seize. The evidence response team unit (ERTU) insisted that every artifact had to be treated as an individual evidence item, requiring separate chain of custody documentation and classification as valuable evidence. That meant completing thousands of green sheets, each with three signatures, for every single item.

The evidence control unit (ECU) at Quantico and I both objected. Just as I didn't have time to sign tens of thousands of documents, they had no interest in receiving that many forms or spending weeks manually entering them into the system. Then the Sentinel team at headquarters weighed in, warning that trying to input such a massive volume of evidence at once could overload the system, potentially disrupting case management across the entire bureau.

Despite these concerns, ERTU wouldn't budge. For them, strict adherence to procedure outweighed the practical realities of the case.

It was one of the most ridiculous meetings of my FBI career. On one hand, I was being told that I *had* to do something. On the other hand (well, two hands, actually), I was being told I *couldn't* do it.

After I diplomatically told the ERTU people to pound sand and thanked the others for their time, Jake and I got back on the phone together. He then sent me an Excel spreadsheet with all the necessary data fields for valuable evidence items: a basic description of the item, the date and location of seizure, the seizing agent, and so on.

It was a start but far from a perfect solution. There was no way multiple people could efficiently fill out complex spreadsheets in the field without inevitably entering data in the wrong fields. We needed something more structured to keep the process organized without creating an administrative nightmare.

In my military life, I had used Microsoft Access, a database tool that allows users to populate tailor-made fields, to build training programs. Drawing on that experience, I spent the next couple of weeks working with Access until I had an evidence registration system that looked viable and ran it by Jake. He agreed that it would do exactly what we needed it to do.

Next I filled out a request for deviation on evidence—because, of course, the FBI has a form for everything—and submitted it to the ECU chief for approval. Once signed off, the deviation allowed us to input any number of evidence items into an Access file and then enter that file into Sentinel under a single green sheet. It was a practical solution that cut down on paperwork while still meeting the bureau's chain of custody requirements.

Day by day the prospective operation expanded to draw in more FBI resources and personnel. The bigger it got, the more it seemed to grate on Greg Massa's nerves. He never objected outright, but every time I updated him on the plan, the "you've got to be shitting me" look on his face said plenty. I couldn't blame him. Greg had enough on his plate managing the day-to-day violent crime problem, and I knew that this was a headache he didn't want to dedicate time and energy to.

On the other hand, ERTU at Quantico was determined to be involved—on their terms. This was the same unit that had insisted I fill out twenty thousand green sheets.

ERTU oversees evidence recovery teams in the field, made up of both FBI agents and professional support staff. These teams are routinely deployed across the country to assist field offices with evidence collection, following a rigid twelve-step forensic protocol—the kind of methodical process you'd see on *CSI* or similar crime shows. But this wasn't that kind of case. We weren't dusting for fingerprints, collecting blood spatter, or swabbing for DNA. Besides, every FBI agent is trained in evidence recovery, and art crime team members would be leading our collection efforts. We needed a flexible, practical approach, not a scripted forensic playbook.

If dealing with their rigid protocols wasn't bad enough, ERTU also objected to evidence collection outside daylight hours, citing trip-and-fall safety concerns. I couldn't believe it. We were bringing in lights and generators, and everyone else was willing to work evening and night shifts. In early April in Indiana, it was dark by 6 p.m. If we limited ourselves to daylight hours, we'd be there for a month.

I didn't want ERTU involved. But they were part of the FBI's case support structure, and Indy field office leadership wanted them included. So did Jake.

As an evidence response team member back in Philly, Jake was loyal to the program and pushed for their involvement. That said, he also knew we had justifiable exceptions to the normal ERTU procedures. So we made major adjustments, streamlining the process to focus only on what was necessary to get the job done.

For example, I compromised and changed the operational plan from 24/7 to 16/7—two eight-hour shifts from 6 a.m. to 2 p.m. and 2 p.m. to 10 p.m., with FBI police securing the site overnight from 10 p.m. to 6 a.m. It wasn't ideal, but it kept the operation on track.

That schedule aligned with the usual 6 a.m. to 10 p.m. federal law enforcement window for executing warrants—a safeguard meant to prevent searches and seizures from unreasonably disrupting people in their homes. But in this case, it significantly tightened our already limited time frame, adding another layer of pressure to the operation.

Despite the countless obstacles we had to navigate, by early March we had a solid operational plan. While Jake and I would continue refining it, we felt we had plugged any major gaps.

What was tripping us up was the lack of a warrant. The US Attorney's Office didn't believe we had sufficient probable cause to justify searching Miller's collection and seizing problematic objects. Without their approval, everything we had meticulously planned—every logistical detail, every contingency—hung in limbo, threatening to unravel before we even got started.

Four

Probable Cause

Seated at her desk, Melissa Curtis, an assistant United States attorney for the Southern District of Indiana, shook her head. "Tim," she said, "I can see how you have probable cause to seize the Spanish cannon, along with a few dozen other objects, based on what you and your subject matter expert observed and from what the two of you elicited from Miller. However, you're contemplating taking thousands of objects you have no specific information on."

"That's true," I replied. "But again, there was no way we could ask Miller about everything in his collection. That would literally take weeks. Besides, we can't keep going back to ask about stuff without arousing his suspicions. And he's so old and frail, he might not live much longer. Either scenario could lead to evidence being dispersed or destroyed. The clock is ticking on this thing. But two-thirds of the objects we did have time to ask about led to statements that indicate unlawful possession. I think that pattern is clear."

"A good defense lawyer would attack that argument in court."

"Maybe so. But you and I both know this case is unlikely to go to trial."

Melissa grimaced. "That's part of the problem here. This office's number one priority is to prosecute cases, and as many successful cases as possible. My bosses make that clear every day."

"I understand that. My bosses would prefer a viable path to prosecution too. This case is outside of everybody's wheelhouse. It doesn't fit with any of our normal performance metrics. But we've still got to do the right thing here, especially about the Native American human remains."

"Drew Northern said the same thing," Melissa said. "I agree with you both and I want to help you, if I can. Those pictures of skulls are definitely troubling." She paused, before adding, "But no one knows how long Miller is going to live, and we have to respect his rights as a suspect and a citizen. He could fight this legally, and you need to have a strong basis for any seizures you want to make."

"We think we do," I said. "Like I've been saying, Miller has commingled lawful and unlawful objects in his collection, and you can't tell which is which on the spot. Only careful investigation and analysis can determine that.

"And once again, there are plenty of situations where a lawful search warrant allows for the seizure of additional, similar items found in the same location. Suppose we traced the dissemination of child sexual abuse material to a specific laptop in someone's home. A search warrant would authorize the seizure of that laptop, but if we discovered another similar laptop nearby, we wouldn't ignore it—we would rightly seize both to determine whether the second one contained evidence of a crime. If the second device turned out to be clean, it would be returned."

Letting that sink in for a minute, I continued. "The same principle applies here. Our warrant would authorize the seizure of specific, unlawful artifacts, but if we encountered other items of the same nature and likely origin, we would have the legal authority—and the responsibility—to seize them as well, while ensuring full respect for Miller's rights throughout the process."

Melissa shot me a look that made it clear she didn't want me launching into another analogy. I kept going anyway.

"Or take another example. Suppose surveillance tracks a cargo theft gang driving a stolen semitrailer full of televisions into a warehouse. You get a warrant, go in, and discover three more trailers packed with televisions and DVD players. You seize them all because they match the nature of the stolen goods. If any of it turns out to be legitimate property, you return it. That's how seizures work."

Melissa said, "We're not as comfortable with those analogies as you are. Everything in Miller's collection is a unique, individual object, and he apparently acquired many artifacts legally. You need specific probable cause for anything you want to seize."

"Come on, Melissa, you know that's not quite right," I said with a grin. "A search warrant doesn't require proof beyond a reasonable doubt—that's for trial. All I need is probable cause, which just means I have a reasonable basis to believe evidence of a crime will be found.

"Think about a drug lab. If I walk in, with a warrant, and see tables full of pills, I don't have to conduct a field test on every single pill before seizing them. I just need to take a couple of exemplars to confirm what they are. The rest fall under the scope of the original probable cause. Same idea here—I don't need to individually prove every artifact is illegal before seizing it. I just need enough evidence to justify taking a closer look."

A hint of a smile appeared on Melissa's face and immediately vanished. We'd sparred over this dividing line on a few previous cases, but always in good spirit. As an FBI agent, and as a cop, I had had countless—sometimes heated—disagreements with prosecutors over it.

The Fourth Amendment of the Constitution, regarding search and arrest warrants, prohibits "unreasonable searches and seizures" and stipulates that warrants must be based on "probable cause, supported by oath or affirmation, and particularly describing the place to be searched, and the persons or things to be seized." Cornell Law School's Legal Information Institute puts it this way: "Courts usually find probable cause when there is a reasonable basis for believing that a crime may have been committed (for an arrest) or when evidence of the crime is present in the place to be searched (for a search)."

The Constitution doesn't define the meaning of "probable cause." According to Cornell's Legal Information Institute, "The Supreme Court has attempted to clarify that meaning . . . while recognizing that probable cause is a concept that is imprecise, fluid, and very dependent on context." Distinguishing between arrest and search warrants, the Legal Information Institute says probable cause for a search warrant "exists when there is a fair probability that a search will result in evidence of a crime being discovered," provided "an affidavit or recorded testimony . . .

support[s] the warrant by indicating on what basis probable cause exists." Moreover, "courts often adopt a broader, more flexible view of probable cause when the alleged offenses are serious."

I told Melissa, "Let's go back to my child pornography example. If I can articulate the basis for a reasonable belief that an electronic device contains illegal images, that belief logically extends to other electronic devices I might find commingled with it. So, the affidavit for the warrant and the warrant itself will refer to seizing 'any and all computers, computer systems, computer software, storage drives,' and so on.

"Or in my cargo theft example, if I've got a reasonable belief that there's a stolen semitrailer in a warehouse, that logically extends to similar things I find commingled with it. So the affidavit and the warrant will typically include 'any and all trucks, trailers, cargo containers, their respective contents,' and so on."

Picking up steam in my argument, I continued, "It's the same with Miller's collection. His own statements, along with what the subject matter expert and I observed, support a reasonable belief that he's unlawfully possessing many of these artifacts and that he committed crimes to obtain them. If that's the case, then it's also reasonable to believe that similar artifacts mixed in with those could be evidence or the fruits of criminal acts.

"We'll have subject matter experts on-site to help make those determinations. But we can't *prove* the commingled evidence is unlawful before we search for it and examine it. Nor do we need to. That's not what the Constitution or case law require."

No assistant US attorney likes to be schooled on the law, particularly not from someone who's not a lawyer. Melissa frowned and said, "Well, Tim, I'll discuss that again with my colleagues. But we feel pretty strongly that you need more for a search warrant than you've got now."

It was a frustrating discussion for both of us, and in early 2014 we had it many times, both in person and on the phone. I was fortunate that Melissa was willing to listen to me in the first place, let alone keep going in circles on the issue of Don Miller's collection.

Melissa was one of the best assistant US attorneys I had ever worked with, and we had built a strong foundation of trust from my work on domestic terrorism cases in Indiana. If I had just walked into the US Attorney's Office and pitched the Miller case to whoever was available, I would have been shut down immediately.

Miller's alleged crimes were serious, and Holly and I had seen and heard enough to establish a fair probability that a search would discover additional evidence of those crimes. My draft search warrant affidavit reflected that reality, seeking the seizure of any and all commingled artifacts that Miller's own statements, relevant documents, or expert opinion gave probable cause for believing unlawful. Proof beyond a reasonable doubt was unnecessary.

The Miller case's unfamiliar context made Melissa and her colleagues uncomfortable with treating his collection as commingled evidence, but I had to find a way to convince them. What really frustrated me, though, was that, as I mentioned in the last chapter, I didn't think we needed the warrant. And even if I got it, I didn't intend to use it.

Although the consensus hope in the field office was that Miller would voluntarily consent and fully cooperate, Drew and the rest of the office's leadership did not agree that we could dispense with search and seizure warrants. With that in mind, I redoubled my efforts to convince Melissa Curtis that seizing commingled material was legally sound, respected Miller's constitutional rights, and aligned with standard warrant practices across a variety of crimes and evidence types.

Once again, I argued that if Miller had two virtually identical artifacts—for example, Anasazi pots of the same design, one clearly an unlawful possession (based on his own statements, which we were obligated to take at face value) and another for which we had no information—then it was reasonable to seize both because they were commingled. Only through careful examination could we determine their legal status and then return anything we couldn't prove was unlawful.

The inherent tension between prosecutors and investigators on this sort of issue is healthy. It helps protect citizens' rights and strengthens the government's arguments. I believe in Americans' constitutional and civil rights, and I never wanted to exercise government power to trample on them. Melissa's skepticism about seizing commingled evidence was understandable, given how far outside her experience the Miller case was. I might have been frustrated by her stance, but I had a lot of respect for her as an able prosecutor with absolute integrity.

Drew helped me untangle the complex web of laws that could apply to different parts of Miller's collection and support probable cause for seizing them. I'd knock on his open office door, and if he wasn't too busy, I'd drop into a chair and say, "Let's talk about NAGPRA" or "Let's talk about the Abandoned Shipwreck Act of 1988." Ten or fifteen minutes later, I'd walk back to my desk with new angles and insights that helped shape the affidavit at the core of my search and seizure warrant applications.

In one of our talks, Drew suggested a commingled evidence scenario to share with Melissa. Suppose a disgruntled ex-employee or ex–romantic partner claims a jeweler is trafficking in stolen luxury watches and currently has a dozen of them in their house. The informant even describes some of the brands and models. You get a warrant, and in a cabinet in the jeweler's house you find a dozen watches, including ones matching the informant's list of brands and models, that would retail for thousands of dollars each. In a different cabinet you find more luxury watches, including many of the same brands and models. The jeweler claims these watches are legitimate inventory from a store they've recently closed. It would be odd not to seize all the watches, assess their origins, and simply return any that proved to be legitimate.

"That's an interesting analogy," Melissa said the next time we talked. "In fact, all your analogies are interesting. But I've bounced them off my colleagues, and we still don't feel you have probable cause to seize thousands of things you don't have specific information on."

Despite our collegial relationship, I couldn't help but grow increasingly frustrated with Melissa over this seeming impasse. I reminded Melissa that we'd be conducting the search with the help of highly credentialed subject matter experts. Beyond the artifacts we already had specific probable cause to seize, we'd take only the items the experts deemed problematic or suspect.

Melissa remained resistant, and I started to wonder how much of that resistance was really coming from her bosses. They undoubtedly didn't want to spend time and resources on property crimes that weren't going to be prosecuted in court, and I was guessing they just weren't willing to take on any risk for what they deemed to be an unimportant case. Or maybe they just didn't see the Native American human remains as troubling.

That might seem odd to think now, but in 2014, there simply wasn't the same level of awareness or concern—at least outside the Native American community—about the ethical and legal issues surrounding such remains. Back then, it wasn't uncommon for them to be found in museums, university anthropology and archaeology departments, and even private collections, with little public outcry. Thankfully, institutions are starting to see things differently today.

As a local cop, I could take a warrant application straight to a judge, and I frequently did. As a federal law enforcement officer, however, I had to have the approval of the US Attorney's Office first.

"I'm expending a lot of time and energy doing battle with the US Attorney's Office," I complained to Drew. "And it's wasted effort, because Miller is going to consent, and we won't need to execute the warrant."

Drew characteristically responded, "You're probably right, but we can't be sure. It'll only really be a wasted effort if we don't have a warrant and Miller won't let us in the door without one."

So it was back to the drawing board, with Drew's continuing help in refining my probable cause argument. But I wasn't just relying on legal theory—support for probable cause was also building through investigative inquiries I was making.

Many of Miller's Native American artifacts had display labels listing the state they came from, and he had told Holly and me about excavations in South Dakota, New Mexico, Arizona, and other states. I followed up by calling the state archaeologists and land-use managers in each of those states. None had a record of Miller ever obtaining a permit to collect archaeological resources on state land.

Likewise, I made similar inquiries to federal land management agencies, and their records showed the same thing. Miller had never been issued a permit to excavate or remove artifacts from federal land either.

Drawing on his law degree and legal experience, I pulled Jake into the warrant debate. He had seen plenty of cases where federal judges upheld warrants allowing for the seizure of commingled evidence, particularly in drug investigations.

Early in his February visit to Indianapolis, he said, "Cynthia Jacob, my thesis adviser, not only teaches cultural heritage and preservation law at Rutgers, she's also a highly experienced litigator in the field. She's fascinated by the Miller case and has offered to help on a pro bono basis. How about flying her out here to review the affidavit with us? Maybe even have her talk to Melissa? Hearing about commingled evidence from a litigator and law professor might carry some weight with her."

It was a good idea, and we brought Cynthia out to Indy, where she volunteered her time and expertise. She gave us some helpful suggestions on the affidavit, but the bigger impact came when we introduced her to Melissa.

As their conversation unfolded, I could see Melissa's confidence growing in the commingled evidence argument. Cynthia's litigation experience and academic expertise lent weight to the legal justification, and for the first time, it felt like we were making real progress.

That feeling grew stronger over the next few one-on-one conversations I had with Melissa. Her tone of voice and expressions gradually suggested that she personally saw the commingled evidence argument as legally sound.

But on the surface, she still disagreed. She kept saying, "We're not comfortable."

Behind that, I heard what she wasn't saying outright: "My bosses aren't comfortable."

The field office leadership and I were now aiming to start the search and seizure operation at the Miller farm on April 1, and that date was fast approaching. I realized Melissa was in a tough position. She might have been willing to approve my request to take the warrant to a federal magistrate judge, but if her bosses opposed it, she couldn't overrule them—no matter what she personally thought.

It's probably obvious by now that I don't like taking no for an answer, especially when the no feels arbitrary. Whenever I'd disagreed with

Melissa in the past, she had always presented a serious, well-reasoned argument for her position, whether it was declining a case or taking a different approach to pursuing it.

About a year earlier, I had brought her a historic document and signature fraud case. A collector in Indianapolis had purchased a collection of documents after confirming that a small sample of lower-value items was authentic. But once he had the full collection in hand, he realized everything else was fake. This kind of scheme—seeding a fraudulent collection with a few authentic low-value pieces—was a common tactic used to deceive good-faith buyers.

I built a solid case before bringing it to Melissa, seeking her approval to take a warrant application to a judge. But she responded that it didn't meet the threshold for involving the US Attorney's Office or pursuing federal prosecution, and she laid out substantive reasons why.

So I handed the case back to the Indianapolis Metro Police detectives who had originally sought my help. I was disappointed by Melissa's decision, but I understood and respected it. At the very least, I knew I had strengthened the case for Indy Metro to pursue on their own terms.

For the Miller case, however, Melissa had never presented a serious legal argument against my commingled evidence reasoning. It was always just, "We're not comfortable."

If "we're not comfortable" really meant "my bosses aren't comfortable," then maybe it was time for a showdown that would ostensibly be with Melissa but would really be with her bosses. I went to see her in her office and ran through the commingled evidence argument one final time.

"I'm sorry, Tim," Melissa said. "We're not going to go forward."

"But we have solid information there are human remains in the house. We have to go in there and get the human remains out."

"I'm sorry," she repeated. "We won't approve the warrant."

"Okay, Melissa, you go ahead and decline my search warrant. That's your prerogative—and your bosses'. But let me tell you what I'm going to do.

"We both know I can't go straight to a judge like I could when I was a local cop, but I can go to the state district attorney's office. I've got pictures of human skulls that informants say are in Miller's house, and I've seen at least a couple of human bones in his house myself. Maybe those skulls are ancestral remains, maybe they're contemporary. I don't know, and neither do the informants. Therefore, I can reasonably suspect that Miller might have killed people, and he's got their bones in his basement.

"I'm going to tell that to the DA and get a search warrant for homicide. And if we have to build this case on a state warrant instead of a federal one, then that's exactly what we'll do."

Melissa stared at me in shock. She knew I meant every word. Finally she said, "Let me share that with my boss, Tim. I'll get back to you ASAP."

I thanked her for that and left her to it. She was mad at me, and I knew her bosses would be furious, as perhaps my own would be. If I did what I said and built an effective case, it would reflect very badly on the US Attorney's Office for the Southern District of Indiana. It's just not kosher for a state prosecutor to have to do a federal prosecutor's job. I didn't like upsetting Melissa, but it was worth it if the office approved my search warrant. And if the US Attorney's Office still wouldn't approve my search warrant application, my next stop was going to be a state prosecutor's office.

Sure enough, however, Melissa called the next morning and said, "All right, Tim. Send me your search warrant packet so I can review it before you go to a judge."

I was still sending revised drafts of my affidavit to Melissa when Jake returned to Indianapolis on Monday, March 17. From that point on, we worked side by side, grinding through twenty-hour days.

I hammered away at the affidavit while Jake ordered supplies and handled logistics for the search and seizure. Then we swapped seats, and he reviewed the affidavit and offered suggestions while I checked over the operational preparations. Things were finally coming together.

Search warrant affidavits follow a standard template that begins with the law enforcement officer's qualifications and experience, lays out a probable cause argument based on relevant statutes, and concludes with the specifics of what the warrant will cover.

In this case, that meant including most of the case information detailed in the first three chapters of this book—everything from Miller's statements and background to how the search and seizure operation would unfold. It also covered the roles of non-FBI, non–law enforcement subject matter experts and student volunteers, ensuring the process would be handled properly.

At around eighty pages (over ninety after including a few single-spaced attachments), the affidavit was as long as one might expect for a complicated financial fraud case. As is standard practice to protect an ongoing investigation, the application package requested that both the affidavit and warrant be placed under seal. It remains under seal to this day. Because of that, I can't quote it directly.

The scope of Miller's collection implicated numerous international treaties and a host of federal laws, including NAGPRA, ARPA, the National Stolen Property Act, the Abandoned Shipwreck Act, the Endangered Species Act, and the Bald and Golden Eagle Protection Act, among others. Tying all of that together—demonstrating probable cause for each legal violation while justifying the need to seize thousands of artifacts—took time and precision. And unlike a financial fraud case, this affidavit included photographs of human skulls sitting haphazardly on a shelf.

On Thursday, March 27, 2014, I took the search warrant package to a federal magistrate judge. I sat in the outer office for over an hour while the judge read it.

Eventually I heard, "Agent Carpenter, come on in."

If a judge sees problems with a warrant, this is when you find that out. But the judge simply said, "Raise your right hand."

I raised my hand, and the judge recited the usual formula.

He signed the warrant and slid it across his desk.

"I have only one question, Agent Carpenter."

"Yes, Your Honor?"

"Did he really do all of this?"

"Yes, Your Honor."

He shook his head and said, "Good luck."

Five

Six Days in April

Part 1

At the presearch briefing in the Indianapolis field office on Monday, March 31, 2014, an agent from the western United States raised a hand. I nodded at him.

"We're executing a search warrant," he said. "What do you mean 'no weapons'?"

Some of the worst media and political blowback from Operation Cerberus Action came from the image of federal agents arriving in force—wearing raid jackets and body armor, carrying tactical gear and long guns—to arrest respected members of their communities. It didn't matter that those federal agents had legitimate operational concerns to warrant that posture. It was the imagery that stuck. To avoid a similar controversy, my operational plan was clear: no raid jackets, no tactical gear, and no visible weapons.

The agent's question exasperated me—not just because I'd already explained, earlier in the briefing, why we weren't going to make a show of armed force, but because I was running on fumes. For the past three weeks, Holly, Jake, and I had been working longer and longer days to keep the search and seizure operation on track for the next morning—all while still handling our regular jobs. That day alone, I had driven two hours down I-65 to teach a two-hour explosives course in New Albany, Indiana, just across the Ohio River from Louisville, Kentucky—then two hours back to be in time for the briefing, with plenty of search-related work still waiting for me afterward.

I stifled my frustration and answered the question.

"Like I said before, those of you who are agents have your personal sidearms. But I never want to see one during this operation.

"Don Miller is ninety years old. There is absolutely nothing to suggest he poses a threat of physical violence. And if he comes out of his house in the middle of the night carrying one of his antique rifles to give us the finger, I don't want anybody shooting him."

I wasn't surprised by the question. Even a ninety-year-old can kill you, and law enforcement has to be prepared for every scenario. These days, it seems to be more difficult to know how to prepare properly. But seasoned law enforcement personnel know how to exercise judgment—when to escalate and, just as importantly, when not to. This is where having police experience benefits an FBI special agent. Street cops learn early on that not every situation calls for a show of force, and in this case judgment mattered more than firepower.

"So let me repeat. We're going to do our work quietly and professionally. No raid jackets, no tactical gear, no long guns. You will keep your personal sidearm concealed at all times.

"Besides, I don't believe we're going to need our warrant," I said. "I think Miller will give us his consent, and this will be an evidence recovery operation with a cooperating subject. We don't need to escalate this into something it's not."

It was an all-hands briefing for everyone with a search and seizure role: FBI agents and non-agent support professionals, experts like Holly, and student volunteers—about 150 people all told. During the briefing I noticed some of them, including art crime team agents Dave Bass, Susan Garst, and Ronnie Walker, looking intently around at the assembled group. Afterward Ronnie told me, "I was trying to take in the full scope of the assets you've marshaled. This is bigger than any FBI operation I've seen before. It must be one of the biggest, longest searches the FBI has ever done. I think a lot of people at the briefing were having the same reaction."

While I was certain the FBI had conducted much larger operations for other types of crimes, I understood Ronnie's point. We had a huge challenge to meet, no question. Jake, our fellow art crime team agents, and I worked late into the night at the field office, making sure the search and seizure convoy was ready to roll in the morning. Meanwhile, Holly was dealing with last-minute issues with her grad students, the subject matter experts, and everything needed for their participation in the operation. I doubt any of us got more than a few hours of sleep that night.

I was grateful my house was a short drive away. Knowing the search was going to push me to my limits, Risa and I had agreed that she would take the kids to her family in Milwaukee. It wasn't easy being apart, but we both knew it was better than me stomping around the house, overtired and irritable, snapping at them simply for existing in my sleep-deprived orbit.

At 9 a.m. on Tuesday, April 1, 2014, I knocked on Miller's door, with Holly, Drew, Jake, and Rush County Sheriff Jeffrey Sherwood standing beside me.

Just a week earlier, Sheriff Sherwood and one of his deputies had told me they had visited Miller socially in the past and had seen his main basement display. They had also heard rumors that Miller had an adjacent climate-controlled room filled with skulls and other human remains. His possession of human remains wasn't exactly a secret—at least not to some members of his community.

We had shared enough evidence with the sheriff for him to know we had solid probable cause for our search and seizure operation. Bringing him along that morning wasn't just a courtesy, however, it was strategic. His presence gave Miller a familiar, friendly face in our group, someone from his own community rather than just a team of federal agents.

I hoped it would help keep the temperature low as we sought Miller's consent.

"Good morning, Mr. Miller," I said, when he opened the door. He glanced at the sheriff before turning his gaze back to me. "I'm FBI Special Agent Tim Carpenter, and I'm here with these folks to explain why I've been coming by to see your collection and ask you about it."

"Oh?" Miller said.

"Yes, sir." Turning slightly to my companions, I said, "Sheriff Sherwood you know, of course. You'll remember Dr. Holly Cusack-McVeigh, the anthropologist who was with me the last time I came by." Pointing first at Drew and then at Jake, I went on, "And let me introduce Supervisory Special Agent Drew Northern, who is our chief division counsel at the FBI's Indianapolis field office, where we both work, and Special Agent Jake Archer, who works with me on the art crime team. Could the five of us come in and tell you what this is about?"

Miller gathered himself briefly and said, "I guess you should come on in." He stepped back, opening the door wider for us to enter.

Sitting in the living room with Miller and his wife, Sandra, I leaned forward and said, "Mr. Miller, I told you I'm an archaeology enthusiast, and that's true. I'm passionate about art and archaeology, and your collection is truly spectacular.

"But you and I both know there are serious problems with it. Some of what you have, you bought. But some of it, you looted. You've desecrated graves. You've taken objects that don't belong to you."

I let the words settle, watching Miller's reaction, knowing this was the moment that would set the tone for everything that followed.

Miller didn't dispute anything. A look passed between him and Sandra that suggested they had thought something like this was always possible.

I didn't sugarcoat it as I continued to explain things. In my mind, there were two possible versions of Miller's legacy. What he decided right there, in that moment, would likely determine what that legacy would be.

He had crossed lines he shouldn't have, desecrating graves and amassing a collection filled with illicit artifacts. But at the same time, he had a choice. He could fight us legally. Or he could cooperate, take responsibility, and help ensure his unlawful possessions went where they truly belonged.

I laid out the two ways he could be remembered. In one version of the story, he was an obsessive collector who had gone too far but in the end chose to do the right thing and worked with us to fix what he could.

The other version was far less forgiving. He could just as easily be remembered as an unrepentant grave robber who refused to take responsibility and left behind a massive, tangled mess for his family to deal with.

His cooperation wouldn't erase the past, but it would allow him to shape his own legacy as someone who, in the end, did the right thing. That was the choice I hoped he would make.

"Well, what is it you want to do?" Miller asked, still outwardly calm but now with a hint of irritation and disquiet.

"Both times I was here before, you shared anecdotes suggesting that many of the pieces you've acquired—both domestically and internationally—are unlawful. Based on her expertise as an anthropologist specializing in Native American culture and history, Holly identified many other artifacts that are also likely unlawful.

"With your cooperation, we'd like to conduct a search to identify problematic artifacts and any associated human remains in your possession. We'd like to have your consent to do that."

Miller's eyes widened briefly at the mention of human remains. "You're here to take everything?" he asked with obvious concern.

"No, sir," I said. "Holly and other subject matter experts will help us determine which artifacts are probably unlawful. Those artifacts, along with any human remains, will be taken into custody for investigation and analysis.

"Anything found to be lawful will be returned to you. Unlawful artifacts and human remains will be repatriated to the tribes and countries they came from."

Miller took that in and then said, "I'd like to call my lawyer now."

"Yes, of course," Drew said.

Miller picked up a cordless landline phone and was soon telling his lawyer, a partner in a prominent Indianapolis firm, that FBI agents wanted his consent for a search and that one of the agents was the Indianapolis field office's lawyer. After listening briefly, he held the phone out to Drew and said, "He wants to talk to you now."

Drew stepped into the foyer to take the call. As he walked out, Miller glanced over at Sheriff Sherwood again, as if looking for reassurance.

The sheriff smiled and said calmly, "The FBI has a job to do, Don."

We followed standard procedure when seeking a subject's consent to a search. Neither Drew, Jake, nor I mentioned the warrant tucked inside my jacket. Revealing it up front could be seen as coercion, pressuring the subject into giving consent under duress. Instead, we mention a warrant only if asked directly by the subject or their attorney.

As Drew later told me, Miller's lawyer quickly asked about a warrant, and Drew confirmed that we had one. But when Drew returned to the living room, he didn't bring it up. Instead, he simply handed the phone back to Miller and said, "Your lawyer is still on the line."

On the advice of his lawyer, Miller agreed to the search. I thanked him for his cooperation and explained that we would begin that morning and complete the search within ten days.

I then offered the Millers the option of staying at one of Indianapolis's best hotels at the FBI's expense while the search was underway. We knew how disruptive it would be and figured that they may be more comfortable in a plush hotel. As expected, they declined. With any luck, Miller would continue sharing useful information about his collection while we were there—just as he had during my previous visits with Bruce and Holly.

With the most pressing business settled, it was time to shift focus and get the operation moving. I told Miller that Drew and Jake would go over the consent forms with him, including his right to revoke consent at any time. As Holly and I stood up to leave the room, Miller stopped me—he had something he wanted me to know first.

"I'm not the digger you think I am," he said defiantly.

"All right, sir," I said, neither agreeing nor disagreeing. We would soon see what kind of digger he was.

Things began to move fast. I stepped outside to the front stoop and called Greg Massa, who would be on-site commander, to tell him to roll in our convoy of equipment and personnel. The convoy was waiting about five miles away in the parking lot of St. Vincent Catholic Church, just west of I-74. The church would also be letting us use the parking lot as a media zone when the press inevitably came to ask what we were doing at the Miller farm.

Holly wanted to immediately survey Miller's basement display area again. But first I had to follow procedure and clear the house. While Holly waited in the foyer, I went through every room to make sure no one else was there. I also checked all of Miller's antique and historical weapons to make sure none of them was loaded before I let Holly know she could go down to the basement—with one caveat. She wasn't to touch or move anything yet. We had to photograph the entire property first.

With the safety sweep complete, I stepped back outside and looked north. The convoy was just turning onto South 850 West, the quiet stretch of road Miller shared with two neighbors.

The convoy was an imposing procession of vehicles, each carrying a crucial piece of the operation. Leading the way was an oversize RV, which served as our mobile command post—the base of operations, BOO in FBI jargon. Another RV functioned as a mobile photography studio, ensuring high-quality documentation of seized artifacts.

Behind them, a semitruck with a fifty-three-foot flatbed trailer carried lumber, lights, and other building materials needed to construct our processing space. A second semitruck with a flatbed trailer hauled several ATVs for navigating the property as well as industrial generators to power our field setup.

Following the trucks, a fleet of evidence response team vehicles rolled in, along with a half dozen marked FBI police cruisers and SUVs for site security. Several full-size pickup trucks towed trailers loaded with DRASH tents, which would serve as our workspace, medical unit, and meal tent. Bringing up the rear, a dozen or so cars and SUVs carried FBI personnel. As you might imagine, the convoy was quite a spectacle in this part of rural Indiana.

The FBI's technical hazards response unit (THRU) specializes in setting up field infrastructure for complex operations, particularly those involving hazardous materials, sensitive evidence, or specialized environmental controls. For this operation, they estimated it would take about fourteen hours to fully assemble our setup. That included laying down floors inside the DRASH tents and connecting them with plywood passageways to create a sealed, climate-controlled environment.

We couldn't risk moving artifacts straight from Miller's relatively stable indoor space into the outside air. The passageways ensured a gradual transition and helped maintain a consistent environment to protect the artifacts from potential damage due to sudden shifts in temperature and humidity.

Since our workday ended at 10 p.m., THRU would likely have to pause setup overnight and finish the next morning. However, before we set up any infrastructure, photographers documented the condition of the Miller compound, including the buildings, north and south driveways, lawn, trees, and other plantings. These photos would serve as a reference for any repairs needed due to incidental damage from our vehicles, foot traffic, and temporary structures. Once the photography was complete, THRU's first priority was setting up the latrines, ensuring they were available for use throughout the day.

Our personnel footprint that day was mostly THRU's setup crew and a few evidence response team members. The full search team—including Holly's grad students and subject matter experts in anthropology and archaeology—wouldn't arrive until the next day.

However, two women from the field office's victim and witness assistance program were part of the convoy, tasked with looking after the Millers. In effect, we treated Don Miller as a cooperating witness to his own crimes. For the duration of the search, our victim and witness assistance professionals cared for the Millers as if they were their own grandparents. They walked and fed their dog, handled laundry, picked up prescriptions and groceries, and even cleaned much of the house—including taking care of the dog's accidents inside. It was a thankless task, one that I will be forever grateful to them for handling with grace.

Also arriving with the convoy were art crime team agents Dave Bass, Susan Garst, and Ronnie Walker. The plan was for Dave and Ronnie to anchor one of our two eight-hour shifts and for Susan and a fourth agent to anchor the other. At the last minute, however, the fourth agent had become unavailable. On my behalf, Ronnie had reached out to another team member, Liz Rivas, to see if she could step in as a replacement. Liz was set to fly into Indianapolis from Los Angeles the next morning.

A couple of times, I stepped away from coordinating setup activities to check in with Drew, Jake, and the Millers. Once the consent forms were completed, we got a set of keys from the Millers. Then, Holly, Jake, and I began a triage survey of the collection, using a color-coded system to classify artifacts:

- Red for items that were certainly unlawful
- Yellow for those that were likely unlawful
- Green for artifacts that Miller could keep

With our system in place, we started the painstaking process of sorting through the vast collection. We had four categories of concern:

1. Human remains
2. Sacred and funerary objects
3. Objects of cultural patrimony, items that belonged collectively to a tribe or cultural group rather than to an individual
4. Everything else

Our immediate priority was locating any and all human remains. That search began with the locked basement room mentioned by the tipsters as well as Sheriff Sherwood and Deputy Sheriff Drake.

Inside the room, a nearly complete skeleton lay on red cloth inside a raised wooden display case with a glass top and sides, allowing visitors to see inside. Though not an actual coffin, the case eerily resembled one in shape and design.

The remains had been carefully adorned with artifacts. Metal armbands encircled the humerus (upper arm) bones, while a dozen thin bracelets wrapped around the radius and ulna (forearm) bones on both sides. A stone-and-bone chest plate lay across the ribs, and arranged alongside the bones were axe heads, a Catlinite pipe, and a knife blade. A ring had been forced onto a finger bone, and a handwritten card nearby read, "Sioux Warrior, 19th Cent."

We later learned from Miller's grandnephew and grandniece that when showing the room to favored visitors, Miller claimed the remains belonged to Crazy Horse, the legendary Sioux warrior who died in 1877. There was no evidence to support this claim. In fact, Crazy Horse's family had buried him in secret, specifically to prevent the kind of desecration-by-display that Miller had engaged in. As time went on, we would learn that the bones themselves told a different story—one that flatly contradicted Miller's claim.

A shelf above and to the left of the display case held twenty-five skulls, and there were a couple of paper sacks with bones on other shelves. We had been expecting that Miller might have the remains of as many as a dozen individuals, but we were already straining that estimate past the breaking point.

We found bones scattered throughout the house, in rooms adjoining the main basement area and other parts of the residence. Among them were several adult skulls with arrowheads hammered into them. Skulls turned up in unusual places, including one tucked between books on a high shelf in the ham radio room, as if it were watching over the space.

While we searched the rest of the residence for human remains, photographers got to work, capturing detailed images of Miller's collection, and the residence itself, to document its condition before anything was moved. Evidence response team personnel began sketching detailed floor plans of all the compound buildings, assigning identifying letters to every room and taping placards with those letters on walls and doorjambs. Meanwhile, THRU personnel were making progress on setting up the DRASH tents and the rest of our infrastructure.

Somewhere in the search supplies, packed on one of the trucks, were Tyvek suits and respirator masks. Instead of interrupting the setup to dig them out, Holly, Jake, and I pressed on with our triage survey. Our attire was suited for meeting with the Millers and securing their consent, not for grubbing around in dusty, moldy closets, storage areas, and crawl spaces throughout the Miller compound.

The more we looked, the more bones we found. It wasn't just that we kept finding more human remains. It was that we kept finding them in increasingly appalling conditions.

Jake and I were both seasoned ex–local cops as well as FBI agents. We'd worked homicide cases and seen our share of gruesome crime scenes. I had been on active service in combat and war zones in the Middle East as a USAF explosive ordnance disposal specialist during Operation Desert Storm and in the years after 9/11. As an FBI bomb tech, I had been deployed overseas on temporary duty assignments, responding to attacks and mass-casualty events. But this was something else entirely.

When you saw dead bodies in those situations, they were the fresh result of dynamic violence—an explosion, a shooting, a bombing. Somehow that was more understandable, even easier to process, than arrowheads hammered into a skull for dramatic effect, a baby's skull repurposed as an apple bowl, and the static accumulation of bones, sometimes mixed with animal remains, scattered throughout the compound.

Bones were strewn across shelves and stuffed into tote bags, plastic garbage bags, paper grocery sacks, and cardboard boxes. They were filthy with grime and black mold, infested with silverfish. Mice had built nests inside skulls with bits of paper and cardboard. For all of Jake's and my combined experience in law enforcement, homicide cases, and combat zones, this was new—as shocking to us as it was to Holly.

Jake later recalled, "Whenever we found another cache of bones, it seemed like a new low in terms of how Miller treated Native Americans' remains. Every time we were like, 'Okay, it can't get any worse than this.' But it kept getting worse. Every new room was full of horror."

The afternoon light was fading by the time Holly, Jake, and I finished searching the Wyman Research Building, where we had found numerous sets of human remains jumbled in boxes and tote bags and scattered on shelves among artifacts.

The fresh air outside was welcome as we headed toward the dilapidated white, two-story farmhouse where Miller had grown up—a structure that likely dated back to the 1920s or earlier. Inside, the ground floor and upper dormer level held little beyond broken-down furniture, buried under layers of dust, dirt, and cobwebs. But in the kitchen, we found a narrow staircase leading down into a low-ceilinged, unfinished basement, where exposed pipes and aging electrical wiring hinted at a space rarely used—at least, not for anything good.

The power was off in the house, and we had to use flashlights to see our way. The damp cinderblock foundation walls and the ceiling were all streaked with black mold. It was a bit of a labyrinth with walls that had apparently partitioned the space into different storage areas like a cold cellar for root vegetables and places for tools. But at the far end of the basement, our flashlights picked out what we were looking for: another staircase.

According to the tipsters, Miller kept some human remains in a fallout shelter he had had built under the farmhouse in the 1950s. The second set of stairs, narrower than the first, took a sharp 90 degree turn down about a half a story to the fallout shelter, a concrete bunker even more dank, filthy, and moldy than the basement. A subterranean passage with almost a foot of dirty, trash-strewn water led to the basement of the Wyman Research Building, where we'd just seen the other end of the passage.

Rickety glass vitrines, empty except for dirt and cobwebs, sagged on either side of the bottom of the stairs. Across from the vitrines, rotting wooden shelves sat on brackets screwed into the concrete wall. On the floor in between several boxes and tote bins held what we thought were probably mixtures of human and animal bones, covered in dirt and mold. Rats and mice were obviously nesting in some of the boxes and tote bins. They had apparently scurried off when they heard us coming down the stairs.

We stood up from those boxes and bins, our flashlight beams partly illuminating our grimaces of shared revulsion amid the dark. Holly turned and cast her flashlight toward the rotting shelving.

"What's that?" she said, spotlighting a large black garbage bag crammed under the lowest shelf. She went over and pulled out the bag, which was covered in mold and grime. We gathered around the bag, each of us involuntarily taking a deep breath before we opened it up. When we did, a large raccoon came flying out between us and darted up the stairs to whatever hole in the wall it used to enter and leave the building. I'm surprised that neither Jake nor I drew our weapons and tried to shoot the damn thing.

The bag was full of bones, including a dozen skulls, mixed with bits of insulation, cardboard, and twigs that made up the raccoon's nest. Everything about the way Miller treated the human remains he had looted was callous and disgusting. But for me somehow this was the worst. What a horrific way to treat the dead.

The three of us managed to maintain our composure, but beneath the surface we couldn't help but feel deeply unsettled. As the week went on, the rest of the search and seizure team experienced the same reaction. No matter how seasoned or professional they were, none of us could remain completely unaffected by what we were uncovering.

When Holly, Jake, and I came up out of the farmhouse bunker into what was now early-evening light, we could see that the infrastructure setup was progressing well. The THRU team had erected all the DRASH tents, with those designated for processing seized artifacts positioned right next to the residence's garage. The latrines, medical tent, and chow tent were a short distance away, ensuring easy access while keeping them separate from the main work area.

Our plan had always been to handle human remains separately from artifacts. We had figured we could collect them within a day or so, then shift our full focus to identifying and seizing problematic artifacts.

But we weren't dealing with a dozen remains, or even two or three dozen. There were hundreds of people's bones scattered throughout Miller's compound. We hadn't planned for that.

We were going to have to find more time for collecting human remains. Jake started for the mobile command post to begin tweaking our plan to account for that.

The distinctive thump of approaching helicopters momentarily distracted us. The roadblocks keeping drivers from South 850 West between State Road 244 and West 900 South—except for residents of the two houses down the road and across from the Millers—were causing only brief detours. But it was clear that word of our operation had already reached local and regional news outlets.

The helicopters overhead belonged to Indy's network-affiliate television and radio stations. It wouldn't be long before the footage they were capturing was airing not just in Indiana but on national and international news as well.

Drew happened to be checking on the final setup of the media zone at St. Vincent's Church when I called him and said, "There are way more human remains here than we anticipated."

"That's not good," Drew replied. "How much more?"

"Hard to say for sure, but there must be bones from over 350 individuals here. I'm guessing even more."

"Oh my God."

"It's kind of overwhelming, Drew. Especially when you see the conditions Miller's been keeping the remains in. They're covered in filth and mold. There are insects, mice, and even raccoons nesting in them."

Shocked, Drew didn't respond for a moment. Then he said, "We'd better keep that quiet from the media while the search is still underway. Miller, his family, and his friends will be watching the local news, and the last thing we need is for him to get upset and revoke his consent. Though, honestly, I think his lawyer would talk him out of it."

"Agreed," I replied. "More importantly, we're going to have to arrange a national consultation with the tribes as soon as possible."

"That thought was just occurring to me too," Drew said. "I'll get Cathy Burton [his paralegal assistant] to send out an email alert for what, 2 p.m. tomorrow?"

"Perfect. Thanks for taking care of that."

"You got it," Drew said.

I joined Jake in the command post to help fine-tune our plan of attack for day two, the first day of actual evidence collection. But before we could finish, two of the techs from the FBI's operational photography unit called us outside. Holly was with them.

"Hey, the seventh floor at Hoover is asking for you to do a quick video to show the site and explain what you're doing. They want to use it to brief the director."

It wasn't a request the techs were conveying, it was an order. As they spoke, they positioned the three of us in front of a tripod-mounted camera, setting up bright lights to compensate for the evening darkness.

James Comey had taken over as FBI director on September 4, 2013. The art crime team had never recorded a video report for him—or for any FBI director, for that matter. But then again, we had never deployed as a full team before, and this search and seizure operation was shaping up to be one for the books. Given the scale of what we were uncovering, a report for the director made sense.

Even before we were covered in dust and grime from the triage survey, Holly, Jake, and I were already exhausted from weeks of preparation. And then the sheer scope of human remains we had uncovered had hit us like a ton of bricks—twice over.

At that moment, I doubted I could spell my own name correctly, let alone deliver a polished report. But we didn't just have to stand in front of the camera and talk. We had to take the crew around the entire property, walking them through the gruesome discoveries we had already made and giving them context.

We pointed out key locations, explained what we had found, and let them shoot B-roll footage for the final video. Somehow, despite our exhaustion, we managed to give a coherent account of both our shocking findings and the otherwise smooth start to the operation. I was told later that the video was a great success with Director Comey, so mission accomplished.

Back in the command post, Jake and I finished the final tweaks to our search and seizure plan. By 10 p.m., THRU had outdone themselves— nearly all of our infrastructure and supplies were in place. The setup crew, having put in an exhausting day's work, packed up and headed to the Hampton Inn in Shelbyville, about fifteen minutes away, where the out-of-town personnel were staying.

After a final run-through of our checklist, Jake and I met with the officers assigned to overnight duty. Though Miller had consented to the search and seizure, his farm compound was still technically a crime scene. We had to maintain 24/7 site integrity—or as the saying goes, "hold the site"—to preserve an unbroken chain of custody for everything we seized. The FBI police were more than happy to assist, and their presence was a welcome addition to the operation, helping ensure tight security throughout the night. Score one for Noel Gil.

Around 11 p.m., Holly, Jake, and I finally headed for our cars, the night air cool and still around us. Jake exhaled, rubbing his face. "Twelve hours from now, we're going to be buried in artifacts."

Holly shook her head. "Buried in something."

I glanced back at the darkened farmhouse, then opened my car door. "Get some sleep," I said. "Tomorrow's going to be a hell of a day."

We were all back at the site before dawn on day two, Wednesday, April 2. Holly and I weren't feeling any effects from mold exposure, aside from maybe a little extra fatigue. Jake, on the other hand, admitted to having a fever and the beginning of a hacking cough, but he waved it off: "It's game time. Let's go."

His commitment was a godsend. Without him, the whole operation would have fallen apart before it even got started.

At 6 a.m., we assembled everyone on the first shift in the chow tent, and I gave them their instructions. Counting FBI agents, support professionals, subject matter experts, and museum studies student volunteers, the first shift totaled about sixty people. Another sixty or so would take over for the second shift, starting at 2 p.m.

Most of the first shift would begin seizing, inventorying, photographing, and packing problematic artifacts. Holly and her fellow subject matter experts would guide the process, working alongside Dave Bass, Jake, and me to ensure everything was handled properly and efficiently.

Because of the overwhelming number of human remains, often mixed with animal bones, we had discovered, I assigned Susan Garst, assisted by Ronnie Walker, to identify and separate the human bones for collection. Before her FBI career, Susan had been a forensic anthropologist. Her expertise in human skeletal analysis was exactly what we needed to sort through the chaotic mix of remains with precision. Both Susan and Ronnie suited up in Tyvek coveralls, gloves, and respirator masks, an essential precaution after what Jake, Holly, and I had experienced the day before.

In Ronnie's words:

> Like everybody else at the search, I had a jaw-drop, "Oh wow" moment when I first saw all the museum-quality artifacts Miller had accumulated. That was followed by sadness and anger over the damage Miller had done in acquiring the artifacts, and then by a focus on making things right.
>
> Being Susan's helper peeled me away from the artifacts and heightened that focus. There were boxes and bags of human and animal bones mixed together, and boxes and bags of only one or the other. You have to be an expert like Susan to quickly and accurately distinguish the human bones, except for the obvious ones like skulls.
>
> Our training and experience enabled us to compartmentalize our emotions and methodically identify the human bones and put labels beside them. But we periodically had to recenter ourselves. For example, we'd go into a room and see a paper grocery sack on a shelf. We'd take the sack off the shelf, and there'd be a person's bones inside. Sometimes the person was a child. That was harder to see and just move on from.
>
> Miller's treatment of the remains was so careless and callous. It was one of the most horrific things I've seen in nearly thirty years of law enforcement.
>
> There wasn't a square inch of Miller's compound we didn't search for human remains. And then we went back over every square inch again to make sure we didn't overlook anything. Every time we poked our heads into a room or a nook, we found more remains.
>
> I still think about being one of the first people to help identify the remains and start them on their way to a proper resting place. It gave us a sense of duty even beyond that for the artifacts.

Reluctant as I was to leave just as the operation was hitting its stride, Drew and I had a 2 p.m. meeting with the tribal community back at the

FBI office in Indianapolis. Jake would brief the second search and seizure shift when it started at the same time. As I pulled away from the Miller farm, news helicopters were circling overhead again, showing that word of the operation was continuing to spread.

In 2014, there were 566 federally recognized Native American tribes—a number that has since grown to 574. Beyond that, hundreds more tribes remain unrecognized by the federal government. The sheer number of tribal nations made it impossible to contact all of them on less than twenty-four hours' notice.

Thanks to our presearch groundwork and outreach efforts by Holly, Charli Champion-Shaw, and Larry Zimmerman, though, we had built a small but crucial list of direct contacts among tribal leaders and tribal historic preservation officers (THPOs) in Indiana and nearby states. At the same time, Cathy Burton had helped spread the word to a wider audience, sending alerts via email to the National Association of Tribal Historic Preservation Officers (NATHPO) and National NAGPRA, a US National Park Service program established to implement NAGPRA after the law's 1990 enactment.

Anyone who could attend the meeting in person at the Indy field office was welcome to do so, with others participating by telephone. Those attending in person included Sally Tuttle, president of Native American Voices of Indiana, and Debra Haza, another member of that organization; Kevin Daugherty, an elder and cultural affairs director of the Pokagon Band of Potawatomi, an Algonquian people with reservation lands in Indiana and Michigan; Marcus Winchester, the Pokagon Band's Tribal Historic Preservation Officer (THPO); George Strack, THPO for the Miami Tribe of Oklahoma; and Charli Champion-Shaw.

Participating by telephone were representatives of tribes in California, Michigan, Minnesota, Oklahoma, Oregon, Wisconsin, and Washington state. Bambi Kraus, NATHPO's founder and executive director, also participated by telephone.

Greg Massa and Melissa Curtis attended the meeting in person. Holly interrupted her work at the Miller compound to join the meeting by telephone, and Bonnie Magness-Gardiner was on the phone from Washington, DC.

Expecting to find only a small number of human remains on the property, we had preemptively reached out to the Pokagon Band of Potawatomi, the closest federally recognized tribe to Miller's property. They had approved the participation of tribal members in cleansing ceremonies for any remains recovered, and Kevin Daugherty and Marcus Winchester were our primary liaisons for that effort.

The demeanor of all the tribal members in the meeting suggested some wariness, and even skepticism, about what we were going to tell them. Bambi Kraus in particular was forceful in demanding to know exactly what we were finding and what we were doing about it. Given the long history of the federal government's treatment of Native Americans, their skepticism was fully justified. They expected what they had almost always received from federal authorities, a high-handed decision made without their input, one they would have no real power to influence or change.

As I explained the situation at the Miller compound, however, my most important message was, "There is a much bigger problem than we anticipated. We need your help and guidance to resolve it." Drew's remarks were in the same spirit.

It was a difficult conversation, and I didn't relish having to report what we had found the day before. The tribal representatives reacted with deep sorrow and outrage upon learning that Miller had looted hundreds of Native Americans' remains and brought them home as trophies. Their expressions and voices carried a mix of grief, disbelief, and anger—not just at Miller but at the long history of disrespect and desecration that his actions represented.

But treating the tribal representatives as guests and equals, and inviting them to partner with us, shifted the atmosphere of the meeting in a positive direction. The initial wariness began to ease, replaced by a sense that, for once, the federal government wasn't just dictating terms—we were listening and working with them.

During the discussion, one of the tribal representatives insisted, "You cannot photograph the ancestral remains," and others seconded that position. I said, "We hear you, and we wish we could refrain from doing that. But we are conducting a criminal law enforcement investigation, and the ancestral remains are evidence. So, we have to photograph them. We have to document them in that way. How can we best do that in a way that is respectful and dignified?"

A consensus quickly emerged: Art crime team members would take only the minimum necessary photographs of the remains—just enough to document their location, condition, and the time they were found. I assured the group that these photographs would not be shared with anyone outside the FBI, unless they were required as evidence in court—an extremely unlikely possibility.

We also agreed that only Holly and the art crime team would collect and package the remains, with the help and participation of several select tribal members, ensuring they were handled with the utmost care and respect. This was a stark deviation from standard FBI policy, but it was the right thing to do, and I was committed to making that happen.

By the end of the meeting, there was undoubtedly still some skepticism—and rightfully so. But there also seemed to be a greater sense of trust that we were taking the issue seriously, treating it with the respect it deserved, and genuinely working on their behalf. A few tribal representatives even expressed appreciation directly, acknowledging our efforts to consult with them early and to begin righting the wrongs of Miller's crimes.

Kevin Daugherty also gave us a concerned warning. "Thank you for what you are doing," he said. "But you must be careful. The spirits of those whose graves have been desecrated are angry, especially the spirits of the children, and that might bring something bad on you or your families."

I didn't have time to dwell on Kevin's warning. But I thanked him and the other tribal representatives on behalf of the FBI, and I promised to keep them informed.

Six

Six Days in April

Part 2

When I got back to the Miller compound after the emergency tribal consultation, the second shift was well underway. Liz Rivas had arrived and was working with Dave Bass and Holly. With Liz on board, we now had the full complement of four art crime team agents, in addition to Jake and me, as outlined in the operational plan.

Jake had briefed the second shift when it started at 2 p.m. As I walked through one of the two registration and photography tents, I noticed that the admins at the registrar's desk were entering information into the Access database differently than how I had instructed them that morning.

"Hey, guys, that's not exactly how you're supposed to enter that data," I said.

"This is how we were told us to do it."

"Oh, okay. But stop doing that now. Here's what I want you to do." I explained the procedure again just as I'd outlined it at the briefing that morning for the first shift. In the other registration and photography tent they were also entering data incorrectly. I corrected it there as well, making sure everyone was on the same page.

As I stepped back outside, I saw student volunteers emerging from the packaging tents, carrying boxes marked with red or yellow stickers—problematic artifacts, already moving through the system.

Dammit, I thought. *I said we weren't going to use those freaking stickers on the boxes.*

During the planning phase, Jake had strongly advocated for using colored stickers—matching our red, yellow, green triage protocol—to mark boxes as they were packaged and moved. Holly and I had disagreed. We saw the stickers as unnecessary at that stage and a potential source of confusion, especially if they fell off during transport or were misapplied, leading to misidentification of evidence. I had vetoed their use outright.

And yet here they were. In my exhausted, sleep-deprived state, I knew I was probably overreacting to something trivial. I was so tired that it was possible I had somehow approved of their use and then forgotten about it. But at that moment, well, it just pissed me off.

I grabbed my radio and called Dave, Jake, Liz, Ronnie, and Susan. "We have to have a powwow. I want to see everybody in the command post in ten minutes."

I couldn't believe those words had just come out of my mouth. The whole operation I'm emphasizing cultural sensitivity and respect, and then I go and call a "powwow." I felt like an idiot. Sadly, my exhaustion-induced idiocy didn't stop there.

Inside the command post, I laid out the issues I had seen after returning to the site. I'm not a micromanager by nature, and I wasn't about to start then. Everyone in that room was a highly capable, experienced agent, and I trusted them to get the job done. But we had a plan for a reason, and as soon as you start deviating from a plan, things have a way of going sideways.

The team defended the adjustments they had made. They weren't making changes just for the sake of it. They had practical reasons for them. But I was concerned that unless it was absolutely necessary, changing our procedures was confusing to the people trying to do the work and might lead to mistakes. I felt we needed consistency, not conflicting directives.

Frustrated, I blurted out, "There can only be one chief out here, y'all."

The room went quiet for a beat—not because I was angry but because of what I had just said. At first, I didn't understand why everyone was suddenly trying not to smile, their expressions caught between amusement and surprise.

Then it hit me. In the FBI, there are unit chiefs and section chiefs, and *chief* is a term we use all the time. But let's be honest—that's not how I was using it in that moment.

Given the context of the Miller case—and my earlier "powwow" remark—I immediately thought, *Oh my God, I can't believe I just said that.*

I shook off my embarrassment over the unintentional stereotype. There wasn't time for that. Instead, I reiterated my instructions, making sure we were all back on the same page and moving in sync with the plan.

Everyone got back to work, refocusing on the task at hand. Jake headed downstairs to oversee operations in the main basement display area, while the rest of the team pushed forward with the search and processing efforts.

At around 5 a.m. on the third day, Jake, Holly, and I arrived back at the site, ready to put in another grueling day. Susan and Liz arrived shortly before 6 a.m. to start the day shift, while Ronnie and Dave were set to come in later for the afternoon/evening shift. At least, that was the plan.

Susan and Liz spent much of their first workdays together in Tyvek suits and respirator masks collecting human remains. In Liz's words, "Two o'clock came on the first day, and Susan and I looked at each and said, 'We're not leaving. What are we going to do, go watch television at the hotel?' So, we stayed until 7 or 8 p.m. that day and well into the evening on every subsequent day."

Likewise, Dave and Ronnie arrived at the site each day hours before their scheduled 2 p.m. start. Ronnie recalls, "The shift delineation got a little fuzzy. As things evolved, it became all four of us there for extended periods of time. We showed up as soon as we could and worked as long as we could stand it."

In our operational planning, Jake and I knew we could count on major efforts by other members of the art crime team. Susan, Liz, Dave, and Ronnie went above and beyond those high expectations every day of the search.

With only minor adjustments, the operational plan held up remarkably well. The basement display area in Miller's residence—his "showroom," as Dave called it—contained the majority of his artifacts, both problematic and otherwise. Two teams worked simultaneously, one in each half of the large room, under the direction of Holly, Jake, me, or one of the other art crime team agents.

In addition to Holly, or in her place when she left to catch a few hours' sleep, at least one or two archaeologists and an anthropologist remained in the basement to help identify objects for seizure. The X-ray fluorescence expert from the University of Georgia used his portable scope to examine every artifact we intended to seize. He detected traces of arsenic, historically used as a pesticide and preservative, on a few objects, but nothing that posed a significant risk.

Once we completed the search and seizure activity in the basement, we moved through the rest of the residence, then on to the Wyman Research Building, the old farmhouse, the barn, and the other outbuildings—ensuring no problematic artifacts or human remains were overlooked.

Once we identified an item for seizure, we tagged it with a preprinted evidence item number on an archival tag and recorded that number on an inventory sheet, along with a brief description provided by Holly or another subject matter expert. Because Miller had grouped artifacts together in shadow boxes and deep picture frames, a single evidence item number often applied to multiple artifacts—sometimes as many as fifty or sixty. This approach helped streamline documentation while maintaining accurate tracking of everything we seized. Later, during evidence reviews, we could separate and catalog individual pieces as necessary.

Photographers took one or two photos of each artifact or group of artifacts, with the archival tag beside it, in situ before anything was moved. These in situ images documented each object exactly as it was found, preserving its original context within Miller's collection for investigative and repatriation purposes. Two student volunteers at a time stepped in to carefully transport the artifacts for further processing. One carried the object—always using both hands—while the other acted as a spotter, guarding against trips, falls, or unexpected collisions with someone rounding a corner.

The first stop on the path from Miller's possession to FBI custody was the garage, which served as the initial checkpoint in the evidence-handling process. There a controller verified each evidence item number on the archival tags against a master list. This step ensured that numbers were assigned in sequence without any being accidentally skipped. If a number had been skipped, the controller voided it on the master list to prevent errors in the documentation process.

The controller then directed the object handlers to one of two registration and photography tents, which sat side by side just outside the garage. These parallel processing stations kept the workflow moving smoothly, preventing a bottleneck of artifacts piling up in the garage.

Inside each tent, the first stop was the registrar's station, where designated personnel worked to double-check each entry as they recorded evidence item numbers and brief artifact descriptions in the Microsoft Access database I had created. Next, the objects moved to one of two photography stations, where additional high-quality images documented each item and its condition. An evidence control technician in each tent ensured that every artifact followed the correct processing sequence before moving on.

The parallel flow of artifacts through the two registration and photography tents merged together in the packaging station in a larger DRASH tent. Every resulting package, box, or crate was then numbered and inventoried. The photographs and packing information were added to the Access database, linked to the evidence item numbers, and another controller checked everything against the master list of numbers.

Finally, the evidence items were loaded onto trucks for transport to temporary storage at the Indianapolis field office. To maintain an unbroken chain of custody for the artifacts, an FBI agent accompanied every truckload.

At the field office, a dedicated team received and stored the packaged artifacts in predesignated locations that Jake and I had scouted beforehand. We had set up carefully labeled plastic shelving in conference rooms, storage areas, and unused offices to accommodate the volume of material. Each box that arrived from Miller's farm had its new location recorded in my Access database and clearly labeled on the outside of the box, ensuring meticulous tracking from seizure to storage.

On our first full day of evidence collection, we processed one hundred evidence items through this system. Again, each evidence item number usually represented multiple objects.

On our second day of evidence collection (the third day of the operation), we collected 300 evidence items. From that point forward, we averaged 320 to 330 evidence items per day—a testament to the efficiency of our system and the discipline of our team. We accomplished this without a single loss or instance of damage, despite handling extremely fragile artifacts, some dating back five to six thousand years.

Honoring our commitment to the tribal community, we treated human remains separately and did not process them through the artifact processing stations. Before we began recovering any human remains, we had everyone except Holly, art crime team members, and tribal representatives from the Pokagon Band of Potawatomi leave the room. The tribal representatives then led a ceremonial prayer, offering ritual food to nourish the spirits of the dead. They also spoke to the spirits, explaining that they were beginning a journey to a proper resting place and would no longer be kept in a place of desecration.

As much as possible, we inventoried and packed human remains where we found them, using special archival boxes, and then left them in place for later collection. If the immediate environment was too filthy because of mold, rodents, or other issues, we carefully relocated the remains outside, where they were properly prepared and then sequestered in a designated collection area. In some cases, this initial handling was deeply unsettling. We had to pour silverfish out of skulls or remove mice nests from inside them, a stark reminder of the neglect and indignity these remains had endured. As a sign of respect and veneration, tobacco pouches prepared by Charli Champion-Shaw and Holly were packed with the remains.

This was a consent search, which meant we couldn't force Miller to leave his property. Nor did we want to—he might reveal valuable information about his collection that could help us understand where artifacts and remains had come from. But that didn't make it any less strange to catch glimpses of him hovering nearby, sometimes literally looking over our shoulders as we worked through the grim reality of his lifelong grave robbing.

On the second day of the operation, which was our first full day of evidence collection, Miller's presence presented its first challenge. We were following our triage protocol, which prioritized finding, documenting, and packaging ancestral remains before shifting our focus to artifacts. The task consumed the entire day, as we carefully worked through the staggering number of human remains scattered throughout Miller's collection.

Miller had been watching us all day. He had seen the steady procession of remains being carefully recovered, cataloged, and packed. Despite the fact that we had explicitly told both him and his lawyer that human remains would be our first priority, he still seemed unprepared for what that actually meant.

By late afternoon, he was agitated. He approached me, visibly upset, and blurted out, "Why are you taking all of my Indians? I thought you were here for the pots."

It was an infuriating statement, steeped in his Manifest Destiny presumption that he had some right to the remains of Native Americans. The day before, Miller had told me he wasn't as bad a digger as I thought he was. But by this point, I had seen enough to know the truth. He wasn't just a bad digger, he was far worse—nothing more than an unabashed grave robber.

I wanted to challenge him right then and there, to force him to confront the reality of what he had done. But I held my tongue, knowing that provoking him might risk him revoking consent and that getting the job done was more important than my anger. Instead, I patiently explained that most people might find what he had done to be offensive, and that my number one priority was to recover the human remains from the property.

Miller sneered, "If it's just a bunch of dead Indians that make you squeamish, go ahead and take 'em."

That hit me like a punch to the gut. Unable to keep quiet, I retorted, "Okay, Don, if that's how you feel about it, then you won't mind if I go down to the cemetery and dig up your dead grandparents and take them home to put them on my mantel?"

Miller stopped in his tracks. He had spent his life on the farm where he was raised. He worshipped at the same church his parents had attended, and he believed that the land he lived on was hallowed by his ancestors and consecrated by the faith he shared with them.

Yet he couldn't admit—not to anyone, and most of all not to himself—that this same truth applied to Native Americans. He looked up at me hard, his eyes widening in shock before they narrowed in anger. His face flushed red, his mouth working as if to speak, but no words came. After a long moment, he turned and walked away.

The emotional and cognitive dissonance Miller had just displayed was at the core of his sixty-plus years of desecration and abuse of human remains. It wasn't ignorance. It was deliberate refusal to see Native ancestors, or any Indigenous peoples for that matter, as deserving of the same dignity and reverence he claimed for his own.

And that was what revulsed all of us on the search team. You can put FBI agents on a blood-splattered triple homicide scene, and they'll go in and do the job without hesitation. But Miller's crimes felt darker, not because of violence in the moment but because of their cold, methodical intent—a lifetime of desecration, carried out over decades, with full awareness of what he was doing.

Although we were soon hitting our stride and meeting our search and seizure benchmarks, things were hardly stress-free. As Dave recalls, "Every once in a while, you'd hear a startled shout, because someone had just opened a box or bag of bones and critters had come spilling out. It was like a Stephen King novel. You never knew what creepy crawlies you were going to find."

If that wasn't bad enough, occasionally Don made his presence felt with organ chords that shook the house. Given the circumstances, it was a bit surreal.

Again, Dave recalls, "The organ was another expression of Miller's obsessive personality. He loved playing the pipe organ so much that he custom-built his house around one." In Liz's words, "It was eerie to hear that music, especially when we were collecting the human remains. It was like being in an episode of *Criminal Minds*. It gave you chills."

Ronnie puts it this way: "You would look to your left or right and see how devasted the tribal representatives were, first by the extent of the human remains, and then by the disgusting conditions they were in."

Meanwhile the local news outlets were hammering us. When reporters first started asking questions, Drew had quickly shut down speculation that this was a terrorism case, domestic or international, or that we were conducting a major drug bust.

As for what was happening, he kept it simple: We were investigating unlawful artifacts, and Miller was cooperating. But the local media took that and ran with it, echoing the sentiment of the surrounding community. They painted Miller as a victim, a real-life Indiana Jones, a kind and generous man who had spent decades welcoming Scout troops and school groups into his home to see his collection. In their version of the story, we weren't seizing stolen cultural property, we were harassing an elderly man who had spent his life preserving history.

Drew and I could only shake our heads, wondering how the local community and media would react if they saw the human remains Miller conveniently left out when showing his collection to Scouts and schoolkids. We both wanted to expose to the media and the world how, as Drew put it, "Miller had completely 'othered' Native Americans." He treated their remains as collectibles, not ancestors. As trophies, not people.

But revealing that would have invited chaos: protests, counter-protests, and a media frenzy that could have disrupted our operation. The truth would come out in time. For now, our priority was clear: remove the looted human remains and stolen artifacts from Miller's possession, ensuring they could finally be returned to where they belonged.

On Friday, April 4, the fourth day of our operation, I had decided not to go directly to Miller's house. Instead, I first stopped at the field office to check on the storage and organization of the seized artifacts that had already come in. Jake was in charge of the day shift at Miller's house.

Things at the field office were calm and under control. The search site, however, was a different story.

During my forty-five-minute drive to the site, my cell phone started blowing up. A few supervisors of professional support staff on-site were not happy—and they wanted to make sure I knew it. Their chief complaints? We were driving their people too hard, the protocol we had put in place to protect the artifacts was too rigid and time-consuming, and some of their people were getting upset when a member of the Art Crime Team insisted they do things the right way.

I groaned inwardly. I really didn't have time for this shit.

There was no question it was a highly pressurized situation, partly because of the operation's enormous scope and demanding schedule and partly because of the extreme duty of care it required. But there was no way to change the parameters of the operation and no leeway to relax our duty of care.

At the same time, I dutifully listened to the complaining supervisors and assured them that I recognized how physically and emotionally exhausting the operation was for everyone involved. I asked the supervisors for their understanding and promised to do a better job of supporting their people and letting them know their work was important and appreciated.

When I arrived at the site, I barely made it up the driveway before being summoned by Greg Massa, who, again, was the overall on-scene commander of the operation. Greg had several logistical issues that needed immediate attention and pulled me aside to go over them.

About twenty minutes later, I began walking the site and checking in with everyone at their work stations to try to rally their spirits, something I'd been trying to do all along. But in hindsight, I was so stressed out and tired that I hadn't been giving it quite as much attention as it needed. For the rest of the operation it moved up on my priority list, and fortunately everyone settled down and kept their shoulders to the enormous wheel we were moving. I will always be grateful for their doing so.

When I saw Jake, I recognized that he was pushing himself much too hard. He looked terrible—pale, exhausted, and clearly unwell. He was flat-out sick with the black mold fever that was hammering him. But he was putting in another eighteen-hour day, pushing through everything to get the job done.

I beckoned him aside and said, "Jake, we know you're sick from breathing in all that black mold. Go back to the hotel and get some sleep—you could really use it. We'll see you back here tomorrow morning, when you're feeling better."

Jake started to protest, and I cut him off. "I can't risk losing you for the rest of the operation because you work yourself so hard you wind up in the emergency room. I don't want to see you back here until tomorrow morning."

It was a tough call to lose Jake's contributions even for a few hours, but the right one. The next morning, he was by no means fully recovered from the black mold infection. But he was rested enough to continue being a star player for the duration of the search.

In truth, Jake was my co-MVP from start to finish. Without him, there likely wouldn't have been a viable operational plan at all. His wicked smarts and collection management expertise were crucial to figuring out how to move thousands of artifacts quickly and safely—without a single loss or damage.

And when we realized that Miller didn't have just a dozen or even a few dozen human remains, but hundreds—blowing apart our initial expectations—Jake was instrumental in adapting our approach. That ensured we could still meet our benchmarks for collecting artifacts while handling the staggering number of remains.

Jake's in-your-face intensity and enthusiasm never dimmed. That fire and passion endeared him to the art crime team and made him damn good at his job. I will always have the utmost respect for Jake and the incredible work he does.

My other co-MVP was Holly. She had also been pulling eighteen-hour days to wrangle her team of grad students, recruit a slate of first-class subject matter experts, and coordinate the nondisclosure agreements and other paperwork necessary for both groups to participate in a law enforcement investigation. That was on top of her invaluable input to the operational plan. She was an integral part of the triage survey with Jake and me, searching through every moldy, debris-laden corner of the Miller compound to identify all the remains. And she was on-site hour after hour, day after day, guiding the work of grad students and subject matter experts and personally taking the lead in the careful, respectful packaging and removal of the human remains. Without Holly and Jake, I don't know how I could have managed the search and seizure.

High stress and exhaustion can push anyone to their limits, making them react in ways they might regret. Late in the operation, a photographer from another field office completely lost it over the fact that there was no lettuce at the mid-shift meal of burritos and tacos from Qdoba or Chipotle. I was briefly off-site, but his ranting and raving upset other on-scene personnel so much that they called me back to deal with him.

Angry over having to take the time for such nonsense, I laid into the guy: "No lettuce? Are you kidding me? Get the hell off my crime scene."

He calmed down, apologized, and stayed on the job. His complaining was a momentary lapse in a high-stress environment, nothing more.

In hindsight, I was too rough on him. As Drew put it, "Even those of us who were agents were upset by all the human remains and their condition." We had made a point of emphasizing the importance of checking in on each other's mental and physical health, and we even had grief counselors on-site to help people process what they were seeing. But I wasn't immune to the stress either, and at that moment I could have been a better leader.

When the last of the human remains were respectfully packed in archival boxes, we loaded them into a dedicated box truck, separate from any artifacts. Before the truck departed for the field office, where the remains would be sequestered in a room by themselves, members of the Pokagon Band of Potawatomi held a cleansing ceremony.

For fifteen minutes, all search activity stopped. The fifty or so people on-site gathered in a solemn circle as the tribal members burned sage, offering chants and prayers to honor the ancestors and guide them to a proper resting place.

Liz describes it best:

> In dealing with the artifacts you could think, *Oh wow, I'm touching this beautiful pot that would be under glass in a museum.* But seeing the desecration of people's remains brought you into the reality of how Miller obtained those artifacts. As a Mexican American I felt a connection to Native Americans, and crawling in the bunker and other parts of the compound collecting bones made me feel dirty.
>
> I only felt a sense of peace with the ceremony before the truck left with all the human remains. It purged the darkness that was burdening me. I felt uplifted at the thought that these souls were beginning their journey to a proper resting place.

While we were still deep in the process of collecting human remains and artifacts, Bob Jones arrived on-site. An SAC personally visiting a field operation is a rare event. They typically oversee from afar, checking in through supervisors rather than showing up in the trenches. But Bob wasn't just there to observe.

"Where do you need some extra help, Tim?" he asked.

Then, without hesitation, he suited up in Tyvek, stepped into the thick of the operation, and worked side by side with the team for a couple of hours. That demonstration of leadership—not just being present but getting his hands dirty alongside his people—was a powerful morale boost. It carried more weight than any speech or pep talk ever could.

Another implicit endorsement of the operation came when Larry Zimmerman forwarded an email to Charli Champion-Shaw, who then shared it with me. It contained a Facebook message from former National NAGPRA director Tim McKeown, adding another layer to the unfolding story.

By then, news of the operation had gone global, and McKeown

wanted us to know something critical. In 2011 and 2012, Miller had reached out to multiple tribes, trying to sell parts of his collection. Among the items? Genealogy information—something he was demanding $70,000 for.

That Miller had actively solicited Native American tribes to buy back what he had looted from them—essentially asking for ransom money—was staggering. If there had been any doubt about the necessity of the search and seizure operation, this erased it. It reinforced what we already knew: We had acted just in time.

By Saturday, the operation was beginning to produce diminishing returns. The human remains had all been safely stored at the Indy field office, and we were nearing the end of collecting problematic artifacts. However, exactly how near we were to wrapping up became a point of contention between Jake and me.

To legally seize artifacts Miller had obtained overseas, we needed a clear legal basis grounded in the laws of the country of origin. By Miller's own reckoning, his most financially valuable artifacts—worth $700,000, he had told Holly and me—were a collection of Danish celts. These stone implements and weapons had come to Denmark from Viking-controlled territories in Ireland and England, areas subject to the Danelaw in the late ninth and early tenth centuries. They were of enormous archaeological significance, offering potential insights into Viking trading networks during that period.

Drew was standing in Miller's basement showroom with several members of the team, when one of the archaeologists shook his head in disbelief. "To find even one Danish celt in reasonable condition would make my career," the archaeologist said. "Miller has thirty absolutely pristine examples."

Despite the strong interest from our academic partners in seizing the Danish celts, I had to say no. Denmark was late to developing a national cultural patrimony law compared to many other European nations. It wasn't until the mid- to late 1980s that the country began strengthening its legal protections for antiquities. Even then, Denmark's Act on Protection of Cultural Assets in Denmark (Cultural Assets Act) of 1986 primarily required that certain protected objects obtain a license before leaving the country. The law did not clearly criminalize possession or transport of those objects, only their export without a license.

So, while Miller's removal of the Danish celts from Denmark was probably technically illegal, on the surface it seemed to be strictly an export violation, not a criminal offense under Danish or US law. And we just didn't have the time to do a deep dive into the matter.

Jake pushed back, arguing that we should seize them anyway. But without a clear statutory basis, I couldn't justify taking them. So, I made an executive decision. We would leave the Danish celts, along with other items that fell into any similar legal gray area.

Before we left, we warned Miller explicitly that just because we weren't seizing certain artifacts, it didn't mean they were lawful for him to sell or keep—only that, for now, we didn't have enough information to justify taking them.

By Sunday, April 6, we felt reasonably confident that we had identified and collected all of the human remains as well as most of the artifacts we believed Miller had obtained illegally or improperly. At the same time, I was keenly aware of the massive resource strain and expense the operation was placing on the field office. With that in mind, I began discussions with the team and field office leadership about wrapping things up ahead of schedule. Doing so would allow us to conserve resources while ensuring we had accomplished our mission.

It wasn't just that we were nearing the end of what we could collect. Bad weather was closing in fast. It had already rained several times while we were on-site, and with around 120 people moving across Miller's yard for six straight days, we had already turned it into a giant mud puddle. The next incoming storm front was going to make things much worse. If we didn't finish soon, we'd be dealing with flooded tents, bogged-down equipment, and a logistical nightmare. It was time to get out while we still could.

With agreement from all decision-makers, we made the call to pull the plug and begin shutting down the operation. Late that Sunday afternoon, we collected the last of the artifacts and started packing up the site.

My early estimates of Miller's collection had been fairly close—his total inventory came in at roughly forty-two thousand pieces. From that, we seized nearly five thousand individual artifacts and approximately two thousand human bones, representing an estimated five hundred people. It was the largest recovery of human remains and cultural artifacts in FBI history—and quite possibly in US history.

The Miller case had reached the end of the beginning, you might say. A whole new set of challenges awaited us.

Seven

Handle with Care

A few days after the search ended, I answered my cell phone and heard, "Special Agent Carpenter, this is Jim Comey. I want to commend you and your team on a job well done on the Miller search and seizure operation."

Since Comey had become FBI director in September, word had spread that he sometimes called agents to congratulate them on good case work. It was such a contrast with his predecessor's practice over the previous twelve years that several agents Comey called had actually hung up on him, thinking it was a hoax.

That was my own initial reaction, but I managed to say, "Yes, sir. Thank you, sir. I'll share that with the team."

"Please share it with everyone who contributed, Tim. But don't worry about alerting your co-case agent, Jake Archer. I'll be calling him myself."

When Jake and I talked next, we couldn't help giving each other a virtual high five over Comey's phone calls. Jake also had some other feedback to share. He was interning with Norman Muller, the Princeton University Art Museum's chief conservator. Norm had given Jake helpful comments on our operational plan, and he'd been eager to hear how things went. When Jake showed him a few photographs of Miller's collection and reported that we'd successfully collected around five thousand artifacts and two thousand human bones, Norm said, "You moved a small museum's worth of precious material in a week and didn't lose or break anything?"

"Yes."

"That doesn't happen. You and Tim should be lecturing to museums about this."

An expert conservator's praise for our careful handling of archaeological artifacts and ancestral remains was really gratifying. But our duty of care was just beginning.

The most pressing postsearch task was pest eradication. During the operation, we had encountered nests of rodents and artifact-destroying insects throughout the Miller compound, and the collection bore the signs of that activity. Insects eat textiles and wood, and they excrete acids that can damage pottery.

To contain the infestation, we isolated everything we knew to be contaminated in a designated room at the field office, sealing it off with plastic. Human remains were stored separately in a room reserved solely for them. Meanwhile, sealed archival boxes filled with the remaining artifacts were tucked into any available space—conference rooms, storage areas, and unused offices.

Adding to my concern, the field office was brand new. We had moved in just a year earlier, leaving behind the old federal building in downtown Indianapolis. Seeing rows of shelving and boxes of evidence stashed throughout our pristine new space tested the patience of some of my colleagues, but it couldn't be helped. We knew we needed an off-site storage facility, but until we actually had a solid count of the material we had seized, we didn't know precisely what size space we would require.

Holly and I began calling curators and preservation experts at the IMA and other museums to ask how to deal with the pest-control issue. The response was always more or less, "You need to freeze everything that can safely be frozen, not just the things with visible signs of infestation."

"Fine. Can we bring you boxes of things to put in your freezer?"

"Hell, no," they said, but in politer words.

Museums typically have one or two specially made chest freezers that are about the same size people often have in their basements or garages. We had thousands of things to freeze. No nearby institution had the capacity to handle that for us.

After some creative brainstorming and suggestions from experts in the field, we explored the idea of renting a refrigerated ("reefer") tractor trailer, like those used to transport frozen food. The experts advised that we needed to take things down to at least -20 degrees Fahrenheit for ten days to eliminate all pests—only a virus could survive that. At -30 degrees Fahrenheit, the same effect could be achieved in just seven days.

I found a vendor with a fifty-three-foot reefer capable of reaching -30 degrees Fahrenheit. Within a week, it was parked in the field office's fenced-and-gated lot, accompanied by a fuel tank and a generator to keep it running 24/7.

We froze everything that could safely withstand -30 degrees Fahrenheit for three weeks—extra time to ensure complete eradication. In total, about 90 percent of the seized material went through the deep freeze. The only exceptions were wooden ethnographic artifacts, which would crack and deform at such low temperatures. Instead, we kept these sealed until they could be carefully cleaned using archivally sound methods.

Freezing wasn't our only tactic in the fight against pests. While deep freezing was the most effective way to eliminate most infestations, we also took additional precautions. We brought in a pest control specialist from a company that serviced museums, scheduling weekly visits at first, then scaling back to monthly inspections.

Even so, complaints arose. My field office colleagues were convinced that the seized material had unleashed a plague of insects into their workspaces. A few even reported suffering mysterious insect bites while at work.

All fingers pointed at the Miller collection—and directly at me. But the experts assured me that no pests could have survived -30 degrees Fahrenheit for three weeks. Each time we emptied a batch from the freezer, we found only piles of dead insects and rodents. Our sealed storage room ensured that nothing was escaping into the rest of the building.

To get to the bottom of it, office management hired a different pest control company to investigate. Their findings cleared the Miller collection—and me. The real culprits were several potted plants that someone had brought in for their cubicle. But convincing everyone that the Miller material wasn't to blame took some time.

HANDLE WITH CARE

A primary responsibility in our duty of care was informing, and consulting with, the Native American community. On April 9, 2014, three days after the conclusion of the search, we held our second tribal consultation. The tribal representatives who had come to the field office for the first consultation were there again, and a larger group than before participated by telephone.

The mood of the meeting was somber but intensely curious. Everyone wanted to know what we had found. How deep was the wound, and what was the FBI going to do about it?

I reported the successful completion of the search and the seizure of approximately five thousand artifacts and two thousand human bones. At that point, we estimated that a third of the artifacts were Native American, a third were foreign, and the rest remained unidentified.

I also outlined our short-term storage plan at the field office, our pest eradication efforts, and the need for an off-site facility for long-term storage and evidence review. Additionally, I announced our commitment to following NAGPRA regulations for the repatriation of artifacts, emphasizing our dedication to restoring dignity to ancestral remains and ensuring respectful repatriations.

Regarding the ancestral remains, we confirmed that no DNA or other invasive testing, such as radiocarbon dating, would be conducted. This decision was guided in part by our internal evidence protocols but even more so by the wishes of the tribal nations. They viewed DNA and radiocarbon testing as a further insult to the ancestors, as it would require drilling into the bones to extract samples. We agreed.

The tribal representatives at the meeting supported our proposal that osteologists take skull measurements using the Howells dataset in hopes of determining cultural affiliation. However, I noted that the Howells dataset (more on this below) could only suggest probable cultural affiliations, meaning we were likely to end up with a significant number of unaffiliated remains.

There was already a general consensus among the tribes that unaffiliated ancestral remains should go to the federally recognized tribe closest to where the remains were recovered. The Pokagon Band of Potawatomi were the closest tribe to Miller's farm, and Kevin Daugherty said they would be glad to receive all unaffiliated remains for reburial on behalf of the Native American community as a whole. During the discussion I explained that the unaffiliated human remains would likely include some that Miller had looted in foreign countries. The Pokagon Band of Potawatomi said they would also be willing to give those remains a secure, respectful resting place.

Those present seemed to welcome the Pokagon Band's generous offer. Over time, I worked to build support for this solution through additional tribal consultations and countless informal conversations with tribal representatives at cultural heritage conferences and other venues.

One question from the tribes that I couldn't answer was whether Don Miller would be charged and prosecuted. Many in the Native American community understandably wanted to see Miller held accountable for his crimes in a court of law.

I said, "It's a little soon to know what is going to happen on that front. The FBI gathers evidence, and then the US Attorney's Office decides whether to bring charges and prosecute them. I will keep you posted as that situation develops."

In our internal discussions, Drew and I still anticipated that Miller's advanced age would make the DOJ reluctant to prosecute him, given that his offenses were, legally speaking, property crimes. If prosecution did not move forward, the government would need to negotiate an agreement with Miller for him to formally relinquish title to the seized material. When the time came to take concrete steps in either direction, we would inform and consult the tribes. Until then, discussing the matter—and weighing the potential benefits and drawbacks for the tribes—was premature.

The tribal representatives were visibly tense over learning about the state of their ancestors' remains, the sacred objects Miller had looted, and the artifacts in his collection. I also sensed their deep wariness—toward the FBI, the government, and a system that had repeatedly betrayed and harmed Native communities. That same distrust had surfaced during the emergency meeting on day two of the search, when I first informed a smaller group of tribal representatives about the sheer extent of the human remains at Miller's compound.

Such wariness was hardly unexpected or unwarranted. Yet, over the course of both meetings, my colleagues and I also sensed a generous willingness to believe that we were sincere in our approach and determined to build an honest partnership with the tribal community. It seemed, just maybe, that the tension and distrust were starting to ease.

In the hallway after the meeting, Kevin Daugherty echoed what he had told Drew and me after the first consultation. "We appreciate what you're doing and that you're keeping us informed. The government is finally getting it right here," he said. Then his tone shifted. "But please be careful. When the spirits of the ancestors are disturbed—especially the spirits of the children—that can come back on you or your family."

So far, there was no sign of anything untoward happening to us or our families, but we deeply appreciated his concern for our well-being.

The art crime team's annual training was two weeks away, April 22–24 in Chicago. As planned, Jake and I arrived early and met for dinner and drinks on Monday, April 21.

I'd asked Jake to get together with me so I could express my appreciation for the fantastic job he'd done in helping me plan and lead the search and seizure. I also wanted to tell him that his becoming a full-fledged member of the art crime team—the timing depended on Bonnie, but the sooner the better—was really going to strengthen the team.

We were on our second beers when Jake brought up the culture clash I'd warned him about. "I think things went pretty well, didn't they?" he said with a smile. "I didn't sing a single Springsteen song."

I laughed and said, "Oh, I don't know. There were one or two moments I thought I was going to have to go full-on country boy with you." I paused before adding, "Stickers being one of them." That elicited his own laugh.

We both knew that in an operation as large and intense as the search and seizure, a few people were bound to walk away with bruised feelings over something. As I told Jake that evening, "I ruffled a few feathers along the way myself, but you can't make everyone happy all the time. The bottom line is I couldn't have done this job without you and your Jersey Jake drive."

Over the next three days, our training included sessions at the Art Institute of Chicago and Leslie Hindman Auctioneers as well as a discussion on cultural heritage and property law with Patty Gerstenblith. Each session was valuable and informative, and the whole program was a welcome break from the exhausting months Jake and I had had leading up to it.

But the dominant topic on the team's mind was the Miller case. Everyone felt an immense sense of pride in what we had accomplished and excitement about what it meant for the future of the art crime team.

It's safe to say that everyone also felt that Jake had fully earned his place on the art crime team, even if that status wasn't yet official, and we embraced him as one of our own. That sense of solidarity only grew as those who hadn't been at the search learned more about how it had unfolded day by day.

As Liz, Susan, Ronnie, Dave, and I recounted the operation, we couldn't help but highlight Jake's enormous contributions—from planning to execution. Holly's contributions had been equally vital. Sadly, since she wasn't an FBI employee, she couldn't join us in Chicago for the training. She was sorely missed, and "The Miller Team," as we were referred to that week, all heaped praise on her expertise and poise under pressure. The rest of the team needed to know how critical she had been to our success.

Humor in the face of adversity is a powerful team builder, and there was plenty of good-natured ribbing about how exhausting Jake's intensity could be. But by the end of the training session, it was clear that everyone on the team needed and wanted Jake in the mix going forward.

Above all, the success of the operation gave the art crime team a new sense of itself as a team and what it could achieve in the future. But it was clear our work was only getting started. I made sure everyone knew to be ready for temporary duty (TDY) assignments to assist with evidence review in Indianapolis and, eventually, with the repatriation of ancestral remains and artifacts.

Meanwhile, my day job never let up. It only grew more complicated and time-consuming.

My regular bomb tech duties continued, including coordinating and staffing special events from auto races to football and basketball games. The Level 3 WMD Stabilization team I had started assembling for the Indy field office in 2013 was now in its full build-out and training phases. I also had to design and teach a forty-hour electronics course for federal, state, and local bomb squads around the country. On top of all that, I had to attend bomb technician training sessions to keep my own certifications up-to-date, along with participating in national training exercises—including one that lasted two weeks in northwest Oregon.

Just when I thought my workload couldn't get any heavier, FBI headquarters mandated that every field office conduct a mall attack training exercise in 2014. This directive was a direct response to the September 2013 terrorist attack on the Westgate shopping mall in Nairobi, Kenya.

In that attack, four members of al-Shabaab—a militant Islamic group based in Somalia—stormed the mall, murdering sixty-seven people and wounding about two hundred more before they themselves were killed. The White House and FBI leadership feared that this could serve as a blueprint for a similar attack on a US shopping mall, making large-scale preparedness exercises a top priority.

The largest owner of major shopping malls in the country, Simon Property Group, is based in Indianapolis. For that reason, the director's office decided that the Indy field office would host the last and largest mall attack training exercise, the capstone event of the nationwide effort.

At the time, I was the only special agent bomb technician in the Indy field office. Therefore, I was responsible for developing training scenarios, designing realistic (but non-dangerous) IEDs, coordinating role players, and providing props such as realistic weapons for added authenticity. Preparing for the event, which was scheduled for August, consumed countless hours.

This was a major undertaking for our relatively small field office—and a significant drain on my time. But given the real threat of a copycat attack in the United States, I had to give the training exercise a maximum effort.

Throughout the remainder of that year, I had to scramble to grab a few hours here and there to work on the Miller case. It wasn't the first time—and wouldn't be the last—that I was too busy to take my full complement of annual leave, a strain on both me and my family.

The good news was that Holly was committed to seeing the case through to the end. Holly could have easily stepped away after assisting with the search operation, but instead she proved to be a rock star, dedicating a tremendous amount of time to helping us properly inventory, condition report, and investigate what we had seized. On top of that, she began working hard to connect us with the right folks in the tribal community to start those early consultations.

Recognizing the value of her expertise, we arranged for her to have her own access card to the FBI facility and extended the consulting contract she'd worked on during the search and seizure, allowing her to come and go as her schedule allowed. Not that the money we paid Holly drove her extraordinary efforts. She put her heart and soul into the Miller case. Her contributions at every stage of the investigation were incalculable, and we were more than fortunate to have her on the team—along with her incredible grad students, who got invaluable real-life experience as part of progress toward completing their degrees.

During the spring and summer, I devoted as much time as possible to reviewing the twenty-four boxes of general evidence we had collected—travel journals, scrapbooks, photos, home movies, and more. A summer intern began the daunting task of organizing over twelve thousand still photos, including prints, Polaroids, and 35mm slides that we had seized from Don. I asked them to identify locations using landmarks in the photos as well as references from the Millers' scrapbooks and other records to help us better understand Don's looting activities. That work resulted in around two hundred digital folders of images, categorized by various US states and foreign countries.

On June 16, we held a two-hour tribal consultation. Because the operation had received extensive media coverage, word had spread quickly throughout tribal communities, generating significant interest and concern about what we had uncovered. As a result, the consultation was well attended, though mostly via teleconference.

I provided an update on our review of photographs and documents as well as our plan to move the seized material from the field office to a separate facility for extended study and efforts at cultural affiliation. I also shared a revised tally of the collection. After a thorough review of our Access database, we now estimated that about half of the artifacts we seized were Native American.

With considerable uneasiness, I described—as delicately as possible—how Miller had disarticulated and mismatched human remains in his possession. He had fixed detached mandibles onto skulls that they didn't belong to, taken random teeth from multiple people and glued them into unrelated jaws to create the illusion of a complete set, and made other equally disturbing alterations. I also carefully detailed the appalling condition of many of the remains when we found them, like the bones and skulls, with a raccoon nesting among them, in a moldy garbage bag in Miller's fallout shelter.

It had to be traumatic for the tribal representatives to hear, largely for the first time, the details of Miller's destructive and disrespectful treatment of their ancestors' remains. But they deserved and needed to know the full extent of the damage and how it complicated efforts to determine cultural affiliation.

To that end, I announced that we were arranging for a leading academic osteologist to make noninvasive measurements of the skulls and attempt to rearticulate the skeletal remains we'd recovered. We continued to believe that the majority of the remains were Native American but were also confident that some of the remains were non-Native. Based on Miller's documents, the Native American remains seemed to be primarily from Arizona, western New Mexico, South Dakota, and the Ohio River Valley.

I also announced our plans for a secure website, where tribes' designated representatives could view photographs of the Native American artifacts we'd seized and submit claims on them. Although the website was still in the conceptual stage, I said that no photographs of ancestral remains would be included and that, apart from designated tribal representatives, access would be strictly limited to those with a legitimate need, such as representatives of foreign countries where Miller had looted and subject matter experts assisting us with cultural affiliation. Additionally, I emphasized that the design we envisioned would appropriately compartmentalize that access. For example, a government official from New Zealand or an expert on Māori artifacts would not be able to view sensitive Native American materials, just as a Native American tribal historic preservation officer would not be able to view potentially sensitive Māori artifacts. Accordingly, Native American cultural objects would be kept separate from foreign artifacts to the extent possible.

As in every meeting with the tribal community, I reiterated our commitment to following NAGPRA regulations for repatriations. And I reaffirmed our dedication to restoring dignity and respect to their ancestors.

In addition to delivering the distressing news about the condition of the ancestral remains, I also addressed the factors weighing against prosecution of Miller. He had turned a frail ninety-one on May 25, and that alone made prosecution unlikely. At his age, there was a real risk that he could pass away at any time from natural causes or a medical emergency, and it was doubtful he would even survive the stress of arrest, booking, and an initial court appearance. Prosecution would also stop repatriation work cold because it would involve a lengthy forfeiture process, with an appraised value required for every artifact before a court awarded judgment to the government or Miller. Even if Miller passed away, the government might be locked in litigation with his estate for years before cultural affiliation work could begin.

Pursuing forfeiture didn't make sense for Miller either. If he chose to contest the seizure and fight for the return of his collection, he would face significant legal costs with little chance of success in court. At his advanced age, he could not realistically expect to live long enough to see the process through. Instead, it would only create a legal and financial burden for his widow and surviving relatives.

I told the tribes that if Miller were fifty, sixty, or even seventy years old, the discussion about charging and prosecuting him would likely be very different. But given his age, both the US Attorney's Office and the bureau believed the better course of action was to negotiate a global relinquishment agreement with Miller and his second wife, Sandra. In exchange for immunity from prosecution, they would formally relinquish title to the seized material and acknowledge the government's authority to retain and repatriate everything—except for artifacts that could be proven to be lawful possessions.

To be sure, we would have done the requisite investigative work and endured the forfeiture process if that were the only way forward. But that wasn't the best path to a just result.

Miller's informed consent, given on the advice of his personal legal counsel, had facilitated the search and seizure. In the same way, his voluntary relinquishment of title, again with legal counsel's guidance and full protection of his rights, would serve the ultimate goal of justice: the respectful repatriation of the ancestral remains and cultural artifacts.

Miller wasn't exactly getting off scot-free. While he had legally acquired much of his collection (remember that we seized only roughly 17 percent of his collection), the pieces he prized most were the fruits of his illicit digging and grave robbing. By seizing them, we had stripped away the crowning achievements of his life's work and obsession.

Moreover, though he might still have the support of a few close friends and like-minded individuals who shared his Manifest Destiny prejudices, his reputation—both in his home community and beyond—was unraveling. Media coverage might still use an Indiana Jones hook to introduce him, but every account of his looting of human remains shattered any illusion of him as a heroic adventurer.

For the most part, the tribal representatives in the meeting responded to my observations with resigned acceptance, though there clearly was frustration that Miller wasn't likely to face criminal prosecution. I explained that we would probably approach Miller and his attorneys to reach an agreement later in the summer and that I would keep them posted about this and other developments.

In July, Drew and I arranged for Indiana University osteologist Jeremy Wilson to conduct Howells Craniometric Data Set measurements on the skulls Miller had looted and kept as trophies. From the mid-1970s to the mid-1990s, Harvard University forensic anthropologist William W. Howells conducted and published comparative studies of 2,524 skulls, representing twenty-eight different population groups from around the world. For each skull, he took eighty-two specific measurements, creating a comprehensive craniometric dataset that remains a key resource in forensic anthropology and bioarchaeology. Today, an osteologist can replicate those measurements and use specialized software called FORDISC to analyze them against the Howells Craniometric Data Set, helping to determine possible ancestry or population affiliation.

The software generates probabilities rather than definitive identifications. For example, it might determine that a particular skull has a 70 percent likelihood of being of Siouan origin, with smaller probabilities indicating possible northern European or Asian ancestry. In some cases, the results may include multiple possible affiliations, none of which exceed a 50 percent probability, highlighting the inherent uncertainty in such analyses.

There would always be uncertainty in using this method to culturally affiliate ancestral remains. Legitimate concerns existed about racial biases in Howells's research, the limited representation of Native American populations in his dataset, and the overall reliability of its identifications.

However, it was, and is, one of the few noninvasive techniques available for affiliating skeletal remains that are also acceptable to the Native American community. In some instances it might provide strong evidence of origin. In others, it could serve as a valuable tool when combined with additional sources, such as the Millers' home movies and other documentation of their digs.

Wilson and a research assistant began measuring skulls at the field office in mid-August, which only heightened my urgency to transfer the seized material to a dedicated facility where osteological work and evidence review could proceed more efficiently.

In July, the bureau had authorized efforts to secure a suitable commercial space, which we planned to lease "covertly"—just a fancy way of saying that, while the landlord knew who we were, we wouldn't be hanging any signs out front that said "FBI," nor would we be chatting with our neighbors about what we were doing.

There were two reasons for pursuing a lease this way. First, renting off the economy was much faster and involved far less administrative bureaucracy than the traditional method of securing government space through GSA. Second, it allowed us to keep quiet about what was stored in the warehouse, reducing the risk of making it a target for thieves or vandals.

Drew was becoming increasingly involved in the Miller case, effectively taking over the supervisory and administrative burden from Greg Massa—something Greg was more than happy to hand off. Together with a realtor, Drew and I began looking at "flex space" warehouses—facilities with office space in the front and a loading dock with warehouse space in the back. Before long, we found a suitable 5,000-square-foot space in an industrial park within a reasonable driving distance of both the field office and our homes. Since Drew would be my backup on everything related to the warehouse, it had to be a location we could both reach quickly if needed.

We left the previous tenant's signage in place to help keep a low profile. As far as our near neighbors in the industrial park were concerned, we were a consulting firm. They were always curious about exactly what we were up to, and I sometimes told them that we were designing a new ice skate or a new kind of ball bearing.

Leasing the warehouse was only the beginning. Once we had the space, we had to bring in a contractor to modify it to meet our needs.

The loading dock was already equipped with a standard dock-height platform for unloading tractor trailers, but we also needed a drive-up ramp. This would allow us to bring a box truck directly into the warehouse, ensuring that loading and unloading could be done discreetly, away from public view.

Beyond that, we required separate, secured storage rooms, each with restricted access: one for human remains and others for Native American and foreign artifacts. The space also needed workstations for the osteologist as well as areas for examining, cleaning, and repacking artifacts. We designated office space for reviewing general evidence, such as Miller's home movies of his digs, and updating an ever-growing case file.

To protect the artifacts, we had to ensure stable climate control, as both excessive and insufficient humidity could cause damage. This meant installing humidifiers and dehumidifiers to work in tandem with the warehouse's heating, ventilation, and air conditioning system as outdoor temperature and humidity conditions fluctuated.

Creating and maintaining near-museum-quality storage and workspaces in a standard warehouse was no easy task. Drew and I knew managing the facility would come with plenty of headaches, but I saw the build-out as a creative challenge—one that I genuinely enjoyed tackling.

The warehouse was also expensive, and securing funding for it became an annual budget battle. Still, it was far more cost-effective than leasing space in a fine art storage facility, and there was no question that it was essential to advancing the case.

By August, I began to make serious headway on the website I'd mentioned at the tribal consultation in June. Again, I had three non-FBI user groups in mind for the website: subject matter experts, Native American tribal representatives, and cultural heritage and law enforcement officials of foreign countries where Miller had also looted archaeological resources and, in a few instances, human remains.

During the search and seizure operation, we had relied on several subject matter experts to help identify problematic artifacts on-site. With the seized material spanning so many cultures and time periods, the need for additional expertise only grew as we moved into evidence review and worked to establish cultural affiliations. However, coordinating in-person visits for potentially dozens of experts in Indianapolis was neither practical nor cost-effective. We needed a better way to give experts access to the artifacts.

Thinking through this problem, it occurred to me that a dedicated website could serve as a way to bring the artifacts to experts in virtual form. The idea was sparked by the National Stolen Art File (NSAF), which allows users to browse images of stolen artworks. However, the needs of this investigation—along with the importance of respecting victim communities, whether sovereign tribal nations in the United States or foreign countries—meant that a Miller case–related website couldn't be open to the public like the NSAF. Access would have to be by invitation only.

To be truly useful, the site also needed far more functionality than the NSAF, which, at the time, provided only a single image of a stolen artwork along with basic details like the artist's name, the date, and the size of the piece. I wanted experts, tribal representatives, and foreign cultural and law enforcement officials to be able to explore multiple images of an artifact from different angles, along with any provenance or provenience information we could extract from Miller's records and our ongoing investigation.

It wasn't as simple as just throwing images up on a site and turning folks loose, though. We needed to ensure that we could control exactly what each invited user could access. It was crucial that non-FBI visitors couldn't freely roam the entire site. Their access needed to be carefully managed based on their role and expertise.

As I envisioned it, subject matter experts would have access only to the specific artifacts we needed their expertise to identify. Native American tribal representatives would be able to view all Native American artifacts but not foreign materials, while foreign users would see artifacts from their respective countries but not Native American objects. Both groups, though, would have access to artifacts that had not yet been culturally affiliated as either Native American or foreign, since we needed everyone's help in fully identifying them. For FBI use only, there would be a separate, restricted section documenting the human remains recovered from Miller.

During a telephone meeting in mid-August, the team at headquarters responsible for managing the NSAF and other bureau internet assets confirmed that everything on my wish list was feasible. To ensure security and allow me to tailor and track user access, each visitor would be assigned a unique password, and every login would require two-factor authentication.

At the time, I assumed this wouldn't pose any issues for the site's intended users. But time would prove me wrong, as I'll explain later. For the time being, I was excited by the prospect of building the site and bringing it online.

I was also intrigued by the thought that the website could help us deal with the complex process for repatriation under NAGPRA. Since NAGPRA's enactment in 1990, the tribes had gotten comfortable with that process, and they wanted us to use it for everything. Insofar as possible, we intended to do that.

That was easier said than done, because not everything we seized from Miller fell under NAGPRA. As I mentioned in describing the challenge of establishing probable cause for our warrant, Miller had looted some of the material before NAGPRA was enacted. Other items didn't fit within its four protected categories: human remains, funerary objects, sacred objects, or objects of cultural patrimony—those items that hold ongoing historical, traditional, or cultural significance to a Native American tribe or community. These objects were never meant to be privately owned, sold, or given away, because they belonged to the tribe as a whole, not to any individual.

Adding to the complexity, Miller was a private individual, not a federal agency or a nongovernmental institution receiving federal funds. That meant he wasn't subject to NAGPRA's regulatory requirements, which govern how federal agencies and federally funded institutions must handle Native American remains and cultural items. The only part of NAGPRA that applied to him was its criminal provision, which prohibits the trafficking of Native American human remains and cultural objects obtained in violation of the law. But that provision didn't exist until NAGPRA became law, long after Miller had already taken many of these items.

Miller had illegally excavated and transported countless artifacts to Indiana, violating numerous federal, state, local, and international laws—but not necessarily NAGPRA. Still, as we worked with the tribes to determine cultural affiliation, it became clear that we needed a single, organized way to present all of the Native American artifacts we had seized.

Even with material we knew, or strongly suspected, fell under NAGPRA, we faced a significant challenge. The law was designed for documented collections held by federal agencies or federally funded institutions—not for private collections or objects seized as evidence in a criminal investigation.

These agencies and institutions must inventory all culturally affiliated materials and submit a Notice of Inventory Completion (NIC) to the National NAGPRA program within the Department of the Interior. The NIC is then published in the Federal Register, a process that generally takes six months or more. After that, institutions must negotiate with the affected tribes and file a Notice of Intent to Repatriate (NIR), which must also be published in the Federal Register before repatriation can proceed. It's a slow, bureaucratic system built on the assumption that cultural affiliations are already well documented—an assumption that didn't fit the reality of Miller's collection.

Most of the Miller collection was undocumented, lacking provenience records apart from what we could piece together from his and his first wife's travel journals, home movies, and other personal materials. Although NAGPRA specifically exempts the Smithsonian Institution and its constituent museums, it has no carve-out for law enforcement. The artifacts we'd seized were evidence, and we were going to have to do a lot of work to establish that they were indeed unlawful possessions and, if possible, culturally affiliate them. Attempting to prepare a NAGPRA inventory with cultural affiliations to specific tribes before this process had even truly begun was simply impossible.

There was no way we could strictly follow the letter of the NAGPRA regulations, but the website offered a way to honor their spirit. By serving as a digital inventory with photos of all the artifacts, it would provide transparency and accessibility.

We would notify all 566 federally recognized tribes (the number in 2014) about the website, effectively launching a national consultation. Tribes could then designate representatives to review the artifacts and submit claims. As cultural affiliations were identified with input from subject matter experts and tribal representatives, we would prepare and submit NICs. From there, our consultations would shift from broad outreach to direct engagement with the specific tribes connected to the artifacts.

I had a number of in-depth conversations about this plan with the office of the National NAGPRA program manager, Sherry Hutt. Fortunately, National NAGPRA agreed that the approach was sound and gave us a basis to go forward.

From Sunday night into Monday morning, August 17–18, 2014, the mall attack exercise took place at a Simon Group mall on the south side of Indianapolis. The event drew numerous foreign dignitaries and law enforcement officials, along with police executives from around the United States, who observed as the exercise unfolded once the mall closed to the public at 6 p.m.

In total, several hundred people were involved. Role players pretended to be mall personnel, shoppers, and terrorists. Multiple state, local, and federal SWAT teams, bomb squads, and even the FBI's hostage rescue team participated. The Indiana National Guard completed the scene by deploying active-bleeder dummies, which lay on the floor, pumping out fake blood. With extensive coordination and high-end special effects, the exercise felt like a full-scale Hollywood production. I was on-site through the night, overseeing the tactical scenarios I had designed and setting off training device explosions to add realism and test the capabilities of the bomb squads and SWAT teams.

Following headquarters' strategic plan, the exercise began with a 911 call reporting active shooters inside the mall. The response escalated quickly from the Greenwood Police Department, which had jurisdiction over the mall, to the Indianapolis Metro Police Department SWAT team, other local law enforcement, and the Indiana State Police. Eventually, the FBI took command as the scenario unfolded and the terrorism nexus became apparent.

It all unfolded effectively and was a great learning experience for everyone involved. By the time the mall opened to the public again at 10 a.m. on Monday, there was no sign that anything unusual had occurred. Months of preparation had paid off, but my role in the exercise had sidetracked me quite a bit from the Miller case.

Later in August, Drew sent a draft of the global relinquishment agreement to Miller and his attorneys. This was far from a standard court-ordered forfeiture, and there was no template for the agreement. Because of her heavy caseload, Melissa Curtis allowed Drew to take the lead in shaping what was, in many ways, a novel concept.

The agreement was straightforward: In exchange for immunity from prosecution for Miller and his second wife, Sandra, they would voluntarily relinquish any ownership claims to the seized material. This meant the government—specifically the FBI—would take full legal possession of the collection and have sole authority over its disposition. However, if any items were ultimately determined to be lawful property, the government would return them to Miller or his designees at its discretion.

The US Attorney's Office naturally had to review and approve Drew's draft. Thanks to him, it was just over two single-spaced pages of straightforward, mostly plain language with minimum legalese. The Millers' attorneys acknowledged receipt of the draft but then went silent. Drew and I agreed that pushing for a quick response would be counterproductive. If we hadn't heard back by early 2015, we would give them a nudge.

The contractors completed their work on the warehouse in October, and I wasted no time outfitting it. I scoured the field office for unused tables, desks, chairs, and storage cabinets, gathering whatever I could. Everything else I needed, I ordered and had delivered to the office.

Working alone after hours with a hand truck, I loaded the field office's box truck and shuttled everything over to the warehouse, one load at a time. Always committed to the case, Holly and her merry band of grad students helped me set up the warehouse and get everything ready to receive Miller's collection. As usual, they were a godsend.

With the infrastructure in place, we were finally ready to move the collection. In many ways, it felt like the Miller search 2.0. From October 27 to 29, Holly, her graduate students, and I used that same box truck to transfer all the seized material to the warehouse. I took care of the loading, unloading, and driving duties, while Holly served as collections manager at the warehouse.

The actual move took about two days, with most of the third day spent placing everything in the designated rooms and workspaces the contractors had built for us. We also logged each box's new location into the Access database. Once again, we managed to complete the transfer without any losses or damage.

Jeremy Wilson and his research assistant continued their osteology work in the warehouse, using the computers and specialized software I had purchased for that purpose. But I had to buy additional computers and monitors to finish setting up the warehouse for evidence review.

Beyond that, I also had to cover the warehouse's monthly rent and utilities and start bringing in art crime team agents on TDY assignments. All of that required funding from headquarters. However, the FBI, like the rest of the federal government, was operating under a temporary continuing appropriations resolution, creating significant budgetary uncertainty, something we were beginning to get very accustomed to.

Congress must pass continuing appropriations resolutions whenever it fails to approve full spending bills by October 1, the start of the federal fiscal year. These stopgap measures allow government agencies to keep the lights on and meet payroll. Since 1977, there have been only three years when Congress didn't have to pass at least one continuing resolution—either for the entire government or for specific agencies.

Unfortunately, the politics surrounding these temporary funding measures seem to grow more intense every year. Federal agencies, uncertain about when or how much funding they'll receive, hesitate to release money to the field until Congress passes a full-year budget. While funding has always been approved eventually out of necessity, no one ever knows exactly when that will happen.

The FBI bureaucracy was overly cautious on this score, in my view. To try to move things along, I wrote a report in mid-November on the Miller case. The report summarized everything that had happened since the original tip, including the tribal consultations and the fact that the website was "nearly ready for live deployment . . . before the end of the year." I sent the report to headquarters and followed it up by going there myself with Drew and Holly in early December.

On Thursday, December 4, Drew, Holly, and I pitched FBI executives on releasing the funds the case needed. For field office personnel like

Drew and me to make such a pitch at FBI headquarters wasn't unheard of, although it didn't happen every day either. For an outside subject matter expert and consultant to join in making the pitch was definitely unusual. But it was important for the decision-makers to understand the full scope and import of the Miller case, and Holly was the best person to fill them in on its scientific and cultural aspects.

I can't say how much it helped, but it certainly didn't hurt. After listening to us, the executives gave the green light to move forward, just as soon as Congress passed a continuing resolution.

With funding secured and FBI executives satisfied, Drew, Holly, and I spent the next day giving our first full presentation on the investigation to a non-bureau audience—aside from the information we had already shared with the tribes. At the Smithsonian Institution's museum support and storage center in Suitland, Maryland, just southeast of Washington, DC, we presented to a group of about twenty-five administrators, curators, researchers, and repatriation specialists from the National Museum of the American Indian (NMAI), using nearly the same PowerPoint slide deck we had just shown at FBI headquarters, except for a few slides that were law-enforcement sensitive.

Although the Smithsonian is a quasigovernmental organization, and about two-thirds of its staff are federal employees, it was quite unusual to discuss an ongoing FBI case outside the bounds of federal law enforcement or direct consultations with the victim community. I had FBI headquarters approval to provide this presentation to this specific group, but I nevertheless admonished the audience not to share any details of my presentation.

The NMAI staffers, several of whom were Native American, were already familiar with the case, both from news coverage of the April search and seizure and from ongoing discussions within the tribal community. Drew, Holly, and I wanted to give them a deeper, inside look for two key reasons.

First, their expertise in repatriation and their close ties to Native communities made them valuable partners. Engaging with them supported the FBI's commitment to ongoing consultation and cooperation with tribal nations on the Miller case. Second, the NMAI and other parts of the Smithsonian could potentially assist in culturally affiliating the seized material, helping to determine where and to whom these artifacts rightfully belonged.

The reaction to our presentation was mixed. On the one hand, the curators, repatriation specialists, and their colleagues were fascinated by the quality of the artifacts we'd seized. They were relieved to know that these cultural items were no longer in Miller's possession and would eventually be repatriated to their rightful tribes. On the other hand, everyone was shocked and dismayed by the sheer extent of Miller's looting and, even more so, by his treatment of Native American ancestral remains. As we left the NMAI that day, we all felt certain that sharing this case with them had been the right decision—not just for practical reasons but for moral ones as well.

Drew, Holly, and I headed home hopeful that the bureau would soon have the budget it needed to fund the case and that the NMAI would become a valuable ally in the cultural affiliation and repatriation process. A week and a half later, Congress settled the funding issue by passing the spending bills for the 2015 fiscal year. With the budget uncertainty resolved, I immediately lined up Jake Archer and Ronnie Walker to assist with evidence review in Indianapolis in early January.

Eight

Disturbed Spirits?

I can't wake Marley up," Risa said over the phone, her voice cracking with the worry we both felt. "It's like she's in a coma."

"I'm leaving for the airport now," I said, trying to keep my own voice calm. "I'll get my ticket changed to the next flight home."

Outside my hotel near Washington Square Park in the SoHo area of Manhattan, I scanned left and right for a taxi. It was 10 a.m. on a mild, cloudy Sunday, June 7, 2015. Glancing to my left, I spotted a cab turning my way, its "Vacant" roof light glowing. Just as I raised my arm to hail it, the light flicked off—it had picked up a passenger around the corner. I cursed in frustration.

Then, just behind it, another taxi appeared, its roof light still on. I threw up my hand and flagged it down.

"LaGuardia Airport, please," I told the driver. "As quick as you can."

I called Risa back. There was no change in Marley, our four-year-old—sandwiched between her six-year-old sister, Ailyn, and her two-year-old brother, Macauley. She was still struggling.

I had flown to New York on Wednesday evening, when Marley's only apparent issue was a severe cough, to participate in a continuing legal education seminar, "Art Crime and Cultural Heritage: Fakes, Forgeries, and Looted and Stolen Art," held at New York University Law School from June 4 to 6. Although I had spoken about the Miller case at the National Museum of the American Indian (NMAI) in December, that had been a closed-door session for a small group of cultural repatriation administrators and research specialists. It was still largely within the overlapping circles of the federal government and the Native American community. The NYU symposium, however, was the first truly public venue where the case was discussed—a sign of how it was raising the profile of the art crime program.

My presentation and panel participation had gone well, but my mind was elsewhere—on Marley. Kids get sick all the time, and I wasn't overly concerned yet, but there was an edge in Risa's voice that told me this wasn't just a run-of-the-mill cold. As I made my way to LaGuardia, changed my ticket, and boarded the next flight to Indianapolis, a conversation I'd had more than once played in the back of my mind.

"We appreciate what you are doing," elders from various tribes had told me in one way or another. "But please be careful. The spirits of the ancestors are angry about what has happened to them, and that could come back on you and your families." Kevin Daugherty of the Pokagon Band of Potawatomi had explained that the spirits of children whose remains had been disturbed were even more likely to be unsettled than those of adults. And we had been spending an awful lot of time with those ancestral remains.

I wasn't thinking about any of that—not directly. But the words were there, lingering just beneath the surface, following me all the way home.

The year had begun with significant progress on the Miller case. On January 4, Jake arrived in Indianapolis for two weeks of evidence review, and Ronnie joined us for a week starting January 6. Additional evidence review sessions—some with them, others with different art crime team agents and a few non-agent support professionals from FBI headquarters—took place in February, April, and later in the year.

We had handled human remains during the search and seizure, but afterward they had been placed in respectful and private storage at the field office, where the osteologist began examining them in August. Now, with an osteology lab station set up in the warehouse, the early months of 2015 marked the first time that Holly, other case team members, and I were in regular contact with the ancestral remains.

DISTURBED SPIRITS?

In January, Jake, Ronnie, and I concentrated on the extensive visual record the Millers had compiled, documenting their digs and their handling of artifacts and human remains. The collection included thousands of still photographs, along with home and travel movies in both analog and digital formats, offering a firsthand look at their activities over the years. To properly analyze the analog footage, we first had to digitize it. Commercial conversion services were prohibitively expensive, so we had to come up with our own analog-to-digital conversion system to process the material in-house.

I bought a standard 8mm reel-to-reel projector on eBay, but to actually convert the films, I needed something more advanced. After a bit of online research, I purchased a relatively inexpensive digital conversion system, a machine designed to convert analog film one frame at a time, capturing the frames as separate still images before stitching them together into a seamless digital movie file.

A typical 8mm film reel contains around 3,600 frames per 50 feet of film, meaning even a small reel requires thousands of individual captures. The used projector's feeder reel could accommodate only three-to-six-inch reels of 8mm and Super 8 film. But many of Miller's reels were much larger—10.5 to 16 inches in diameter, holding up to eighty minutes of footage on 16mm film.

A quick fifteen minutes in my woodworking shop was all it took to modify the setup. I built a pivoting wooden arm attached to a plywood base, allowing the projector to handle the larger reels by positioning them in a custom slot, making it possible to digitize the bigger films with ease. To me, this was just a simple quick fix to get us up and running. But, to this day, Jake still brags about my "amazing woodworking skills," telling everyone that I'm a master carpenter because I built this rig.

What can I say? City people . . .

Every evening before we left the warehouse, we set everything up to digitize one of the longer reels of film overnight. A few times, we arrived the next morning to find the film had jammed, forcing us to start over. But for a hacked-together setup, it mostly worked surprisingly well.

Much of the footage was irrelevant to the case. For example, Miller had gone to the Indy 500 on several occasions and recorded entire races.

Many reels and tapes contained footage of other innocuous public events or family gatherings, often interspersed with shots of digs or of Miller and his first wife, Sue, at home with looted artifacts and human remains.

Taken as a whole, the footage and photographs revealed just how obsessive Miller was about documenting his activities and interests. The films, tapes, and images captured Don and Sue Miller—along with their accomplices—in and around Native American graves, often mugging for the camera with skulls and other bones.

Similar images showed them and their accomplices at Indigenous burial sites on Easter Island and in New Guinea as well as in other parts of the world. Whether in the American Southwest, the Ohio River Valley, Central or South America, on Pacific islands, or at home, their treatment of human remains was the same—casual, heartless, and deeply disturbing.

At home, Don and Sue were pictured smiling as they cleaned skulls and bones, preparing them for display. Some images were even more disquieting, such as baking human skulls in their kitchen oven—as casually as if they were making dinner—to speed the hardening of shellac they'd applied as a preservative. Images from digs showed Don lying in freshly unearthed graves, side by side with the remains he was about to plunder, his expression amused rather than reverent.

In image after image, whether handling stolen human remains, digging into sacred burial sites, or desecrating the dead, Don and Sue wore ear-to-ear grins, as if none of it carried the weight of real human lives and histories. The sheer callousness captured in these photos was staggering.

These images certainly said something about Don and Sue Miller as individuals. But they also reflected Manifest Destiny and colonial attitudes to Native American and other Indigenous cultures that many pothunters and other people share. The images proclaimed, "We have the right to take these human remains and artifacts and do with them as we please." The gleeful desecration, recorded for later viewing and reminiscing, wasn't happenstance. It was a fundamental part of a process of remorseless cultural appropriation, of turning archaeological treasures and ancestral remains into private trophies and trinkets.

DISTURBED SPIRITS?

The global relinquishment agreement was still sitting with the Millers and their attorney. Drew maintained occasional contact with the attorney but applied no pressure.

It was clear that Don Miller was reluctant to sign away title to what he saw as his life's work, and we didn't want to risk pushing him to the point of withdrawing his cooperation. Keeping him engaged, even if at a slow pace, was wiser than forcing a confrontation.

At the beginning of March, Don and Sue Miller's attorney informed Drew that they had both signed the relinquishment agreement. He would soon be sending it to the bureau with his own signature added. When it arrived, we would no longer have need of our unused search and seizure warrant, and it would go back to the court of the magistrate judge who signed it.

On March 17, 2015, the General Counsel's Office at FBI headquarters received and countersigned the agreement. Five days later, on March 22, Don Miller passed away, just a little over two months shy of his ninety-second birthday at the end of May.

As is typical with any relinquishment of title agreement, there was a thirty-day estoppel period during which a counterclaimant could come forward and assert ownership of the seized material. But in this case, there was no one who could legitimately claim title to looted artifacts and human remains, aside, of course, from the victim communities or lineal descendants. Nevertheless, we still observed the waiting period.

In due course, full custody of the artifacts and remains irrevocably transferred to the federal government—and for all practical purposes, my colleagues and me. We were now responsible for what happened next. If disturbed, angry spirits of the dead were seeking someone to target, and Miller was no longer alive, that left us—even though everything we were doing was in service of ensuring their rightful return and final rest.

The first unsettling event for my family involved our Belgian Malinois, Brogan. I had gotten Brogan as a puppy in 2005, during my second year in the FBI. Having worked with K-9 dogs as a local cop, I initially thought I might train him for the bureau's small K-9 team, but that never came to pass. Even so, Brogan played an important role in my life. He was with me through the early years of my career, and he became an unexpected point in my favor when I met Risa. Like me, she had grown up with dogs and loved them, and Brogan quickly became part of our life together.

By spring 2015, Brogan was ten years old and a beloved member of the family. He seemed to be in his usual fine shape—active, strong, and full of life, enthusiastically chasing away the occasional coyote that ventured too close to our farmhouse.

But one day in March, he suddenly began limping. By the next day, a tumor had appeared, bulging from his shoulder. The decline was shockingly fast.

Putting him down to spare him from suffering was devastating for all of us. We mourned Brogan for about a month before Risa announced, "This family needs a new dog."

I wanted to hold off. The Miller case evidence review had ramped up significantly, piling on to an already overwhelming workload. On top of my usual bomb tech duties, I was training two other agents to become special agent bomb technicians. In the long run, that would ease my burden. But in the short term, it only made things more demanding.

But Risa was firm. "We have to get another dog."

"Okay," I said. "But I can't deal with training a puppy right now. Let's look for a nice, older rescue dog so we don't have to start from scratch."

Not long after, Risa spotted a notice for a rescue dog adoption event at a pet store in the Indianapolis area. She took the kids, hoping to find the right addition to our family. There, they saw a big mastiff, advertised as "very kid-friendly." But when Marley reached out to pet the dog, it bit her on the face. Risa rushed her to the emergency room, where she needed stitches over one eye.

When adopting a rescue dog, there's no way to know what past experiences might trigger certain behaviors. Risa and I understood that as lifelong dog people, but that didn't make us any less upset about Marley being bitten.

What troubled us most was the rescue group's carelessness—not just in labeling the mastiff as kid-friendly but in failing to properly monitor its interactions at the event. Worse, right after the bite, the group packed up and left—as we later learned, taking the mastiff and the other dogs to another adoption event at a different location. Even more disturbing, they were still advertising the mastiff as kid-friendly, despite the fact that it had just bitten my daughter in the face.

Under Indiana state law, any dog that bites someone must be quarantined, but no one at the pet store knew where to find the rescue group. In the end, we had to trust the store's assurance that all participating dogs were up-to-date on their rabies vaccinations, as required for the event.

Marley's health was our biggest concern, but we also worried about the long-term impact—would she develop a fear of dogs? That only made Risa more determined to bring another one into the family—and soon.

"I think we have to get a puppy, Tim," she said. "A little fur ball in the house will do us all good."

I grumbled at that, but I gave in. In May, we got a Fox Red Labrador puppy from well-established breeders in the area and named him Coby. Some carpet and furniture mishaps gave me plenty to complain about—and even rant and rave over—but before long, Coby settled down and became a beloved part of the family.

The week before the NYU symposium, Marley started coughing intermittently. She had mild asthma and was prone to upper respiratory infections, something we were used to managing. They had never been a serious issue.

However, while I was in New York, Marley's cough worsened. By Friday morning, she was struggling to breathe and couldn't eat.

Fortunately, school was out for the summer, and one of our regular teenage babysitters was available to watch Ailyn and Macauley while Risa took Marley to the pediatrician. At the doctor's office, Marley received a dose of albuterol through a nebulizer, helping to ease her cough and congestion. The pediatrician also prescribed prednisone, a steroid to calm her immune system and reduce inflammation in her lungs.

Risa kept me updated through texts and calls, but the news wasn't good—the steroid wasn't helping Marley's cough. Neither had gotten much sleep that night.

Early Saturday morning, Risa called the pediatrician, who referred her to a pediatric pulmonologist. She left multiple messages, pleading for a callback. When the pulmonologist finally called later that morning, his recommendation was underwhelming. "Let's treat Marley with a dose of Benadryl," he said.

Risa and I were both concerned about giving Benadryl, an antihistamine whose active ingredient is also a strong sedative, to a four-year-old. But pediatricians commonly prescribe it, and the pulmonologist assured Risa that the dose would be appropriate for Marley's age and weight.

The Benadryl worked like a switch, shutting off Marley's cough almost instantly. As the pulmonologist had warned, it also made her groggy and drowsy, so Risa put her to bed. We were both hopeful that a good rest would set everything right.

But on Sunday morning, Risa couldn't wake Marley. "I shook her. I spoke to her loudly. I even clapped in her ear," Risa told me over the phone. "She won't wake up."

"The half-life of Benadryl can only be six hours or so," I said. "It shouldn't put her out for this long."

Based on what the pulmonologist had said, we agreed we shouldn't panic. But we were both worried enough to agree that I should head straight to the airport and catch the next available flight home rather than take my scheduled late afternoon flight.

As soon as I got home, I went straight to Marley's room. Risa was there, crying.

I already knew from our call after my plane landed in Indianapolis that Marley had finally woken up while I was in the air—nearly twenty-one hours after taking the Benadryl. But her vicious cough had returned with full force.

When Risa got the pulmonologist on the phone again, he suggested another dose of Benadryl. He reassured her that if it put Marley into a deep sleep again, it wasn't cause for concern. So Risa gave her the Benadryl. Just like before, it shut the cough off instantly—and just like before, Marley slipped into an almost comatose state.

I shook Marley's shoulder and spoke to her, but she was completely unresponsive. It was so unlike a normal, restful sleep that my anxiety spiked to match Risa's. But although Marley was unresponsive, she was breathing evenly and steadily, and her pulse was strong. Given what the pulmonologist had said, we decided to let Marley sleep and not try to wake her until the morning. Neither of us got any sleep that night.

By Monday morning, Marley was still sleeping—completely unresponsive. No matter how firmly we shook her shoulder, how loudly we spoke, or even clapped in her ear, she wouldn't wake up.

As a cop, I had sometimes used interorbital pressure points around the eyes to rouse someone who was intoxicated or unconscious. It was a last resort, something that usually provoked a reaction.

I tried it with Marley.

Nothing. No movement. No response.

Finally, I tried a sternum rub, rubbing my knuckles firmly up and down her sternum bone. It's a technique that causes significant discomfort—enough to rouse even someone in a deep unconscious state.

That woke her up.

But when we got her to sit up in bed, it scared the shit out of us. The left side of Marley's face was drooping like you see on elderly stroke victims. Her eyes were swollen almost shut, and her eyelids sagged, heavy and unresponsive.

I urged her to get out of bed. "Come on, Marley. You have to stand up and move around. You need to get some blood flowing."

She answered me. But her words were so blurred they were almost incomprehensible, more babbling than speech. At four years old, she could normally communicate well, but now, forming clear words seemed beyond her.

She was also having trouble seeing. She wasn't blind, but everything was blurry. When I held up my fingers in front of her face, she couldn't tell how many there were.

I asked her to walk down the hallway. She tried her best, but overnight, she had lost a shocking amount of muscle control. She looked drunk, staggering unsteadily, bouncing off the walls from one side to the other as she struggled to stay upright.

Risa and I were terrified about the state she was in. I told Risa, "I'll stay here with Ailyn and Macauley. You get Marley in the car and go straight to the doctor"—the pediatrician, we agreed, not the pulmonologist.

Given Marley's impaired muscle control, facial drooping, and vision problems, the pediatrician suspected a possible stroke. She told Risa to take Marley to the emergency room at Riley Hospital for Children in downtown Indianapolis.

You can imagine Risa's state of mind. And you can imagine mine when, strapping Marley into her car seat, she called to tell me what the pediatrician said. Neither of us had ever heard of a young child having a stroke. It's incredibly rare—a .00006 percent chance—but it does happen.

Risa was flying down the highway when a police officer pulled her over. He took one look at the situation and said, "Follow me."

I'd been in his position before, back when I was a patrol cop. You pull someone over and realize they're in the middle of a medical emergency. In that moment, you have to make a call. Do you make them wait for an ambulance? Let them continue on their own, risking an accident? Or do you clear a path and get them there safely?

The officer made the right call. He flipped on his lights and siren and gave Risa and Marley a safe, fast escort to Riley Children's Hospital—exactly what they needed in that moment.

The attending physician in the emergency room quickly ruled out a stroke based on clinical signs. But when it came to what was wrong, he hesitated—hemming and hawing instead of giving a clear answer. That didn't sit well with Risa. Her microbiology training and strong temperament meant she was never shy about challenging a medical professional, especially when it came to her child. She got right in the doctor's face and demanded, "What is your worst-case scenario?"

"I'm concerned that Marley might have a tumor of the cerebellum," he finally said.

As terrifying as it had been to hear the pediatrician suspect a stroke, this hit even harder—a punch to the gut that knocked the wind out of us. A stroke was rare enough in a child, but a brain tumor? That was an entirely different kind of nightmare.

They took Marley for a CT scan, blood tests, and, worst of all, a lumbar puncture to look for signs of cancer in her spinal fluid. I've had my own lumbar punctures, and they're no picnic.

Before I could join Risa and Marley at the hospital, I had to figure out long-term care for Ailyn and Macauley. It was clear we'd be back and forth from the hospital for the foreseeable future, and we needed someone we could count on to look after them. Risa and I had no family in Indiana, so on the way to the hospital, I called some of our extended family to see who might be able to come help.

Risa grew up in Milwaukee with her mother and stepfather. But her father, Herschel, lived in Los Angeles with his second wife, Ruth, and their three daughters. Though they lived far away, they had always been a steady part of her life, and we knew we could count on them. Ruth generously offered to fly in with Risa's half-sisters on Monday to care for Ailyn and Macauley—a huge relief in the midst of all the uncertainty.

The good news after the CT scan, blood tests, and lumbar puncture was that Marley did not have a brain tumor. The bad news was that they had no idea what was wrong with her. They immediately admitted her to Riley's ICU, where the rooms have fold-out beds so parents can spend the night with their children.

Riley put a massive team on Marley's case, but no one could figure out what was wrong. We mentioned the dog bite, which had happened just a couple of weeks earlier, prompting the state health department to track down and finally quarantine the dog. It was too little, too late, and in the end, it didn't matter. The dog was found to be healthy, with no signs of rabies or any other known issue that could clearly be connected to Marley's condition.

At the same time, specialists checked our home—surrounded by farmland outside Indianapolis—for toxic pesticides and herbicides. It was the time of year that local farmers sprayed their fields for weeds and pests, so there was some concern that Marley might have had an exposure that we didn't know about. That, too, turned up nothing that could explain Marley's symptoms.

With each passing day, the lack of answers about Marley's condition left Risa and me more worried and frustrated. Still, we clung to hope.

The doctors and nurses were clearly dedicated, and Riley Hospital for Children had a sterling reputation. Part of the Indiana University Health System, Riley consistently ranks among the best children's hospitals in the country—and the world.

We were also amazed and touched by how the FBI rallied around us. Up until that point in my FBI career, my biggest complaint had been the lack of camaraderie compared to my time in the military and police. In those settings, I spent social time with my fellow airmen and officers—even if I didn't like them. It was just part of the life. We all had to trust each other in tough and dangerous situations, and socializing with one another outside of work was a key part of building that trust.

That same trust exists among FBI agents, but there's a difference. Agents tend to be older, with families they want to get home to after work. The job still demands loyalty and teamwork, but the social bonds aren't always as tight.

I was friendly with fellow agents and other FBI coworkers. But we weren't part of one another's lives outside work. I felt the culture of the bureau was a little cold and distant.

To my surprise, when word got out about Marley, lots of folks from the field office stepped up, even some I had barely spoken to in my four and a half years in Indianapolis. They brought food to Risa and me at the hospital and to our kids, Ruth, and her daughters at home. They offered to run errands, clean the house, and mow the grass—anything to help lighten the load. For the first time in my bureau career, I truly felt part of a community.

The situation gave me a new appreciation of how fortunate we were that I was a federal employee. In addition to our excellent health insurance, I had plenty of accumulated leave along with the freedom to use it. When Marley was admitted to the hospital, I called my supervisor, Leslie Lahr, and simply said, "I'll see you when I see you."

Leslie replied, "Whatever you need." And she meant it. No doubt it was through her that word spread across the field office.

If I hadn't had enough accumulated leave, I could have received donated leave from other federal employees. The leave donation program allows colleagues to transfer their own leave to employees facing medical or family emergencies, ensuring they don't have to choose between work and being there for their loved ones. There was simply a lot more leeway and support for me to take time out for a family medical emergency than there would have been in any private sector job. It would be more than six weeks before I returned to work, and that was completely okay with the bureau and with my bosses in the field office.

In the hospital's ICU, which had become our home for a while, I couldn't help but notice another room that I passed by regularly as I came and went. In that room was a young girl, a toddler younger than Marley, who was frequently crying and always alone, save for the occasional nurse attending to her.

Struggling with our own situation, I stopped one of the senior nurses in the ward one afternoon to inquire about something that was totally none of my business. I told her I thought it was a shame that this poor child—who couldn't have been more than eighteen to twenty months old—was always alone and seemed frightened. Then I asked, "Would it be okay if I went in to spend a little time with her?"

The nurse must have recognized that I was genuinely distressed about the child being alone and that I was also channeling my frustration over not being able to do more for my own child than sit beside her. She gently explained that I couldn't enter the child's room unless I became part of the hospital's volunteer program, which required extensive screening. Being an FBI agent didn't grant me any shortcuts—the usual lengthy background checks for volunteers still applied. I hadn't told anyone in the ICU that I was an FBI agent, but it was in the file, and that information had clearly gotten around.

And then the nurse told me, "The child's mother is a single parent. She's working two full-time jobs to pay for her daughter's care and support her family, with no sick leave, no vacation days, and no health insurance. She can spend only a few hours with her daughter every night. Can you imagine the torment and guilt she goes through when she has to leave her sick child alone all day?"

That was a good smack in the mouth to wake me up. *Holy shit, this is what privilege is*, I thought. It was a sobering moment, realizing that not everyone had the freedom to be with their sick child all day, like I did.

Not everyone had the job security, the leave, or the support that allowed me to be there for Marley without question.

Just as important to Risa and me emotionally was the outpouring of support from the tribal community, who learned of Marley's illness through Larry Zimmerman and Holly. Within a day of Marley's admission, Larry and Holly were passing along emails and phone calls filled with concern and encouragement. It felt almost like a church group rallying around a family in need—except this wasn't just one group. We were receiving support from entire communities within the tribal nations, lifting us up when we needed it most. And, of course, we were getting that same support from Holly, Larry, and Charli as well.

As word spread, we began receiving offers from the tribal community to perform a cleansing ceremony at our home, using smudging and prayers. Elders from several different tribes reached out, wanting to help in any way they could. We were deeply grateful for the offers and the genuine concern from the tribal community. Just knowing they were lifting us up and doing everything possible to help meant the world to us.

Sincerity is a fundamental value among Native Americans. When I dealt with the tribal community, I always spoke from the heart and strove to match my actions with my words. For the tribal community to reciprocate as it did was a very meaningful, powerful gift to my family and me. We'll never forget it.

Seven days into our ordeal of uncertainty and worry, a neurologist—one who had not yet seen Marley—came through on morning rounds with a group of medical students. After examining Marley and reviewing her chart, she said, "This is a long shot. What I'm thinking of most often affects males between forty and seventy, though it can also occur in females. There are reported cases in teenagers, but I've never heard of one in a child as young as Marley. We've never seen a case of it in this hospital."

"What do you think it might be?" Risa asked.

"Marley's symptoms match something called Miller Fisher syndrome, or MFS. It's a variant of Guillain-Barré syndrome, GBS. Both are autoimmune disorders that attack the myelin, the protective covering around nerve cells. What happens is that something—like Marley's cough—triggers the immune system. But instead of shutting down once the infection is gone, the immune system keeps attacking, this time targeting the myelin.

"Think of it like stripping the insulation off electrical wires that are bundled together. Without insulation, the electrical impulses running through them interfere with each other and get crossed up. The same thing happens in the nervous system. Signals misfire, and the body loses control of itself."

After letting that sink in, the doctor continued, "The symptoms of MFS are exactly what Marley has: ataxia, the lack of muscle control she's suffering from in her movement and speech; areflexia, her lack of any reflex response when we tap below her knee with a rubber hammer; and the ophthalmoplegia that's paralyzing the muscles that control her eye movements and giving her pain behind the eyes.

"Similar things happen with GBS. But GBS tends to show itself first in the lower body and then move up, whereas MFS tends to show itself first in the upper body and brain stem and then move down, which is what we're seeing with Marley."

The neurologist's diagnosis, delivered so clearly, was music to our ears. At last, someone had a good idea what might be wrong with Marley. Of course, we needed more than that, and we asked, "Is there a way to confirm that she has MFS? Can you treat it?"

"We can confirm it with a blood test, although the blood will have to go to a special outside lab and we won't know the results for a few days. In the meantime, there is a way to treat MFS, and we could start to do that right away.

"The treatment is intravenous immunoglobulin therapy, IVIG. What we would do is give Marley antibody-rich globulin by IV for ten hours at a time over the course of three days."

"Could that hurt her?"

"The procedure is safe, but it can be a bit uncomfortable. We would want to sedate Marley to ensure she tolerates it well."

Risa and I looked at each other, and we knew—without a word—that we were in complete agreement. The hospital should do the test and start the treatment. Then we heard what the sedative of choice was. Benadryl.

We freaked out. "Benadryl is part of what started this nightmare!"

It took some time, but the doctors talked us off that ledge. They explained that Marley's condition wasn't caused by the small doses of Benadryl the pediatric pulmonologist had prescribed. The real culprit was her immune system's overreaction to her cough—a chain reaction that had nothing to do with the medication.

As we sat with Marley during her first ten-hour IVIG treatment, we went online to read more about Miller Fisher syndrome. That's when we saw something that made our stomachs drop—MFS is fatal in 10–20 percent of cases. The reason? The ataxia can slow breathing to the point where a person essentially dry-land drowns, suffocating from lack of oxygen.

Over the past week, we had spent countless hours watching the monitors tracking Marley's vital signs. By now, we knew what her numbers should be, and it was reassuring to see the familiar readings and steady green lights.

To our dismay, Marley's breaths per minute (BPM) began to decrease about three to four hours into her treatment. Her BPM fell to just two or three breaths a minute, fluctuating at that very low level without rising again. Then the monitor began flashing red and emitting warning beeps. Risa and I were both panicking, although I managed to stay outwardly calm, keeping my voice steady and calm as I spoke.

"The nurses have to be seeing this at their station," I said. "I'm sure they'll be in here soon."

Seconds felt like minutes. Then actual minutes passed—and no one came to check on Marley. I stepped out into the hall and looked toward the nurses' station.

They were just standing around, chatting.

My high-stress career had taught me to compartmentalize and stay focused on the task at hand, no matter the situation. But in that ICU ward hallway, I was an emotionally overwhelmed, overstressed parent.

"What the hell's wrong with you?" I yelled at the nurses. "My daughter needs help in here!"

Other parents came to the doorways of their children's rooms, concerned by how and what I was yelling. A young nurse glanced at her colleagues and walked down the hallway without any hurry or sense of urgency.

DISTURBED SPIRITS?

The nurse came into Marley's room, looked at the monitors, and said everything was okay.

"Everything is most certainly not okay!"

She said, "Calm down, sir. I know what I'm doing. I'm the one who's had eight hours of training on this equipment."

To me that didn't sound like much. "Are you kidding me? Eight whole hours?"

She looked at us and said, "It's my job as a nurse to monitor the equipment and take action, if it's needed. It's your job as parents to be here for your daughter."

I thought Risa was going to climb across Marley's bed and kill her. Risa didn't actually attack the young nurse, but she completely lost it, screaming, "Get out of this room! You're fired! Don't touch my daughter, and don't come back in here!"

The tumult didn't end until a bunch of doctors and other nurses came in on rounds. The most senior physician calmly said, "Your daughter is not in any danger. The low BPM is fairly normal. We should have prepared you for that. It's like sleep apnea. As long as Marley's getting a couple of breaths per minute, she's fine."

"Why didn't you warn us about that? Why didn't the nurse explain it?"

"We should have done that. I'm sorry we didn't."

Risa and I calmed down, but I didn't feel too bad about how we reacted. Any parent would have done the same. The nurse was young and still learning, but she should have been trained to show more empathy with her patients and their families.

Despite all the chaos, the IVIG therapy continued, and almost immediately, we saw positive results. Marley began regaining muscle control. The left side of her face lifted, her speech became clearer, and she could see better.

A couple of days later, the lab results confirmed that Marley had MFS. We could finally see light at the end of the tunnel, and it was getting brighter. The worst was almost behind us. After another week in the ICU, and continued rounds of IVIG therapy, Marley was able to sit up in bed and eat pizza, her favorite food.

After nearly thirteen days in the ICU, followed by a few days in the general pediatric ward, Marley was transferred to inpatient rehab. Her body was healing, but her legs were too weak to support her on their own and she had to relearn how to walk. With leg braces strapped on, she took her first unsteady steps, slowly rebuilding the strength and control she had lost.

Thirty-three days after she was admitted to the hospital, we were finally able to take Marley home. By then, she was about 50 percent recovered. She still had a long road ahead. She wore leg braces for another two months, and it took several more months for her eyelids to stop drooping. In a way, her youth was a blessing. She accepted everything as it came, adapting without falling into fear, anxiety, or frustration the way an older child or adult might have.

Today, Marley is probably 95 percent recovered. Her eyes are still sensitive to light, and for a while, she wore sunglasses in the classroom to help. But she hasn't needed them in a long time. She also permanently lost her reflex response, though the doctors assured us it's no big deal—even some Olympic athletes lack reflex responses.

Her gait is still slightly awkward, but that hasn't stopped her from diving into dance, gymnastics, and cheerleading. She refuses to let any of it hold her back.

People who get Miller Fisher syndrome have a 30 percent chance of recurrence at some point in their lives. That thought stays with us, and whenever Marley comes down with a cold or fever, we can't help but worry.

But we know how fortunate we are. A little boy was admitted to the hospital within hours of Marley, with similar symptoms. His parents were on the same agonizing search for answers, hoping for good news. But his diagnosis was far worse. He actually had a brain tumor. Tragically, he passed away while we were there.

There was nothing fair about it. His family deserved the relief we felt when Marley started to recover. Instead, they left the hospital with an unbearable loss.

We were lucky.

DISTURBED SPIRITS?

Marley was still early in her recovery when my father, Terry Carpenter, passed away in mid-August from a heart attack at age fifty-nine. Exactly four weeks later, his mother, Idalee "Toni" Carpenter, passed away at age eighty-eight after a long battle with late-stage Alzheimer's. Their health struggles had started long before the Miller case, but losing my dad and grandmother back-to-back only added to what was already a brutal year for my family and me.

By design and to keep our commitment to the tribal community, only a small group of people involved in the Miller case had intimate contact with Native American ancestral remains. As the case progressed through 2015 and beyond, however, several others in that small group, or members of their families, experienced very troubling issues that arose out of the blue. A few of these issues were life-threatening, and some are ongoing. For reasons of privacy, I can't share names or details.

On the other hand, some team members who had close contact with the remains experienced no issues at all.

Was there a cause-and-effect relationship between contact with the ancestral remains in the Miller case and the problems experienced by some members of the case team or their families? Or was it all just a series of coincidences?

I don't know, and I guess I never will.

Nine

"Bury Me with My Indian"

Measuring Bones and Consulting the Tribes

I want you to bury me with my Indian."

That's what the tipsters said frail, elderly Don Miller told them, before they became estranged. The tipsters knew "my Indian" meant the full skeleton lying, with assorted artifacts, on red felt in a glass-sided and topped wooden case in a locked room off Miller's main basement display area. Miller opened that room only for himself and his closest family and friends. No one else could view the most prized possession—emotionally if not financially—in his entire collection. A handwritten paper label in the display case identified the skeleton as that of "Sioux Warrior, 19th Cent." But Miller loved to boast that the individual in question was the most famous of all Sioux warriors, Crazy Horse.

Miller's boast held a key to his obsession with Native American artifacts and ancestral remains but also with Indigenous artifacts in general. And the significance of that key lay not just in Miller himself but in what he represented.

We generally think of solving a crime as discovering who did it. When we consider motivation, especially in the case of a serial offender still on the loose, it's usually to help identify and stop them before they commit another crime.

In the Miller case, there was no mystery about who was responsible. From the start, it was clear that if crimes had been committed, Don Miller was the one behind them. And at his age, he was no longer a threat to commit more of the same.

By the time the search and seizure ended, Miller's motivations were no mystery either. He was an obsessive collector, no different from countless others who amass baseball cards, stamps, artwork, or historical memorabilia. Some members of the art crime team had the collecting bug themselves and understood it firsthand. All of us had seen it play out in previous art crime cases.

There was nothing unusual about how collecting, piece by piece, became a habit for Miller and, in his own words, "an addiction." Not every collector has the time and money he did to build such an extensive collection. Not all seek the added thrill of acquiring something forbidden, as Miller did when he looted Indigenous archaeological sites. Not everyone is willing to cross moral and legal boundaries to feed their obsession, as he was. But the basic psychology of Miller's collecting—the excitement of the hunt, the rush of acquisition, the persistent craving for the next find—was nothing out of the ordinary.

The horrific side of Miller's collecting, treating human remains as trophies, gave us all pause, to be sure. But as we seized some two thousand human bones, most of them jumbled together in appalling filth and mold, that grim reality became clear enough too.

We saw it in the way he treated the bones with utter disregard, disarticulating and mixing remains so one person's teeth could fill the gaps in another's jaw for display, hammering arrowheads into a skull for effect, even using a child's skull as an apple dish. We heard it in the stories he told without a trace of remorse about using backhoes to dig up graves; in his bitter complaint, "Why are you taking all of my Indians?"; and in his contemptuous remark, "If it is just a bunch of dead Indians that make you squeamish, go ahead and take them."

As Drew said on a few occasions, "Miller has 'othered' Native Americans to the point where he doesn't recognize them as fully human." Or in Ronnie's words, "It's this continuation of Manifest Destiny attitudes, that anything Native American is there for the taking."

Fortunately, those attitudes are not as strong as they once were and continue to fade. But they still persist in American society. Thousands of pothunters and many others share them. Whatever quirks existed in Miller's personal psychology, they pale in comparison to how his crimes reflect some of the darkest threads in American history and culture as well as some of the most troubling aspects of our national psyche.

People often excuse their crimes by blaming the victims. Rapists claim their victims, whether adults or children, were "provocative" or "wanted it." Justifying collective crimes against humanity, such as the enslavement of Black people or the US government's often genocidal treatment of Native Americans, relies on portraying the victims as inferior beings who somehow deserved their fate or even benefited from it.

Apologists for American slavery argue that enslavement was good for Black Africans, minimizing or ignoring the pervasive violence that defined the system. Likewise, the Manifest Destiny vision of expanding the United States from the Atlantic to the Pacific rested on both the belief that "the only good Indians are the dead Indians," as Teddy Roosevelt put it, and the conviction that it was right to force Native American children into residential schools to strip away their cultural identity.

For Miller, possessing the bones of a great Native American warrior like Crazy Horse was an implicit victory for Manifest Destiny. Having those bones buried with him in his own grave would make that victory permanent. He had no way of proving that his "Sioux Warrior, 19th Cent." was Crazy Horse, but the possibility thrilled him. It allowed him to inflate his own importance and impress others.

This mindset aligned with his approach to all the Indigenous archaeological sites and graves he looted, both in the United States and abroad. By reducing human remains and associated cultural artifacts to mere trophies, he justified and deepened his enjoyment of the spoils.

Solving the Miller case was never about figuring out who did it, or really even why. It was about determining, as much as possible, when and where he had excavated his finds so they could be returned to the peoples and cultures they belonged to. In that regard, "Sioux Warrior, 19th Cent." was exhibit number one.

Could "Sioux Warrior"—Individual 10, as our inventory had to put it for lack of any reliable identifying information—really be Crazy Horse?

The broader collection of evidence we seized from the Millers, including home movies, photos, travel diaries, itineraries, and scrapbooks, gave us strong confidence that they had excavated Individual 10 with their friends the Mitchells, as the prologue describes. These materials helped us pinpoint the location of the dig at the confluence of the White and Missouri Rivers near Chamberlain, South Dakota, in the summer of 1961. There was no doubt that Individual 10 was Native American.

The Missouri curves in a broad southeasterly arc before meeting the White River's tributary waters. Archaeological surveys have identified the land beneath this arc as a favored burial ground, chosen for its striking beauty and the rich natural resources provided by the two rivers. Generations of people who lived in the surrounding area laid their dead to rest there.

During the colonial era and the early years of the United States, this burial ground primarily belonged to the Arikara, Mandan, and Hidatsa tribes. All three suffered devastating population losses from smallpox epidemics, and by the 1830s, the expanding Sioux tribes pushed them northward. From that point on the region became Lakota land, until white European Americans sought to displace and confine the Sioux after the Civil War.

The Arikara harbored deep resentment toward the Sioux, to the extent that some Arikara men served as scouts for Custer's forces at the Battle of the Greasy Grass (the Battle of the Little Bighorn in non–Native American memory). In the years following Custer's defeat, many Sioux children were forced into a nearby residential school, where outbreaks of cholera and influenza claimed lives in the late nineteenth and early twentieth centuries.

Don and Sue Miller knew enough of this history to conduct secret, unauthorized digs in the area over several summers starting in the late 1950s. They were there precisely because it was a good place to look for Native American graves.

But was it a good place to look for Crazy Horse's grave?

A member and war leader of the Oglala Lakota, Crazy Horse was born around 1840. He died more than two hundred miles west-southwest of Chamberlain at Fort Robinson in northwest Nebraska in 1877 at the age of thirty-six or thirty-seven. That May, he had surrendered to the US Army at Fort Robinson, marking the end of the Great Sioux War of 1876 and 1877. The war had been triggered by the rush of European American miners into the Black Hills, a region sacred to the Lakota.

On September 5, 1877, under arrest at Fort Robinson, he was fatally bayoneted in the back after reportedly struggling to resist imprisonment in the fort's guardhouse. He died hours later.

Crazy Horse's parents carried his body about fifty miles east to Camp Sheridan, Nebraska. In keeping with Sioux tradition, they placed him on a temporary burial scaffold. A month later, they secretly laid him to rest, either in the same area or in a location known only to them.

It is remotely possible that Crazy Horse was buried much farther east, near Chamberlain in central South Dakota. However, it seems at least as likely, if not far more so, that his final resting place was near Camp Sheridan in northwestern Nebraska, in the western Dakotas, or in eastern Wyoming or Montana—regions where accounts of his life and movements most often place him.

The evidence seized from the Millers, along with additional research, provided no reason to believe the ancestor identified as Individual 10 was Crazy Horse. But the evidence also did not entirely rule out that remote possibility. Our only other potential source of insight into Individual 10 was noninvasive forensic osteology.

IUPUI osteologist Jeremy Wilson submitted his report on Individual 10 on September 10, 2015. Despite the hundreds of individuals represented by the two thousand human bones we seized from Miller, Individual 10's was the only near-complete skeleton. The bones were "well preserved," and except for "a left ulna from a second individual," they all belonged to the same person.

The formation of the pelvis and the skull both indicated that this person was male. And the length of the humerus in his left upper arm correlated with a likely height of five feet ten, with a margin of error range of an inch or two. Descriptions of Crazy Horse give his height as around five feet nine or five feet ten.

The skeleton of Individual 10 had thirty-one of thirty-two teeth, missing only the top left wisdom tooth, a third molar. However, the skeleton was also missing four of seven cervical (neck) vertebrae and some hand, finger, foot, and toe bones. The report noted, "This level of recovery for smaller skeletal remains is common in situations where skeletal remains have been exhumed by untrained excavators with a limited or nonexistent background in human osteology; smaller bones of the hand and feet are often missed." Although Don Miller prided himself on his archaeological knowledge and technique, he fell far short of accepted practices and standards.

In 1870, Crazy Horse was shot in the face by another Sioux man over his relationship with the man's wife. In addition to leaving a large scar on the left side of his face, the bullet fractured Crazy Horse's left upper jaw, according to the testimony of his close friends and associates. But osteological examination found no healed fracture line, or other signs of trauma from a bullet's impact, on the left upper jaw of Individual 10.

Even more telling was Individual 10's estimated age at death. Until a person's skeleton fully matures, and the long bones of the arms and legs stop growing, there is a strong correlation between age and bone development. Estimating the age of an older individual, however, is more difficult. Once bone growth ceases, skeletal changes become less pronounced, occurring mainly due to injury, disease, or the effects of aging.

The bones at the base of the back of the skull fuse together completely between sixteen and twenty-two years of age. Individual 10's were completely fused, meaning that he was over sixteen at the time of death.

The long bones of the arms stop growing between seventeen and twenty-two years of age. At that point, the ends of the bones close up and fuse over, as do the joint surfaces that those long bones fit with. Individual 10 was nearing the end of that process when he died. The ends of his arm bones had not yet closed up completely and fused over, but the related surfaces of the elbow joint had closed up and fused over, as "is characteristic of a late adolescent or young adult."

The same pattern, with slightly different age ranges, holds for the pelvis and legs. Here again, the osteological evidence indicated that Individual 10 was a late adolescent or young adult male.

In addition, the inner ends of the clavicles (the collarbones), which connect to the sternum and finish growing between twenty-three and thirty-one years of age, were also still open and had not yet fused over, showing that Individual 10 was probably younger than twenty-three when he died. Finally, Individual 10's wisdom teeth showed very little wear from chewing, indicating that they had erupted through the gums not very long before his death.

Together these findings provided "a high degree of accuracy and precision" for estimating that Individual 10's bones had almost finished growing and he was seventeen to twenty-two years old at the time of his death. He was much too young to be Crazy Horse.

The fact that Individual 10 was not Crazy Horse in no way lessened the crime of desecrating his grave and taking his bones home as a trophy. However, it was a relief to know for certain that Don Miller's fantasy about Crazy Horse, one of the most important Native American leaders of the nineteenth century, was false.

The next question to answer was whether Individual 10 was a member of the Sioux or of one of the tribes that occupied the middle Missouri River valley in earlier times—the Arikara, Mandan, or Hidatsa. Again, the only noninvasive way to try to culturally affiliate skeletal remains is through osteological measurements of the skull. Forensic osteology uses twenty-seven measures of the skull (the position of the eyes, ears, and nose; the distance between the eyes, ears, and cheekbones; the maximum length and breadth of the skull; and so on) and a statistical software program to compare skulls of unknown individuals with reference groups of skulls of known origin.

For our in-warehouse osteology lab we had bought the FORDISC program, which originated with the Forensic Data Bank at the University of Tennessee-Knoxville. FORDISC's reference groups are the Forensic Data Bank, which contains skull measurements of fifty-nine Native American males and thirty-two females, predominantly from the American Southwest, and the Howells Craniometric Data Set, which has measurements of 2,524 skulls from around the world. The Howells dataset includes measurements of relatively small numbers of skulls from three Native North American populations: the Arikara of the middle Missouri River valley, the Inuit of Alaska, and the Chumash of Santa Cruz Island, one of the Channel Islands off the coast of Southern California. For example, there are forty-two skulls of Arikara males represented in the Howells dataset.

As I've also already mentioned, there are legitimate questions about possible racist biases in comparative osteology and the small size of the reference groups in the available datasets. Section 2.5 of the osteology report on Individual 10, "Ancestry/Population Affinity," implicitly acknowledged such questions, noting that "ancestry is a conceptual and operational term used by anthropologists with the full recognition that biological races of human beings do not exist."

Using FORDISC to compare the twenty-seven measurements of Individual 10's skull with the reference group in the Forensic Data Bank yielded "statistically reliable" similarities "only . . . to American Indians and Hispanics." On that basis, the report concluded that Individual 10 "falls among the modern range of craniometric variability for known American Indian males." Left unspoken is that this range of variability does not necessarily exclude males from other population groups.

Somewhat stronger evidence came from comparing Individual 10's skull measurements with those in the Howells dataset. FORDISC crunched those numbers and came up with a 45.2 percent probability that Individual 10 had affinity with the Arikara, 28.2 percent probability of affinity with a Norse population, 20.3 percent probability of affinity with the Zalavar people of what is now Hungary, 3.4 percent probability of affinity with a northern Japanese population, and 2.9 percent probability of affinity with an Egyptian population (the total of all the probabilities is 100 percent). Knocking out northern Japanese and Egyptian males from the comparison raised the probability of population affinity with the Arikara to 51.3 percent.

The report noted that of the forty-two known Arikara males in the Howells dataset, FORDISC could correctly identify thirty-eight of the forty-two as Arikara using the twenty-seven measurements of each of these skulls that Harvard anthropologist William W. Howells himself made during his research from the 1960s through the 1980s. That success rate indicated "a moderately strong predictive capability" for affiliating Individual 10 with the Arikara.

A final question for osteological examination was how long ago Individual 10 had died. Radiocarbon tests, which could have provided a date range, were not an option for the Native American remains. These tests require extracting material from within the bones, making them invasive and therefore unacceptable for analysis.

Individual 10's bones showed little sign of weathering while in the ground, a sign that they had been buried in soil with low acidity, like the plains around Chamberlain, South Dakota. The longer that bones are buried, the lighter they become, as inorganic material replaces collagen, and the weight of Individual 10's bones was greater than would be expected if he had been buried in the distant past. Although an older age could not be ruled out except with a radiocarbon assay, the available evidence suggested that Individual 10 "was interred in the ground within the past millennium and . . . more probably within the past 500 years. . . . In short, the high degree of preservation and the weight of the bones suggest a historic-era burial that cannot refute . . . [an] attribution to the 19th century."

It wasn't decisive information, but it was the best we were going to get. Given that the Millers' photographs and other dig-related material showed they had dug up Individual 10 near the confluence of the White and Missouri Rivers, we had to consult on repatriation of these remains with all the modern-day tribes with links to the middle Missouri River valley: the Sioux and the Three Affiliated Tribes of the Arikara, Mandan, and Hidatsa.

Other Indigenous tribes, such as the Otoe-Missouria and Pawnee, also have historical ties to regions along the Missouri River, particularly farther south in present-day Missouri. While their primary territories were not centered on the area targeted by Miller in this dig, I want to acknowledge the broader context of their presence along the Missouri River.

A key part of my plan for tribal consultation was the website I described earlier, which featured descriptions and photographs of the artifacts seized from Miller's collection. But when it launched in early 2015, serious problems for its users immediately emerged. Looking back, I might have predicted these problems, but my cultural ignorance and mistaken assumptions kept me from seeing them in advance.

Naively, I thought that if we built the site, users would come, much like the famous line from *Field of Dreams*. As I mentioned earlier, we had three main groups of users in mind: representatives from Native American nations, cultural heritage officials from foreign countries where Miller had looted artifacts, and subject matter experts who could help with identification.

To accommodate these groups, we designed the site with three sections—Native American artifacts, international artifacts, and unknown artifacts—so we could tailor access accordingly. Native American users could view the Native American and unknown artifacts, foreign officials could access the international and unknown artifacts, and subject matter experts received access based on their expertise. For security, the FBI unit responsible for managing the bureau's websites required unique user passwords and two-factor authentication for logging in.

When the website was ready to go online, the FBI sent letters to the tribal historic preservation officers and government leaders of all 566 tribes that were then federally recognized. The letters invited each tribe to nominate two or three representatives for access to the site.

The response was disappointing. Fewer than forty tribes showed interest and nominated representatives, usually the tribal historic preservation officer along with one or two elders. The preservation officers were often younger and depended on the elders' knowledge. I created accounts for everyone the tribes nominated, but only half ever logged in. Of those, only a handful returned more than once. Considering the challenges they faced using the site, I could hardly blame them.

My main mistake in planning the website was assuming that everyone could get online whenever they wanted to. It never occurred to me to ask what sort of internet service was available on rural reservations. The poor response rate to our letters of invitation was a wake-up call I shouldn't have needed, telling me, "Lots of people don't have broadband. Lots of people don't have *any* internet, you dummy."

I also should not have been surprised that many tribal elders on remote reservations might not be familiar with technology or have the necessary equipment to access the site, even if they had internet service. Like internet users of all ages everywhere, they often misplaced or forgot their passwords.

Two-factor authentication, which was not widely used in 2015, proved challenging for both Native American and international users. The emailed security codes often ended up in spam folders, and even when users found them, the codes expired so quickly that they were frequently useless.

To make matters worse, the FBI unit managing the site optimized it for Google Chrome and could not allocate resources to ensure compatibility with other browsers. This made access especially difficult for those using Windows Explorer or Mozilla Firefox. This was truly a dumb problem that the FBI had created and was seemingly unwilling to fix.

Although the number of people I created accounts for was relatively small, I spent hours upon hours trying to coach people through the process. I also sent out extremely detailed instructions, with screenshots of every step.

These efforts did little to improve engagement because there was another major issue. While I still believe the site was a good idea in theory, and it functioned as intended once users logged in, it was overwhelming. The sheer amount of information made navigation difficult. Even with a search function that allowed users to look up keywords like tribal names, sifting through the entries was tedious. Given that, it was not surprising that most users who managed to log in spent only ten or fifteen minutes on the site before leaving and never returned.

Each evidence item on the site included a comments section. We had hoped this would encourage tribal representatives and foreign cultural heritage officials to engage in a virtual dialogue with subject matter experts, helping us make accurate cultural affiliations. That did happen to some extent. For example, Kelley Hays-Gilpin, an anthropologist at Northern Arizona University in Flagstaff, provided valuable insights on all the Southwest materials seized from Miller's collection. However, the site never gained enough traction to spark the broad discussions we had envisioned.

We also hoped the website might spark general suggestions for improving our cultural repatriation efforts. The four pages of detailed instructions for visiting the site that we sent to users, most of them Native Americans, ended with the following in bold type: "Please remember that this website is a partnership between the FBI and the nations represented by the authorized users. We welcome any feedback, positive or negative, that you may feel will help us improve the website or communicate more effectively with the affected nations."

Our intentions for the website were good. But good intentions couldn't surmount the obstacles that confronted users. It turned out that virtual consultations were no substitute for the direct, personal kind.

With the osteology report on Individual 10 in hand, I emailed the tribal historic preservation officers and leaders of the Three Affiliated Tribes in North Dakota as well as the Crow Creek Sioux and Lower Brule Sioux in South Dakota. These tribes had the strongest ancestral and geographical ties to the land surrounding the confluence of the White and Missouri Rivers, where Don and Sue Miller had looted Native American graves starting in the late 1950s.

Native Americans buried in that area during the nineteenth century were almost certainly members of either the Three Affiliated Tribes or the Sioux. Fort Thompson, the capital of the Crow Creek Sioux Tribe's reservation, was just twenty-six miles north of Chamberlain.

I invited representatives from all these tribes to a consultation, with the time and place to be arranged mutually, to discuss the potential repatriation of Individual 10's nearly complete skeleton, the partial remains of nine other individuals from the same burial grounds, and the associated funerary artifacts. The Lower Brule chose not to participate. However, after a series of emails and phone calls, representatives from the Three Affiliated Tribes and the Crow Creek Sioux agreed to meet on October 22, 2015, in Fort Thompson.

On October 21, Drew and I flew from Indianapolis to Rapid City, South Dakota, where we met Holly, who had taken a different flight. From there, we drove east on I-90 to Chamberlain. The next morning, we made the short trip north to Fort Thompson, where the Crow Creek Sioux were hosting our meeting at the Lode Star Casino.

A few Native American tribes have gained wealth through oil holdings or casinos, but the realities of tribal gaming vary widely. Thriving resort destinations like the Seminole Tribe's Hard Rock–branded casinos and hotels in densely populated southern Florida are a world apart from the Crow Creek Sioux's Lode Star Casino and Hotel, located at the junction of South Dakota state highways 47 and 249.

Unlike the glittering "Guitar Hotel" featured in commercials for the Seminole Hard Rock Casino and Hotel in Hollywood, Florida, just north of Miami, the Lode Star Casino in Fort Thompson had a far more modest appearance that was in keeping with its rural surroundings. From the outside, it resembled a big-box retailer or supermarket, aside from the casino signage. Inside, the slightly worn furnishings reflected the tough economic realities faced by many Native American tribes in the Dakotas.

In a small conference room in the back of the Lode Star Casino, Drew, Holly, and I were cordially welcomed by Darrell Zephier, the tribal historic preservation officer for the Crow Creek Sioux; his father, Clark Zephier, a tribal elder; and Pete Coffey-One Feather, the tribal historic preservation officer for the Mandan, Hidatsa, and Arikara Nation. To attend the meeting, Pete had driven four hundred miles from the Fort Berthold Indian Reservation in northwestern North Dakota.

There was a brief setback before we could start the meeting, as the conference room was not equipped for multimedia presentations. After some scrambling, we managed to set up a way for me to show a slide deck on the Miller case and the specific ancestral remains and artifacts under discussion for repatriation. I made a mental note never to attend another consultation without bringing a portable projector.

As I did every time I spoke to a tribal community about the case, I presented Miller's desecration of Native American ancestral remains in a straightforward, respectful manner—adult to adult. In my experience, victims of serious crimes do not benefit from, and often resent, any trace of condescension. What they do deserve is honesty, compassion, and tact.

Drew, Holly, and I walked the group through the case's progression since late 2013. We also explained how the available evidence and osteological analysis pointed to the remains of the ten individuals, along with their associated funerary objects, being of Arikara or Siouan origin.

Darrell Zephier, Clark Zephier, and Pete Coffey-One Feather responded in the same spirit. As my internal FBI report on the meeting put it, "Initial indications were that the Arikara, who will likely have the most claim over the remains and associated burial goods, were willing to work with the Crow Creek Sioux in their repatriation effort. . . . The Indianapolis Division expects . . . efforts to rebury the remains [on Crow Creek tribal land] as close to the original burial site as possible."

As my internal report also noted, I asked the three tribal representatives "to draft appropriate tribal resolutions indicating the wishes of [their] two tribes with regard to the disposition of the remains and associated burial goods." I told the tribes that after receiving those resolutions, I would then draft the notices of inventory completion that NAGPRA requires for repatriation of any remains or artifacts the statute covers.

More consultation would follow before the repatriation could occur. But Drew, Holly, and I were happy to leave the Lode Star Casino knowing there was going to be a fitting final resting place for "Sioux Warrior, 19th Cent.," along with the remains of the other individuals from the same burial ground. Instead of Don Miller's funeral desire ("Bury me with my Indian") being fulfilled, we had the satisfaction of helping to achieve a victory over, rather than for, the poisonous legacy of Manifest Destiny.

Through the rest of the fall, I continued pushing the Miller case forward, including the repatriation efforts in South Dakota, while balancing my other investigative and bomb tech duties. As 2015 came to a close, I was also preparing for a trial run as the art crime program manager in late January and early February 2016.

If the trial run went well, it would improve my chances of becoming the first art crime program manager to come from within the art crime team itself. It would also make me the first to focus solely on art crime rather than handling it as a secondary duty alongside major theft or La Cosa Nostra program management.

Since long before the Miller case began in the fall of 2013, the core members of the team had been discussing the need for one of us to step into the role of program manager. Nearly a decade after its formation, the team still operated as an initiative within major theft rather than as a fully recognized FBI specialty program.

If that was ever going to change, we needed a leader with firsthand experience handling a variety of art crime cases and, just as important, the ability to supervise them effectively. We also needed someone with the passion and determination to navigate the bureau's formal processes and push for the program to achieve full specialty status.

That meant the leader had to come from within the team. Despite our history of successful, high-impact cases, none had been large enough to convince the bureau that art crime warranted its own full-time program manager or that one of us was the right fit for the role—until the Miller case.

One evening in April 2015, a few of us on the team sat down to discuss who should apply for the program manager position when Tim DeMann's temporary assignment ended in the spring of 2016. We gathered around the table in the office section of the Miller case warehouse, wrapping up a long day of reviewing evidence.

For hours, we had been piecing together connections—matching the artifacts and ancestral remains we had seized with the documentation from Don and Sue Miller's illicit digs. Home movies, photographs, travel journals, and scrapbooks provided crucial details, as did their passports and other travel records. A whiteboard on the wall was covered with notes and diagrams as we worked to trace the full scope of what they had done.

When our discussion shifted from the case to the future of the art crime program, I repeated what had become my usual refrain: "If we are going to pull the team out of the shadows at headquarters and become a fully recognized specialty program, one of us has to go there and lead that fight."

Dave Bass responded, as he had in past conversations, "I think you know we all agree with that, Tim." He shot me a knowing smile. "And I think you know we also all agree that you're the man for the job."

"I don't know about that," I said. "There are others on the team who could do it. Some of them are sitting at this table. What about you? Or Ronnie? Or Liz?" I glanced at each of them as I spoke.

"Maybe so," Dave said. "But you're the best candidate we've got. The Miller case is what put the team on the radar with the top brass, and you're the case agent. We've all been following your lead.

"And I've seen how tough it is to get things done at headquarters. You've got the moxie and the savvy to go fight for the art crime program in that environment—and a real chance at winning."

Ronnie and Liz nodded in agreement.

The praise was flattering, but I wasn't fooled. I knew exactly what was happening. None of them wanted to go to headquarters and have their souls drained by the bureaucracy, so they were rallying behind the one idiot who might be willing to take the plunge.

I wasn't eager to uproot my family and transfer to headquarters, even if I got the job. I was already buried in the Miller case, and trying to keep it moving while also managing and growing the art crime program would be an even bigger lift than what I was already carrying.

On top of that, Risa and I loved our home outside Indianapolis. She was happy in her teaching job, and the kids were in good schools. Disrupting all of that wasn't something I took lightly.

But deep down, I knew Dave, Ronnie, and Liz were right. I just wasn't ready to admit it yet.

Some weeks later, the four of us were on a conference call with Jake and our fellow art crime team agent Chris McKeogh.

"I know I'm speaking for everyone on the team, Tim," Jake said. "You have to go to DC and take over when Tim DeMann leaves the program manager's desk."

Earlier that year, during our annual art crime team training in

Washington, DC, in February, I had pitched unit chief Jay Bartholomew on two key points. First, the art crime program was ready to stand on its own as a full specialty program with a dedicated program manager. Second, the next program manager should come from within the art crime team.

I did not mention myself as a candidate, but I laid out my argument clearly: "The art crime team's profile has never been higher, and that gives us a real opportunity to establish ourselves as a specialty program. We need to take that step because our caseload keeps growing. It's not just the Miller case—we are handling bigger cases and a broader range of investigations. The team needs a leader and an advocate here at headquarters who understands that firsthand and has the credibility to push the program forward."

Jay was receptive and told me it made sense. Not long after, with Risa's support, I spoke with Tim DeMann about the possibility of applying to take over the program manager role when he stepped down. Tim was just as encouraging. He agreed that the program needed someone from within the team to lead it and said he would bring it up with Jay.

Several months passed as Tim continued in the role, but as he neared the end of his tenure, the conversation resurfaced. Later in the year, I received an invitation to step in for a trial run—an opportunity to see firsthand what the job entailed and to prove that the program was ready for a full-time, dedicated leader.

These trial runs, or "test drives" as they are known in the bureau, are an informal but practical approach used by leadership. Headquarters is a challenging environment, and no one wants to invest time and resources in promoting and transferring someone to DC, only for them to be miserable and underperform.

A short temporary duty assignment, usually two weeks to a month, is a low-cost way to give candidates a taste of the job and life at headquarters. At the same time, it allows the unit considering them for the position to assess their leadership style and suitability for the role before making a long-term commitment.

My test drive was set to begin in late January 2016, and over the Christmas and New Year holidays, I found myself genuinely looking forward to it. Balancing the demands of the Miller case while managing and trying to elevate the entire art crime program would be no small task, but the chance to shape the program's future was exciting.

I also realized that stepping into the program manager role could directly benefit the Miller case. Even under the best circumstances, culturally affiliating and repatriating everything we had seized from Miller would take years, and securing funding would always be a struggle. Learning how to navigate headquarters from the inside could give me the leverage and insight I needed to keep the case moving forward.

Ten

Charges to Bring, Changes to Make

From Miller to Malheur to Running the Art Crime Program

TUESDAY, JANUARY 26, 2016, 3:45 P.M.

I found a seat in the far back corner of the Strategic Information and Operations Center (SIOC) briefing room, on the fifth floor of FBI headquarters. There were only a handful of people in the room, but I was a newcomer to the twice-daily crisis meetings that had been going on in SIOC for the past three and a half weeks. In fact, it was my first day at headquarters for my two-week test drive of the art crime program manager's desk. Although I knew I had to speak up at some point in the meeting, I wanted to see how it was operating and listen to its regular participants before I did so.

As the minutes ticked away to the meeting's scheduled 4 p.m. start, more and more people entered the room. I wondered if, when I was ready to raise my hand and ask to speak, I'd be laughed out of the room or listened to.

CHARGES TO BRING, CHANGES TO MAKE

I had arrived in Washington, DC, six days before on Wednesday afternoon, January 20. As my flight from Indianapolis neared Ronald Reagan Washington National Airport in Crystal City, Virginia, across the Potomac River from the capital, the pilot informed passengers that air traffic control was eager to get us on the ground because of bad weather.

Only an inch of snow fell that day, but it quickly froze into black ice on the roads. There were so many accidents during the evening commute that local media referred to the situation as "Carmageddon." I was unpacking in my room at the Crystal City Marriott when La Cosa Nostra and art crime program manager Tim DeMann called and said, "Don't come to headquarters tomorrow morning. A Category 5 storm is on the way, and they're declaring states of emergency from Kentucky and Tennessee to Delaware, and from Georgia to New York. Federal offices are closed as of this evening. We're all stuck at home, and you're stuck in your hotel, until further notice."

With so little snow so far, I wondered if this was an overreaction. But through the weekend, what *The Washington Post* dubbed "Snowzilla" dumped one and a half to over three feet of snow on the mid-Atlantic states, with fifty-five associated fatalities. Washington, DC, came to a standstill, and federal offices remained closed until Tuesday, January 26.

From Thursday through Monday, I tried my best to work on the phone. There was little I could do except strategize with Ronnie Walker. On Wednesday evening, not long after Tim DeMann told me not to try to come to headquarters the next day, Ronnie called from the Portland, Oregon, field office, where he was stationed throughout his time as an FBI agent.

"Are you tracking the situation out here?" Ronnie asked.

By "here," Ronnie didn't mean Portland. He was referring to Burns, a ranching town in eastern Oregon's Harney County, and the nearby Malheur National Wildlife Refuge, managed by the US Fish and Wildlife Service. For the past eighteen days, since January 2, an armed militia of self-proclaimed "sovereign citizens" had occupied the refuge headquarters.

Their leader was Ammon Bundy, son of Cliven Bundy, the Nevada rancher known for his 2014 standoff with the Bureau of Land Management (BLM) over grazing rights and fees. Continuing his family's campaign against federal authority over public land, Ammon Bundy had come to Oregon to rally behind father-and-son ranchers Dwight and Steven Hammond, who were set to return to prison for arson in their own dispute with federal authorities.

The Hammonds, however, had disavowed any connection to Bundy and rejected his help. Undeterred, Bundy demanded that the Fish and Wildlife Service and BLM relinquish control of the Malheur refuge and surrounding land, insisting it should be returned to what he called its rightful owners—longtime local ranching families.

"I'm not really following it closely, but I've been seeing stuff on the news," I said.

Ronnie quickly brought me up to speed on the occupation. Since armed militants had seized federal property and were openly defying US government authority, the FBI was leading the response. The domestic terrorism operations unit within the Counterterrorism Division took charge of the operation, as the situation fell under the bureau's mandate to investigate and counter domestic terrorism threats.

More than two hundred FBI agents and support personnel were deployed, primarily from tactical units like the hostage rescue team and SWAT, given the risk of armed confrontation, and the bureau was using a small plane for aerial reconnaissance. It was also coordinating closely with the Harney County Sheriff's Office and the Oregon State Police, both of which had a strong presence, to contain the situation and prevent further escalation. Local law enforcement had jurisdiction over many aspects of the situation, but with federal land and agencies directly involved, the FBI had primary responsibility for managing the crisis.

As Ronnie observed next, however, one of the big reasons the FBI was in standoff mode was that nobody knew what to charge the occupiers with. There was, and still is, no federal felony for trespassing on federal land. Under applicable laws, such offenses are treated as civil misdemeanors rather than serious criminal violations.

The identified occupiers all appeared to be legal gun owners, and there were no readily apparent firearms violations to charge. Complicating matters further was the issue of optics—there was legitimate concern about escalating the situation into a violent confrontation over misdemeanor offenses, especially since these violations fell under the civil Code of Federal Regulations rather than the criminal code.

Ronnie went on. "New militia groups—militia tourists, you might say—are arriving to join the occupation, and all these people are roaming over the area around the refuge headquarters on foot and in ATVs and other vehicles. They've established defensive positions. On Monday last week they took down a fence that separates the refuge from one of the local ranches. And on Thursday they used a bulldozer to cut a new road."

"I saw news reports about the fence and the road."

"The thing is, Oregon has documented and registered that whole area as an archaeological site, and it's a sacred burial ground for the Burns Paiute Tribe. It is hard to say for certain, but there is a strong possibility that they damaged artifacts in the process or even disturbed ancestral remains. Fish and Wildlife issued a statement Friday that they're putting cultural resources at risk. The tribal chair sent a letter the same day to the FBI, the US Attorney's Office, and Fish and Wildlife calling for protection of those resources under ARPA and the tribe's 1868 treaty with the United States."

I sat up in the chair at the little desk in my hotel room. "Really? If the occupiers are disturbing or destroying anything on the site, that possibly gives us ARPA felonies to charge. We need to get you and the rest of the team out there as soon as possible. Can you get me a copy of the state archaeological survey ASAP?"

"Will do."

When Ronnie emailed the survey, I saw what he meant. While I was riding out the winter storm in my hotel, I used the downtime to start brainstorming with Ronnie. We discussed at length how ARPA might apply to the occupiers and what that could mean for the FBI's efforts. We also went over how the art crime team should proceed—if the FBI leadership decided to involve us.

When federal offices in Washington, DC, reopened on Tuesday morning, January 26, I spent the first few hours dealing with the usual hassle of starting work in a new place. In addition to checking in with HR, Tim DeMann, and Bonnie Magness-Gardiner, I had to get my computer profile transferred so I could access Sentinel from the desktop in my assigned cubicle on the third floor of headquarters.

By midmorning, though, I was finally able to sit down with Tim in his cubicle for a conversation about the Malheur occupation.

Tim told me that the various divisions involved in the operation were meeting with FBI executives in SIOC twice a day, once in the early morning and again in the late afternoon, as was typical for major operations. Since the morning meeting had already wrapped up, the afternoon session would be my first opportunity to propose ARPA charges at Malheur and request what would be the art crime team's second major deployment, following the Miller search and seizure.

During my two-week test drive as art crime program manager, I was expected to handle whatever came up, as long as I kept Tim in the loop and he had no objections to any actions I wanted to take. He was more than happy to let me take the lead on the Malheur issue.

"It'll be baptism by fire for you up there in SIOC," he said with a chuckle. "Better you than me."

TUESDAY, JANUARY 26, 2016, 4 P.M.

SIOC's briefing room had filled up with around fifty people by the time the deputy director walked in and opened the meeting.

For about an hour, the deputy director received updates from the heads of all the various units. Occasionally, someone would suggest a possible felony charge, such as, "One of the occupiers painted our aircraft with a laser, so that might be a charge." But any initial interest in these ideas quickly faded as it became clear how weak the legal footing was.

The deputy director scanned the room with an expression that seemed to ask, *Is that it?*

I raised my hand. When he nodded in my direction, I said, "I've got charges."

"Who are you?" he asked.

"I'm the art crime guy."

Smirks spread across the room, and no one bothered to hide them.

The deputy director's expression shifted to something closer to *Is this man serious?*

I said, "Sir, I run the art crime program, and you're going to want to hear what I have to say. This is an Archaeological Resources Protection Act, or ARPA, case. The Malheur National Wildlife Refuge sits on an archaeological site registered with the Oregon State Historic Preservation Office. It's a documented Native American burial site, and it's sacred ground for the Burns Paiute Tribe. The occupiers are tearing up the site and destroying protected archaeological resources. And ARPA's felony charges come with forfeiture," I continued, "which means we can go in and seize any personal property they are using to commit those crimes, including their personal vehicles."

That got everyone's attention.

I gave a brief background on ARPA, explaining its relevance to the situation. Then I turned to the deputy director.

"You're going to want my team out there. The whole world is watching. The media are filming everything. And our own tactical teams are riding ATVs just outside the occupiers' perimeter, which is also sacred burial ground. They're disturbing the site just like the occupiers are."

Letting that sink in for just one minute, I pressed my point. "Imagine if one of our people disturbs a human skull or an important burial object, casually picks it up and tosses it aside, or worse runs over it, and that footage ends up on all of the national networks. It would be a public relations disaster."

To my surprise, and to their credit, everyone in the room was nodding in agreement. The smirks had vanished.

I built up my pitch to close the deal.

"This is exactly the kind of rapid deployment situation the bureau created the art crime program to handle. Let us embed a team with the tactical units. If it gets to the point where the bureau has to assault the occupiers' defensive positions"—everyone in the room knew that was a real possibility—"the art crime team can guide the tactical teams on how to avoid desecrating the site.

"We can also take the lead in consulting with the Burns Paiute Tribe. If the bureau works alongside the Paiutes, Fish and Wildlife, and the state historic preservation office to assess damage, prevent further harm, and plan for remediation, it turns a potential public relations nightmare into a win."

The deputy director immediately agreed: "Get your people there."

I explained to everyone in the room that Ronnie, one of the most senior agents on the art crime team and based in the Portland office, was already in Oregon and would be taking the lead for our program. I would be deploying additional art crime team agents to support him.

Back at my cubicle, I emailed Ronnie to let him know that the deputy director had approved the deployment of the art crime team to Malheur. I told him I would soon be briefing top executives in the Criminal Investigative Division and would start reaching out to the team to see who was available to join him in Oregon.

At any earlier point in the art crime team's history, they probably would have laughed me out of the SIOC briefing. But the Miller case had elevated the team's profile, and because of that, the deputy director gave me the chance to explain how we could contribute to the response at Malheur.

Well before Snowzilla hit, some FBI executives were already aware of Fish and Wildlife's January 15 statement about the risk to Malheur's cultural resources as well as Burns Paiute Tribe Chair Charlotte Roderique's letter citing ARPA and the 1868 treaty between the tribe and the federal government.

But until I spoke up, ARPA was just as unfamiliar and remote to the people in that SIOC meeting as the 1868 treaty itself.

This remained true even though Burns Paiute tribal leaders had condemned the occupiers for trying to "hold their history hostage" and Chairperson Roderique had formally requested ARPA charges in her letter to federal agencies, stating that if the occupiers "disturb, damage, remove, alter, or deface any archaeological resources on the refuge property," they should be held accountable.

It was also true despite the fact that the occupiers themselves had drawn attention to the issue by posting a misleading video on Facebook with the sensational caption, "SHARE! BREAKING UPDATE BURNS OREGON BLM LEFT NATIVE ARTIFACTS TO ROT IN MICE DROPPINGS!"

Beyond the fact that Fish and Wildlife, not the BLM, managed the refuge, nothing about the occupiers' claim was true. The Native American–related materials they pointed to had not been left in mice droppings, nor were they even part of the refuge's archaeological resources.

In reality, these items were objects that members of the public had purchased from pawnshops and trading posts, then later brought to the refuge, believing they had historical or cultural value. Carla Burnside, the Fish and Wildlife archaeologist stationed at Malheur, used them as teaching aids when speaking to schoolchildren on class trips and other visitors.

Making matters worse, the occupiers' video showed them inside a room where Burnside, who worked closely with the Paiutes, kept artifacts under lock and key on the tribe's behalf. These were not discarded objects but culturally significant items recovered from approved archaeological digs at the refuge. Burnside preserved them exactly as they had been found, in accordance with professional standards and the wishes of the Burns Paiute Tribe, for whom moving them elsewhere would have been sacrilegious.

For the tribe, Burnside, and anyone with real knowledge of the artifacts, it was deeply upsetting to see occupation spokesman LaVoy Finicum and others casually handling them while misrepresenting how they were stored. Burnside's careful stewardship of the refuge's archaeological resources also included clear signage marking where employees and visitors could safely walk without disturbing sensitive areas—including the very spot where the occupiers had cut their road.

The occupiers' supposed concern for Native Americans rang hollow. While Ammon Bundy and LaVoy Finicum claimed to be standing up for tribal interests and protecting artifacts, Ammon's brother Ryan was openly speaking to the media in Manifest Destiny terms: "We . . . recognize that the Native Americans had the claim to the [refuge] land, but they lost that claim."

The lessons we learned from the Miller case made all the difference. They helped Ronnie and me understand how ARPA applied to the Malheur occupation and gave me the ability to explain in the SIOC meeting why the FBI needed a knowledgeable and effective liaison with the Burns Paiute Tribe. Those same lessons made it clear why the art crime team was the right group for the job.

A few hours after that meeting, events took a dramatic turn, making the need to safely end the standoff and bring the entire situation to a close even more urgent.

In the late afternoon of January 26, Oregon time, Ammon Bundy and other occupation leaders left the Malheur refuge to attend a meeting with sympathizers in Grant County, just north of Harney County. The FBI and Oregon State Police (OSP) moved in, arresting most of them at a traffic stop. But LaVoy Finicum sped away in his pickup, tried to swerve around a roadblock, and crashed into a snowbank. When he exited the truck and reached for a loaded pistol in his jacket pocket, OSP officers shot and killed him.

Later, Paiute elders told Ronnie they had feared something bad might happen to Finicum after seeing footage of him disrespectfully handling sacred artifacts at the refuge. Their words echoed what tribal elders had said about the dangers of disturbing the human remains seized from the Miller compound.

The next day, Ammon Bundy released a statement through his lawyer urging the remaining occupiers to leave Malheur. By January 28, only four militia members remained at the refuge.

Desperate to strengthen their defenses, they used a bulldozer on-site to dig two long, deep trenches as additional fortifications. We believe these trenches constituted the largest illegal archaeological excavation in US history. One stretched more than sixty feet long, while both were at least forty inches deep, with some sections reaching depths of fifteen feet.

The trenches cut through and destroyed archaeological strata dating back ten thousand years, reaching some of the earliest human inhabitants of prehistoric North America. At least some of these layers contained burials.

The Burns Paiute Tribe was understandably saddened and outraged by the destruction. However, even worse news about the trenches was still to come.

Once we had received approval from FBI leadership, Ronnie had established close consultation with the Burns Paiute Tribe and Carla Burnside. As I had told the deputy director he would, Ronnie used those discussions to help guide the FBI's tactical teams, ensuring they minimized further damage to the site.

In Ronnie's words, "I was working with the tactical commanders on their plans to take back the refuge and clear its buildings, one by one, if the FBI decided to assault the occupiers. Imagine telling seasoned tactical commanders where their people can and cannot walk, or can and cannot drive their ATVs, and how they have to treat artifacts. Normally that would be insanity to them. Because of the Miller case, the art crime team had the credibility to not only argue that the tactical plans should respect the integrity of the site but be listened to and see our advice reflected in those plans."

In early February, art crime team agents Jake Archer, Donny Asper, Dave Bass, Susan Garst, Liz Rivas, Meredith Savona, and Leslie Wilson began arriving in Oregon to work on the case alongside Ronnie. As much as I wanted to be there myself, I couldn't join them because I was preparing for a four-week bomb tech deployment to teach post-blast training and electronics courses in Bangladesh and India.

While still at headquarters, I attended several more SIOC briefings to update leadership on the art crime team's progress at Malheur. Ronnie and I stayed in regular contact, discussing developments and adjusting our response as the situation evolved. I continued to coordinate what I could, working closely with Tim DeMann, even after I had returned to Indianapolis before heading overseas.

On February 11, the last four occupiers surrendered to authorities, bringing an end to the forty-one-day standoff. With the immediate crisis over, the art crime team shifted its focus from assisting the FBI's tactical teams to assessing the damage and collecting evidence at what was now a cultural heritage and property crime scene. These efforts were a crucial step—not only in remediating the destruction but also in building a case to hold the perpetrators accountable.

In addition to documenting damage inside the refuge buildings—especially ensuring that no artifacts had been damaged or stolen—much of the art crime team's work had to be done outdoors, in the harsh conditions of an Oregon winter. As evidence response team members as well as art crime team agents, Dave and Jake had FBI-issued gear for all weather conditions. But the other team members at Malheur had only their personal clothing. That made it clear that properly equipping the art crime team for field deployments needed to be a priority. Tim DeMann and I immediately began working to secure the necessary funding.

In the meantime, the team made the best of what they had and got on with the job.

The Burns Paiute Tribe asked Ronnie if two tribal archaeologists could be on-site as observers during the crime scene evaluation and evidence collection. Given our experience with the Miller search and seizure, this request made perfect sense.

During that operation, we pioneered a new approach, working side by side with archaeologists, subject matter experts, and even non-FBI and non–law enforcement personnel at a crime scene. It had proven to be an invaluable model, and Malheur was another opportunity to apply it.

Ronnie accordingly replied, "I don't want your archaeologists to observe. I want them to be on the team and partners in the search."

While some members of the art crime team worked with Carla Burnside inside the refuge buildings, others donned Tyvek overalls and entered the occupiers' trenches alongside the Paiute archaeologists. What they found in the trenches was appalling.

For two weeks, the occupiers had been using one of the trenches as a latrine. Throughout the occupation, militia members had also left feces on the surface of other archaeologically sensitive areas. As Burns Paiute Tribal Council member Jarvis Kennedy told *The New York Times*, "Imagine if someone went to Arlington National Cemetery, went to the bathroom on the graves, and rode a bulldozer over them."

With DNA testing, the feces could be linked to specific occupiers. So, the team bagged it all as evidence.

The crime scene work extended far beyond the trenches and the refuge buildings. Ronnie and the rest of the team also coordinated evidence collection at a number of other locations across the refuge, ensuring a thorough assessment of the damage and potential violations.

When that work concluded, Ronnie recalls, "The Burns Paiute Tribe came out to do a cleansing ceremony." Ronnie alerted everyone involved in the search, and about seventy-five people went through the ceremony, one by one approaching a smoky sagebrush fire, where a tribal elder wafted smoke over them while other members of the tribe chanted traditional prayers and sacred songs.

The Burns Paiute Tribe later repaired the trenches with great care, working entirely by hand without the use of machinery. Once the restoration was complete, they held a cleansing ceremony at sunrise, bringing together representatives from all the Paiute tribes in the region. Ronnie and his family were honored to attend as invited guests, witnessing the tribe's resilience and commitment to healing the land.

The art crime team had more than justified its deployment. In my view, the team could have had an even greater impact if the US Attorney's Office in Portland had followed our recommendations and pursued charges under ARPA, as the Paiutes also wanted.

Unfortunately, the US Attorney's Office declined to do so, largely out of concern that they would not be able to prove the knowledge requirement necessary for an ARPA conviction. Instead, they charged the occupiers with depredation of government property.

Initially, twenty-six occupiers were indicted on various charges. While a handful were acquitted in the first trial, every one of them was eventually convicted in later trials or pleaded guilty to avoid trial and the risk of a harsher sentence. A major factor in several of those convictions was the art crime team's evidence from the trenches.

Charging under ARPA might have resulted in more convictions. It would also have sent a stronger public message that Native American artifacts, ancestral remains, and other cultural heritage and property deserve respect and protection.

Let me give Ronnie the last word on this aspect of the Malheur occupation and its connection to the Miller case: "Manifest Destiny ideology is what made Ammon Bundy and his followers believe they had right on their side, just like it made Don Miller believe he had a right to commit the crimes that he committed. It's a complete misunderstanding of our country's history. During the occupation there was an editorial cartoon in *The Oregonian* newspaper, I think it was, that showed a militia leader saying it was time to give the refuge land back to its rightful owners, meaning white ranchers. Off to the side there's a Paiute saying, 'Great. You know where to find us.'"

Even with the Malheur case and my upcoming deployment to India and Bangladesh putting a serious strain on my time, I still pushed the Miller case forward whenever I could.

On February 3, 2016, while still at FBI headquarters, I held a phone meeting to follow up on the in-person consultation we had at the Lode Star Casino in October 2015. Drew and Holly joined by phone from the Indianapolis field office. Bonnie Magness-Gardiner was also on the line, along with Joe Carpenter (no relation to me), the supervisory special agent for the FBI's Indian Country unit.

Although the Indian Country unit was not typically involved in NAGPRA-related efforts, they maintained ongoing communication with tribal communities related to their wide-ranging Indian country violent crime responsibilities, and we kept them informed of developments in the Miller case. Joe sat in on the meeting as an observer.

From North Dakota, Pete Coffey-One Feather of the Three Affiliated Tribes called in. Darrell Zephier and Clark Zephier joined from South Dakota, again representing both the Crow Creek Sioux and the Lower Brule Sioux. Also joining the discussion for the first time was Tribal Historic Preservation Officer Russell Eagle Bear of the Rosebud Sioux, calling in from South Dakota.

Everyone at the meeting agreed that we should repatriate Individual 10, the remains of nine other individuals looted from the same burial grounds, and the associated funerary objects as soon as possible to the Great Plains Tribal Chairmen's Association. (Because human remains and artifacts often cannot be affiliated with a specific tribe, it is common for tribes with shared geographical ties to form an association to handle repatriations collectively.) It was also agreed that the Crow Creek Sioux would take responsibility for reburying the remains on behalf of all the affected tribes.

The next step in the NAGPRA repatriation process was for each affected tribe to prepare formal resolutions outlining their wishes. Once I received those resolutions, I could draft a Notice of Inventory Completion (NIC) and submit it to National NAGPRA for publication in the Federal Register.

In the unlikely event that anyone else wanted to make a claim on the remains or associated funerary objects, the NIC would provide them with an opportunity to do so. Absent any objections, the repatriation could move forward.

On moving the Miller case materials to a dedicated warehouse facility, we had announced that tribal representatives could visit it upon request. Before the phone meeting with the North Dakota and South Dakota tribal representatives concluded, they became the first to express interest in doing so. They proposed sending a delegation to Indianapolis to conduct a ceremony to prepare the spirits of the dead for their journey to South Dakota. We were fully committed to honoring our open-door promise and welcomed their visit.

I left for Bangladesh and India on February 19. Four exhausting weeks later—including a brutal case of "Delhi belly" that left me so dehydrated I had to receive IV fluids at the US embassy medical clinic in New Delhi—I finally flew home to Indianapolis. I had just two days to recover from the illness and shake off the jet lag before the delegation from the Dakotas arrived.

On March 22, Drew, Holly, and I welcomed a delegation of ten people at the Indianapolis field office. Among them were Pete Coffey-One Feather, Darrell Zephier, Clark Zephier, Russell Eagle Bear, and other representatives from their respective tribes. Because the tribes were victims of Miller's looting, we were able to use the bureau's victims' assistance funds for the delegation's travel.

After a brief introduction to SAC Jay Abbott, we gathered the group and set out for the warehouse storage facility in two large SUVs. The drive gave us time to talk, helping to set the tone for what we knew would be an emotional and significant visit.

At the warehouse, the delegation became the first tribal representatives to see how we were storing the remains and artifacts seized from Miller's collection in safe, secure conditions, with proper temperature and humidity control. They also saw that we were keeping remains and artifacts separate, following the guidance we had received from the tribal community at the time of the search and seizure.

Before the tribal elders in the delegation conducted their planned ceremony, we held a brief meeting to discuss the repatriation that would take place later in the year. An issue that remained unresolved was how to treat a sizable collection of Catlinite pipes we'd seized from Miller.

Named for the American painter George Catlin (1796–1872), renowned for portraits of mid-nineteenth-century Native Americans, Catlinite is a brownish-red pipeclay found only in a few quarries in Minnesota, Wisconsin, and Ontario, Canada. Catlinite's softness makes it ideal for boring out and shaping to make smoking pipes. The tribes of the middle Missouri River valley, including the Mandan, Hidatsa, Arikara, and Sioux, have historically used Catlinite to fashion utilitarian and ceremonial smoking pipes.

The Millers' photographs confirmed that some of the seized pipes were directly connected to the remains slated for repatriation. There was also evidence that Miller had acquired many other pipes from the same geographical area.

The unresolved question, one we had previously discussed in South Dakota and on our phone calls, was whether we could reasonably assume that these additional pipes were also associated burial goods covered under NAGPRA.

The discussion around the circular table in the office section of the warehouse wasn't exactly heated, but it was certainly passionate. One of the delegates insisted, "My ancestors never buried these pipes with the dead. It wouldn't have been done."

Other delegates offered a different perspective. "Burying these pipes with the dead was common," one said. "We have lots of burial context for them."

They went back and forth on that point, each expressing strong beliefs rooted in their respective oral traditions. Drew, Holly, and I remained spectators, listening as the discussion unfolded.

Later, I would witness similar debates about a wide range of Native artifacts among representatives of different tribes. A clear consensus never emerged, highlighting the diversity of customs and perspectives within the Native American community.

At the very least, the discussion at the warehouse that day led to one point of agreement—the artifacts recovered from the display case with "Sioux Warrior" should be repatriated along with those remains.

With the discussion settled for the time being, the tribal elders in the delegation turned their focus to the ceremony they had come to perform. Gathering around the remains, they conducted a smudging ritual, wafting sagebrush smoke through the air as they sang, prayed, and drummed. They also symbolically fed the ancestors, ensuring they were sustained for their journey back to South Dakota, more than fifty years after Miller had taken them from their graves.

Before departing, the elders presented us with specially blessed blankets to cover the remains during transport. They also expressed their gratitude for the care and respect we had shown in handling the remains and artifacts and for ensuring that their visit and ceremony could take place.

It was highly unusual for the FBI to open an evidence facility to victims in this way, but given the unique nature of the Miller case, it was entirely fitting. It also marked a meaningful step in turning a page in the bureau's relationship with Native communities.

Immediately after the ceremony, we took the delegation to the Eiteljorg Museum of American Indians and Western Art for a private tour and a catered dinner in the museum's boardroom. The museum's leaders and curators graciously welcomed the visitors and joined us for the dinner.

It was especially significant that John Warren, chairman of the Pokagon Band of Potawatomi, with other members of the tribe, were there to receive the delegation from South Dakota and North Dakota. During the dinner, Chairman Warren reaffirmed the Pokagon Band's commitment to reburying any remains that could not be culturally affiliated with a specific tribe or region, on behalf of the Native American community as a whole. As the closest federally recognized tribe to the Miller farm, the Pokagon Band had stepped forward to ensure that those remains would be laid to rest with dignity.

Ninety days before Tim DeMann was scheduled to leave headquarters, the FBI's HR department formally posted the position and began soliciting applications for an eighteen-month temporary duty assignment as art crime program manager. It was the first time the bureau had specifically sought a supervisory special agent dedicated solely to art crime rather than assigning the role to someone as part of managing the major theft or La Cosa Nostra program.

To encourage field agents to transfer into supervisory positions at headquarters, the FBI's Headquarters Staffing Initiative provided housing subsidies and a per diem expense budget for the length of the eighteen-month stint. Nearly every supervisory special agent assignment at headquarters started this way, even in the rare cases—like mine—where the agent intended to make the move permanent.

I had no desire to promote beyond this role and saw myself staying in the job long-term, quietly envisioning the rest of my FBI career as art crime program manager. But taking the temporary duty route was the standard path, and passing up the financial benefits that came with it wouldn't have made sense.

Since we were fairly certain we wouldn't be returning to Indianapolis in eighteen months, Risa and I put our house on the market and began looking for a place to rent in Arlington, Virginia, just west of Washington, DC. Given the steep housing costs in the DC area, we hoped the TDY housing stipend would allow us to find a place that would give me a short commute to headquarters. We planned to move at the beginning of June, timing it so that Tim DeMann's kids and our kids could finish out their school years before the transition.

What we didn't plan for was Mother Nature. On May 1, disaster struck when a tornado swept directly across our house outside Indianapolis.

We huddled in a bathroom on the ground floor, in the middle of the house, since our home had no basement or storm shelter (unusual for Indiana). The tornado roared through like a freight train, shaking the entire house. The walls rattled, and the roof groaned and creaked as the updraft threatened to rip it away.

In truth, it was a relatively weak tornado, likely no stronger than an EF1 or EF2, but it was more than enough to make us never want to experience another. A stronger storm could have leveled the house and taken us with it.

Even so, this one was hail wrapped, and when it finally passed, our home looked as if a helicopter gunship had circled overhead and raked it with a barrage of rounds. It was a disaster, and we had to scramble to replace the roof and siding just in time to close the sale.

Having found a suitable house to rent in Arlington, we packed up, moved, and began settling into our new routines. Risa started a teaching job in Arlington, the kids adjusted to their new schools, and I stepped into my new role at headquarters as art crime program manager.

On my first day, I had at least some basic ideas about the problems the program faced and maybe even a few solutions, but I wasn't entirely sure how to put them into action. I also understood that in a highly politicized environment like headquarters, I couldn't start running with anything until I had first learned how to walk.

My agenda began with a fundamental issue—almost twelve years after its inception, the FBI's art crime program was, technically, still the "art theft program," and even that was little more than a courtesy designation. Officially, art theft remained an initiative under major theft, which gave the impression that we focused solely on stolen art cases.

In reality, the program covered much more, with theft accounting for only 20 to 25 percent of our caseload. The rest involved fraud, looting, money laundering, smuggling, forgery, trafficking, and numerous other cultural heritage violations.

Step one? Change the name to the "art crime program" and formally establish it as a stand-alone program within the organized crime section.

Furthermore, there was still no formal training or certification process for becoming an art crime team agent. In other specialty programs—such as bomb tech, WMD, SWAT, evidence recovery, and polygraphy—agents were required to complete a basic training course and earn a certification that, if properly maintained, remained with them throughout their FBI careers.

For art crime to be recognized as a legitimate specialty program, its agents needed to meet the same formal training and certification standards. Without that structure, the program would never carry the same weight as other FBI specialties.

Over the years, the team's caseload had steadily grown and become more diverse. For that trend to continue, we needed more agents and a larger budget. Eventually, I hoped to secure headquarters-managed positions for some art crime team agents, ensuring that their art crime responsibilities could not be overruled or eliminated by a field office's SAC. Reaching that level was a high bar, and securing funded positions for such a small program was unlikely—but I always loved a good challenge.

These and other changes were essential for the art crime program to fully address the scope and impact of art crime today. Those of us on the art crime team understood this reality well, but FBI leadership was nowhere close to appreciating just how much the nature of art crime had evolved. It was no longer just about theft or trafficking in illegally obtained artifacts and antiquities.

Legitimately purchased art had become a favored vehicle for tax evasion and money laundering, whether for purely criminal enterprises, terrorism financing, or sanctions evasion. And in many cases, like the Miller case, crimes involving cultural heritage and property could not simply be measured in money. The victims were often cultural groups and sometimes even entire nations.

The team had steadily expanded its expertise and effectiveness across a wide range of successful investigations. The Miller case had put a spotlight on our abilities, and Malheur had further strengthened our reputation within the bureau. These successes, along with progress we were making on the counterterrorism front, positioned us to start turning our aspirations for the team into reality.

However, an unavoidable truth for any organizational entity in a bureaucracy is that it must keep growing or it will begin to decline. If leadership fails to seize a favorable moment, progress slows, and everything starts drifting toward stagnation and collapse.

The art crime program had momentum and a real opportunity to advance, but resistance remained. There were still plenty of naysayers and institutional obstacles within the FBI.

Ironically, one of our greatest assets over the previous decade had now become my most immediate challenge.

I mentioned earlier that the art crime program would not have survived its early years without Bonnie Magness-Gardiner's de facto leadership, which extended well beyond her official role as a management and program analyst. Bonnie provided a critical bridge to the art world and academic community, filling a gap in expertise under a series of program managers who often had little to no background in art crime. Whether they were supportive of the program or indifferent to it, most were content to let Bonnie quietly run the show.

She had done this with remarkable bureaucratic savvy and steely resolve, skillfully outmaneuvering and outlasting any antagonistic supervisors who cycled through on eighteen-month temporary duty. As I have often said, she thrived in the dark, like a mushroom farmer, and for the most part, the art crime program benefited from her approach. But for the program to seize the moment and continue to grow and evolve, someone had to pull it into the light and fully professionalize it.

Bonnie's limitation within the FBI was that she was not a special agent. While the bureau relies on a wide range of expertise and support personnel, its leadership structure is primarily composed of law enforcement agents, particularly at operational levels below the director and deputy director. This is not just a matter of bureaucratic policy but a reflection of how the FBI's mission is structured, balancing law enforcement responsibilities with the need for specialized expertise in programs like art crime.

For example, as the art crime program's caseload grew larger and more complex, it required expert case supervision and management. Having a law enforcement background, combined with art crime expertise, was crucial to providing the investigative oversight and guidance needed to handle cases effectively.

Bonnie's immense contributions to the program were not based on criminal investigative experience, but in other areas that were just as vital. She was an astute guide on the art world and a key connection to academic subject matter experts. She was also a compelling spokesperson on art crime matters and a skilled navigator of bureaucratic politics—all of which helped sustain the program at a time when few in the FBI fully recognized its value. In the process, she had built a small but influential sphere of control, shaping the art crime team by deciding who joined it and serving as its public face at conferences and in meetings with international law enforcement partners.

For the art crime program to reach its full potential, she had to accept a shift in that influence and control. That kind of change would be difficult for anyone, and I tried to make a point to approach it with respect and sensitivity. But again, the need for change was both statutory and practical.

When I began traveling internationally as art crime program manager, I quickly learned that many of my foreign law enforcement counterparts believed Bonnie was an FBI agent. The first time I heard a foreign official ask about "Agent Bonnie," I assumed it was a language issue. But soon I heard the same thing from officials who were fluent in English, and I heard it a lot.

When I explained that Bonnie was not an agent but rather a support professional, foreign law enforcement officials were often shocked. Some even expressed concern about the sensitive law enforcement information they had shared with her, assuming she was also an oath-sworn, duly empowered law enforcement officer.

To be clear, I am not suggesting that Bonnie ever misrepresented herself as an FBI agent—she was far too smart for that. But I suspect she didn't go out of her way to correct the assumption when others made it. That was simply part of her modus operandi—operating in the shadows and working around FBI policies that didn't align with her approach.

Bonnie knew change was coming and likely understood it was necessary, but she was accustomed to doing things her way. One of our first struggles was over titles and how she presented herself externally. As the new program manager, I saw her role as executive officer, supporting the program within the bounds of her management and program analyst position. But I wasn't surprised that she resisted giving up her self-anointed title of art crime program manager.

To be fair, the FBI had been complicit in Bonnie's calling herself the program manager, largely because of the positive publicity she generated. There are still FBI web pages and press releases referring to her as managing the art theft or art crime program.

When I arrived at headquarters, Eric Ives was still in the section as a unit chief, and he made it clear that he had pushed back on this issue before. He told me on several occasions how he had corrected Bonnie when he heard her refer to herself as program manager. "No, you're not, Bonnie. You're the program analyst," he would say. He should know. He had hired her for the position.

Bonnie and I also had a battle of wills over the National Stolen Art File (NSAF). At the time, the NSAF existed only on the hard drive of Bonnie's office laptop. If something happened to either, the entire database could be lost forever.

Beyond that, Bonnie was slow to update the file. New entries often took an extraordinarily long time to be added, and recovered artworks lingered in the system long after they should have been removed. A large stack of unprocessed updates sat on her desk, waiting for attention.

The NSAF needed modernization in multiple ways. But in the meantime, access to the file ran through Bonnie alone. She understood that information is power, and she was reluctant to give up this part of her power base.

The NSAF needed to be readily accessible not just to art crime team agents but to every FBI agent who might encounter stolen art in the course of their investigations. The only practical way to achieve this was to integrate it into Sentinel, the FBI's case management system.

Bonnie pushed back. Without offering any clear justification, she insisted that this wouldn't work. However, when the file eventually became part of Sentinel, it worked seamlessly.

This was just one of several issues that we had different views on. Bonnie was rapidly approaching retirement, and despite the tensions that came with this transition period, I respected her, liked her, and hoped she would stay. She had been instrumental in keeping the art crime program alive for years. Hell, I was in the program because of Bonnie. Still, times had changed, and the program needed to move in a new direction.

I wasn't surprised when she decided to put in her retirement papers. It was a huge loss for both the art crime team and the FBI as a whole, but it was also time to bring the program fully into the light and establish it as a professionalized, modern specialty within the bureau.

In October, while the situation with Bonnie was still moving to its conclusion, Drew, Holly, and I drove to Fort Thompson, South Dakota, in a rented SUV. In the back, carefully covered with the blankets the Dakotas delegation had left with us in March, were Individual 10, the partial remains of nine other individuals, and their associated burial goods, just as we had been instructed.

At the Lode Star Casino, we completed the paperwork to formally transfer the ancestral remains and artifacts to the Crow Creek Sioux. Since our consultation at the casino the previous October, we had built enough trust and respect with the Sioux and the Three Affiliated Tribes that they invited us to witness most of the reburial ceremony.

It was Monday, October 10, 2016—Columbus Day, of all days, for such an event to take place. Five years later, President Joseph Biden would proclaim that Columbus Day would also be recognized as Indigenous Peoples' Day, although the official federal holiday on the second Monday of October remains Columbus Day.

In a beautiful spot on the rolling plains of the Crow Creek Reservation, under a bright, broad sky, our hosts had dug a hole big enough to hold all the remains and burial goods. Three generations of tribal members conducted the burial rites, which included songs, prayers, and drumming. As Drew, Holly, and I stood in silent witness, a small herd of buffalo came to the top of a nearby hill and a lone hawk circled overhead.

Before the reburial ceremony reached its most sacred moment, when the remains were about to be placed into the ground, our hosts asked us to withdraw beyond the ridge to where we had all left our vehicles. The final interment was not for any outsider to see.

Elders from the affected tribes—the Three Affiliated Tribes, along with the Crow Creek, Lower Brule, and Rosebud Sioux—stood in a line, thanking us one by one as we passed. Later, Drew told Holly and me that a Sioux elder had said to him, "We only think of members of our nation as insiders. We think of everyone as brothers, but not as insiders."

Drew wondered where this could possibly be going. Then the Sioux elder continued, "What you've done has brought us so close together with the Arikara"—historical enemies of the Sioux in the eighteenth and nineteenth centuries—"that we think of them as insiders now."

With the reburial ceremony complete, we all returned to the Lode Star Casino for a buffet lunch. During the ceremony, Drew had been especially struck by the singing of a young man wearing a vintage NBA jersey. The two of them struck up a conversation, and afterward, Drew, who had played basketball at Indiana's Wabash College, told Holly and me, "He only wanted to talk about basketball and the NBA, which I was happy to do as a typical Hoosier basketball nut. Yet he was also willing to stand up in front of outsiders like us with the other singers and sing traditional sacred songs for his ancestors.

"It's easy for somebody like me to romanticize Native Americans and forget that they live in the modern world just like everybody else. Yet they can be connected to the past in a way most of us never experience. That juxtaposition is something I don't want to lose sight of."

He hasn't lost sight of it. When Drew later spoke with me about the Miller case for this book, that juxtaposition remained one of his most vivid recollections.

As we left lunch in our rented SUV, I suggested to Holly and Drew that we try to find the spot where Miller had looted "Sioux Warrior" and the other remains that had just been reburied.

They were skeptical that I could pinpoint it, but I was confident. I drove, retracing the same route Miller had taken all those years ago.

We headed south out of Oacoma on County Highway 6, following the paved road as it wound through the landscape. Eventually, the pavement gave way to dirt, and we continued on, driving deeper into the countryside. Finally, we reached a spot I recognized from my study of the Millers' "Sioux Warrior" photographs and travel diary.

I got out and walked about a hundred yards onto the open plain. Beneath some thistle, I spotted sunken depressions in the earth. Turning to face north, I could just make out the bridge over the Missouri River between Chamberlain and Oacoma.

This was the place.

"Come over here," I shouted to Holly and Drew.

Taking in the beauty of the scene in front of us, we took a few photographs and later confirmed that we had found the exact spot by comparing them with the Millers' snapshots from the scene.

We had brought some of Miller's stolen artifacts and skeletal trophies full circle. There was still much more to do to fully resolve the Miller case in the years ahead.

But this was a crucial stage in that journey, and we had seen it through.

Eleven

Adventures in Cultural Diplomacy

From the American Southwest to the
People's Republic of China

Let's just close the case. It's time to shut it down," Greg Massa said.

"You want to close the Miller case?" I said, dumbfounded on the other end of the phone call.

Managing the Miller case from six hundred miles away at FBI headquarters was never going to be easy. But I also never expected to hear Greg, then in his second year as an ASAC at the Indianapolis field office, say we should shut it down.

It was late summer 2016, two months into my tenure as art crime program manager, and I was still getting my feet under me at headquarters. I had called Greg to follow up on my need for someone in the field office to serve as the case agent for the Miller investigation.

"I just need a 10 percent case agent, Greg," I said. "I'll still run the case and handle almost all the case agent's work. But there has to be someone in Indy to sign paperwork for Holly and her grad students, make sure the warehouse bills get paid, and check in if an alarm goes off. And even then, it'll probably just be the humidity control system needing a reset."

"No can do, Tim. I don't have the personnel," Greg had insisted in our first conversation. Now he was going further, first by suggesting, "We should transfer the case to another agency. We've gotten everything we can out of it, and it really fits better over at Interior. Let's send it to Bureau of Indian Affairs or Fish and Wildlife."

"Come on, Greg. No other federal agency is going to take this case off our hands. It's too complex, it's too expensive, and it's going to take a few more years to resolve." At that point, I was hoping to complete the case in 2020.

"Yeah," Greg admitted. That was when he said we should shut down the case because of its complexity, cost, and time frame.

After my initial stunned question, I had to force myself to take a breath before responding further. Laying into Greg wouldn't help.

"Let's think this through," I said. "This is the FBI's case, and it's the Indianapolis field office's case. We have a moral, legal, and statutory responsibility to take it to the end. Right now, the warehouse holds thousands of artifacts and hundreds of human remains awaiting repatriation. What happens to them if we close the case?"

I took another breath. "And what happens to us if we close the case?" Internally, I chafed at saying "us" and "we." If Greg moved to close the case, I'd fight tooth and nail to stop him. But now I was trying to persuade him, not blame and shame him.

I continued, "What happens when tribal communities and the governments of the countries Miller looted start asking questions and pushing for answers? There's bound to be publicity—statements of concern from all sides. We could even see an FBI Inspector General's review or hearings on Capitol Hill. None of us want to find ourselves explaining this in front of a congressional committee, right?"

Greg grunted but didn't respond directly. I shifted to a more positive angle. "The Miller case has brought the bureau a lot of goodwill and positive attention, both here and abroad. We shouldn't squander that. If we see this through, we can build on that momentum and do even more good for the bureau."

I didn't mention that the case had been good for both our careers. It was the main reason I was now at headquarters, with the chance to develop the art crime team to its full potential. Greg was a highly capable agent, and his promotion to ASAC was based on a strong record of achievements. But being part of the largest artifacts case—and one of the biggest, most successful searches in FBI history—had to have helped at least a little.

Greg dropped the idea of closing the case. As for assigning a case agent, his response was still, "I don't have the personnel."

It was not the last time someone in the FBI, whether at the field office or headquarters, suggested shutting down the Miller case or cutting its funding. In those moments, I often wondered how different the response would be if the FBI had discovered that someone robbed the graves of five hundred white people, taking their clothing, their shoes, their wedding rings, and their very bones as trophies. I had no doubt that in that scenario, the bureau would spare no expense, committing whatever money and manpower were needed for as long as it took to resolve the case.

At the time, the art crime program was part of the La Cosa Nostra and major theft unit at headquarters, which gave me access to a dedicated pool of funds specifically for major theft task forces in the field. That money covered salaries and equipment, including vehicles, for local law enforcement officers assigned to joint FBI teams. These partnerships gave field offices extra personnel and the flexibility to assign agents where they were most needed. They also provided local officers with valuable experience and training. And when an operation succeeded, both the bureau and the local department got to share the credit.

"How does this sound?" I pitched Greg later. "I supply funding for four joint task force officers, and you assign a 10 percent agent on Miller. So long as the task force officers put some points on the board for major theft now and then, you can use them however you want."

That got Greg's attention, and, as I suspected he would, he jumped on the opportunity. However, the funding hinged on Indy's field intelligence group raising major theft from a "band one" to a "band three" priority. The bureau used four priority bands to classify the various threats field offices handled, whether related to crime or national security. Field offices could adjust a case category's ranking within their region by following a set protocol. This should have been a routine change, but the field intelligence group refused to cooperate. They did not believe major theft was a significant enough threat to warrant the increase.

In his capacity as ASAC, Greg could have put pressure on the intel folks to get this done. But internal politics being what they are, I suspect he didn't see the effort worth the political capital it would have required, and he let the whole matter die.

Around the time the deal fell through, Leslie Lahr was nearing the end of her seventh year as a supervisor. FBI policy limited supervisory agents to seven years in that role before they had to either promote or return to field agent status. Leslie was not ready to retire and planned to stay in the Indianapolis field office. She had been interested in the Miller case from the start, having approved my preliminary investigation. Greg, albeit grudgingly, agreed to assign the case as one of her new responsibilities.

Having Leslie take over as case agent lightened my load on paper, but in practice, it didn't feel that way. I was still working twelve-hour days, often six days a week, juggling everything my new role demanded. The transition to headquarters was a shift in more ways than one. For the first time since joining the military at nineteen, I no longer had bomb tech duties in the United States or deployments to conflict zones abroad. While I missed the camaraderie of other bomb techs, I didn't miss the work itself.

Fortunately, Drew Northern was still overseeing the Miller case in Indianapolis. If Greg had tried to transfer it or shut it down, Drew would have stood firmly with me in opposition. Holly was also carrying a heavy load as a contractor, balancing her roles as chief subject matter expert and collections manager. The case provided her top museum studies students with invaluable hands-on experience, benefiting both them and the bureau.

Through it all, Drew, Holly, and I worked closely together, leading the consultations with the Native American community on repatriation. We had become a team, each of us committed to seeing the case through.

I was also fortunate that my unit chief at headquarters, Jay Bartholomew, understood the significance of the Miller case, the need to professionalize the art crime program, and the reality that our work was expanding beyond the traditional boundaries of the La Cosa Nostra and major theft unit. I couldn't have asked for a more supportive boss.

When I applied for the role of art crime program manager, I told Jay up front that I planned to make major changes. "The program has been operating in the dark for too long," I said. "I'm going to turn all the lights on." When I got the job, Jay made it clear he had my back. "I trust you, Tim," he said. "Whatever help you need, let me know."

I didn't check in with him on every decision, but I kept him informed. We stayed in sync throughout the rest of his time as unit chief, and his support made all the difference.

Jay's support was crucial because our section chief at the time, Max Marker, saw things differently. The La Cosa Nostra and major theft unit fell under the Transnational Organized Crime East section ("East" referring to the eastern hemisphere), which Max had been leading since 2014. (TOC West, by contrast, focused almost entirely on fighting drug cartels throughout the Americas.)

When Max asked about my vision for the art crime program, I told him that in five years, it would be its own cultural property crime unit, not just a program. It was a bit of a ridiculous goal—no one was likely to approve it as a stand-alone unit with its own unit chief and multiple supervisors—but that wasn't really the point. My statement was meant to send a clear message: The program was going to grow.

Max's reaction made it clear that he would have been happy to knock the art crime program and me down a notch or two. I don't think Max necessarily disliked the program. He just didn't see it as terribly important. I had to stay on guard, pushing back when I could and rolling with the punches when I could not.

Until he retired from the FBI in January 2017, Eric Ives was a great mentor and role model, both in navigating the infighting at headquarters and driving meaningful change. As major theft unit chief from 2003 to 2007, he had been the one to bring the art crime team into existence, along with Bob Wittman and others.

Eric followed three guiding principles. First, no one would ever say he lacked imagination in solving a problem. Second, he used whatever was available to get things done, without asking for permission—or forgiveness—until after the fact. Third, he always found a way to yes. We got along well because I was cut from much the same cloth, especially when it came to refusing to take no for an answer.

No longer directly involved in the art crime program, Eric's final act before leaving the bureau was to create and run what he called the global threat financing program on his own. It focused on how organized crime groups, tax and sanctions evaders, and terrorists launder money through commodities with subjective value and changing prices, such as diamonds, luxury goods, and art. In these trades, the actual worth of the item is often just a small fraction of the amount being laundered.

Eric gave himself the title director of global threat financing, and in late 2016, he chuckled as he told me that, for the first and probably only time in history, the FBI had two directors—the official one who ran the entire bureau and him.

As I mentioned earlier, Bonnie Magness-Gardiner adopted the title of program manager on her own, taking on the many roles and responsibilities that came with it. She handled the job capably, and though the title was never officially designated, no one challenged it—except Eric, who had hired her as a management and program analyst, her true title. Say something enough times, and eventually, it just becomes true. By the time she left, her title was universally accepted across the bureau and throughout the government. This, too, was a good lesson in taking action and asking forgiveness later.

Because supervisors tended to rotate out every eighteen months, it was often possible to simply outlast an unsympathetic or hostile higher-up. Even long-serving unit and section chiefs tended to avoid direct confrontation, preferring to resist change in quieter ways. In true bureaucratic fashion, conflict was usually waged through passive-aggressive maneuvering. In that environment, stubbornness and thick skin were essential for survival.

Generally speaking, if an agent remained a program manager, unit chief, or section chief for an extended period, it usually meant one of two things—their career had stalled or they were not interested in climbing the leadership ladder. Like corporate management, the FBI's executive promotion system prioritized broad experience across a series of short-term assignments, quick rotations designed to check boxes in different areas and build a résumé for the next step up.

The longer I stayed the art crime program manager, the more it limited my ability to do anything else in the bureau. My family also paid a heavy price for my twelve-hour days at headquarters and my brutal travel schedule for tribal consultations, art crime conferences, and liaison with foreign law enforcement. But I was where I wanted to be, and that was enough for me.

There was no real formal process for separating art crime from major theft and making it an independent program. This was going to be one of those situations where, if I said it out loud enough, it'd just become true. I was going to have to pull it out by sheer force of will.

In June 2016, FBI executives, official documents, and even our external web pages still referred to art *theft* rather than art *crime*. When I started using the term *art crime* and argued that the program needed to stand on its own outside major theft, some people pushed back. I ignored them and kept saying "art crime" in every conversation and meeting, and I used it in every document I wrote. Over the next two years, as the management ranks around and above me heard and read the term often enough, it gradually became standard.

Since its inception, the art crime team had generally opened its cases under the major theft classification. The FBI assigns numerical designations to cases based on crime type, which determines which program they fall under. Major theft cases, for example, were classified under a specific number tied to property crimes. But theft accounted for only about a quarter of our growing caseload. Forgery and fraud made up about half, while antiquities trafficking, along with some money laundering, tax evasion, sanctions evasion, and terrorist financing, comprised the rest. If the program was going to stand on its own, it needed a case classification that accurately reflected the work we were doing.

The FBI's Resource Planning Office managed case classifications and other administrative details. When I requested a dedicated classification for art crime, they instructed me to submit a formal proposal outlining the need for it and any relevant subclassifications. In time, the Resource Planning Office approved the request, creating the first classification in bureau history dedicated solely to art crime. It covered not just theft but also art-related fraud, trafficking, money laundering, and the full range of criminal threats the program investigated.

I was not done yet. With the new classification in place, the next step was to draft a comprehensive policy guide to formalize the art crime program and align it with other stand-alone programs across the bureau. For most of its history, the FBI had been weak on formal policy development and implementation, but that began to change in the late 2000s with the adoption of a standardized policy process. Now, any new program required clear guidelines, and I worked closely with the Internal Policy Office to develop the necessary policies and ensure they were implemented across all field offices.

Making sure these changes took hold—and weren't blocked or reversed—required results, and the art crime team delivered. High-profile cases reinforced the need for a stand-alone program. In 2017, the team recovered Norman Rockwell's *Lazybones* after it had been missing for more than forty years, drawing national attention. In 2018, agents successfully recovered the iconic ruby slippers worn by Judy Garland in *The Wizard of Oz*, which had been stolen from the Judy Garland Museum in 2005. The continued progress in the Miller case was just as critical. It not only strengthened my push for change but also helped secure the funding needed to keep the case moving forward.

On May 1, 2017, Drew, Holly, and I flew to Albuquerque, New Mexico, where we met Kathleen Magnafici, an art crime team agent based in the field office there. Together, we went to Old Town Albuquerque's Indian Pueblo Cultural Center, which is operated by New Mexico's nineteen pueblo nations. Our purpose was to begin consultations on the first repatriation from the Miller case to tribes in the Southwest.

The proposed repatriation included the partial remains of sixteen individuals and 219 artifacts, some of which were funerary objects. The craftsmanship and designs of the artifacts were characteristic of several Southwest tribes, and we had tentatively linked some to specific groups. However, osteological analysis of the human remains did not indicate a clear tribal affiliation. Instead, traces of soil matrix and coloration, along with evidence from Miller himself, suggested they likely came from within a hundred miles of St. Johns, Arizona—one of his primary starting points for excavations in the region.

Without invasive radiocarbon assays, we had no way to estimate when the individuals had been buried. That meant we had to cast a wide net in our consultation. For the meeting in Albuquerque, we invited forty-nine federally recognized tribes, including those that currently held land around St. Johns in Arizona or New Mexico, as well as others with historic ties to the area. Several tribes accepted the invitation, including the Acoma; the Hopi; the Salt River Pima-Maricopa Indian Community (SRPMIC); the Gila River Indian Community (GRIC), which included both Pima and Maricopa peoples; and others.

The Gila River Indian Community and the Salt River Pima-Maricopa Indian Community had reservations on the southern and eastern edges of Phoenix, respectively, and their representatives did not travel to Albuquerque. Since they were both in the Phoenix area, they opted to join the consultation by telephone. Unfortunately, technical issues caused their call to keep dropping. We held off on substantive discussion for more than half an hour, hoping to resolve the problem, but eventually, we had to move forward with the meeting for the sake of the other tribes.

As we did in every tribal consultation, Drew, Holly, and I started with a brief update on the Miller case. We then shared the evidence linking the remains and artifacts to the area around St. Johns. To help with the repatriation process, we asked the tribes to visit the Miller case website, where they could view photos of the artifacts and submit claims for any items connected to their communities.

We explained why we could only establish a regional connection for the ancestral remains and asked the tribes to reach a consensus on which of them should take custody on behalf of the group. The Hopi stepped forward, offering to rebury the remains on their large reservation in northeastern Arizona. After some initial discussion, the other tribes at the meeting welcomed the Hopis' offer, pending further conversations.

On June 2, at the request of Acoma Pueblo Tribal Historic Preservation Officer Damian Garcia, we held a follow-up phone consultation. Representatives from Laguna Pueblo, which borders Acoma, along with the Hopi and another tribe, joined the call.

Damian got straight to the point. After further discussions among the pueblos, they had reached an agreement—the Acoma would speak on their behalf regarding the repatriation. He also reaffirmed their support for transferring the unaffiliated ancestral remains to the Hopi for reburial. It was a smooth, practical resolution, the kind that didn't always come easily in these consultations.

The Gila River Indian Community and the Salt River Pima-Maricopa Indian Community did not have representatives on the follow-up call, though we had once again invited all forty-nine tribes to participate. However, we were in ongoing discussions with both communities, working around their schedules to ensure they had a voice in the process.

On August 25, as part of those efforts, GRIC and SRPMIC sent a delegation to Indianapolis to tour the warehouse facility. Tribal representatives were always welcome to arrange visits, and this one provided an opportunity for direct engagement. Holly and Leslie hosted the group, answering questions and addressing concerns. The visit was cordial and productive, reinforcing our commitment to accommodating each tribe's needs in the repatriation process.

By that point, I had begun coordinating with the Hopi to schedule the repatriation of the sixteen sets of remains for spring 2018. They already had a reburial planned for an unrelated repatriation around that time, and it would be more practical to include these remains in the same ceremony. This approach not only eased logistical challenges but also ensured the reburial was conducted in accordance with their traditions.

However, at a later conference in California, representatives from the Gila River Indian Community made it clear—loudly and forcefully—that they were unhappy with the plan. They felt that we had not given them or the Salt River Pima-Maricopa Indian Community a fair opportunity to participate in the Albuquerque meeting or the follow-up call.

But their frustration ran deeper than scheduling conflicts. The two tribes had a long and difficult history with the Hopi, marked by past conflicts that still carried weight. The GRIC representatives did not mince words. "We cannot allow any ancestors of the Pima and Maricopa peoples to be buried on Hopi land," one of them declared.

Although we had been unable to affiliate the remains with a specific tribe, the area around St. Johns was once Anasazi land. Among present-day tribes, the Hopi and the pueblos along the Arizona and New Mexico border had some of the longest historical ties to the region.

Trying to avoid derailing the entire effort, I simply asked the GRIC representatives if they had any evidence connecting the remains to the Pima and Maricopa peoples.

They did not have any evidence, but that did not change their position. They insisted that even if there was only a 1 percent chance the remains were connected to the Pima and Maricopa peoples, neither they nor the Salt River Pima-Maricopa Indian Community could agree to a reburial on Hopi land.

The opposition from the two Phoenix area tribes halted any hope of a spring 2018 repatriation to the Hopi. Resolving the diplomatic impasse between these sovereign tribal nations would not be easy, and that is a story I will have to finish in the final chapter.

Our international repatriations of material from the Miller collection usually garnered at least some positive press in the United States—sometimes a great deal more. In the receiving countries, however, they were always major news.

We kicked off a series of soft diplomacy wins for the bureau and the United States on April 12, 2017, when we delivered two ancient clay cuneiform tablets to the Iraqi embassy in Washington, DC. In a way, this repatriation brought the art crime team full circle. The team had been formed in response to the 2003 thefts from the National Museum of Iraq in Baghdad, making this return a symbolic moment in its history.

On June 6, we returned seventy-five pre-Columbian artifacts to the Peruvian embassy in Washington, DC. Along with them, we repatriated a large religious painting that had been stolen from a church in Cuzco. The art crime team had recovered the painting after it was sold through a gallery in Santa Fe, New Mexico.

There was a heart-stopping moment for Holly and me before the repatriation ceremony and reception. We had already formally transferred possession of the artifacts to Peru and were watching as embassy staff sorted through the boxes, deciding which pieces to display for the media and invited guests. Their handling was casual, almost careless, and we had no choice but to stand by and watch.

Then came the moment that nearly sent Holly over the edge. A staffer reached into a box and lifted an ancient pot with one hand, gripping it by the lip—the most fragile part. Holly stepped forward, her body reacting before she could stop herself. One wrong move, and the pressure could have snapped the lip, sending the entire pot crashing to the floor in a cascade of shattered clay.

For a split second, I thought we were about to witness a disaster. But somehow, the pot held. The staffer set it down without incident, completely unaware of how close they had come to destroying a piece of history. I leaned over to Holly and whispered, "We can't say anything. The material is all theirs now."

She exhaled slowly, eyes still locked on the table. Correcting an embassy staffer in that moment would have been poor diplomacy. We just had to hope everything made it through the day in one piece.

The pot survived intact, and the ceremony was a great success, generating positive media coverage in both countries. Much of that was thanks to Peru's Patricio Lindeman, who had worked closely with me on the arrangements.

The joy on the Peruvian side was nothing new—it was the kind of response we saw with every repatriation. Seeing how important the return of cultural patrimony was never got old, and we never took it for granted. It just increased our motivation to carry the Miller case through to a proper ending.

That was especially true when human remains were involved.

The first time I saw Miller's basement display, I noticed an empty glass case with a mount labeled "Shrunken Head, Peru." The case was still empty when I returned with Holly, and I wondered what had happened to the artifact.

During the search, we got our answer. On a shelf behind some pottery on the other side of the basement, we found what looked like a shrunken head. It had been tucked away, out of sight, but there was no mistaking what it was.

A shrunken head from an Amazonian tribe fit right in with Miller's macabre fascination with the dead. The anthropologists at the scene believed it likely came from the Amazon region, but they also suspected it was a fake—one of the replicas made for the tourist trade. Locals often used monkey heads or wrapped pigskin around a mold, shrinking it in boiling water before stitching in human hair to make it look authentic.

But when we sent the head for testing, the results came back with an unsettling confirmation. It was a real shrunken human head.

The Peruvian embassy was grateful to have it returned, though not as part of the public ceremony. Instead, the handover happened quietly, behind the scenes—an appropriately respectful end to a disturbing find.

On June 30 that year, Drew Northern retired from the FBI, a tough loss for our case team. With his departure, the last of the key decision-makers in the Indianapolis field office who had made the Miller case possible—Special Agent in Charge Bob Jones, Assistant Special Agent in Charge Kevin Lyons, and Chief Division Counsel Drew—had all moved on and been replaced.

The changes weren't limited to Indianapolis. The executives at headquarters who had approved funding for the case in its early years had also moved on, replaced by a new group of leaders with no direct connection to the case or its history.

I had to explain the Miller case repeatedly to each new wave of decision-makers to secure the funding needed to operate the warehouse and carry out repatriations. As I've said, the case cost at least $300,000 a year—money that did not directly support the FBI's traditional investigative priorities. Some executives saw its importance, both for the bureau and the nation. Others did not.

From late 2017 to early 2019, we repatriated material from the Miller collection to Canada, Cambodia, Colombia, Mexico, and Spain. Although most of these repatriations did not involve many items, that did not diminish the care we devoted to them. The material was all significant for its rarity, historical value, and/or exceptional beauty, such as three magnificent Khmer bronzes we transferred to the Cambodian embassy in Washington, DC.

The largest international repatriation during this period was to the People's Republic of China. When we invited foreign cultural heritage officials to review the material seized from the Miller collection, most gave it only a brief glance on our website before responding with some version of, "That looks like part of our cultural heritage. We'd like it back."

Wen Dayan, director general of China's National Cultural Heritage Administration (NCHA), took a far more thorough approach. Starting in late 2016, Dayan worked closely with his colleagues at the NCHA to carefully examine the artifacts, ensuring that each claim was supported by rigorous research and documentation.

To start with, they weren't satisfied with the image quality on the website. At Mr. Wen's request, I supplied a portfolio of high-resolution pictures. Over the next several months, he oversaw a meticulous review process. The NCHA's experts carefully examined every potentially Chinese artifact, assessing its origins and significance. For each item, they produced a brief report, usually about half a page but sometimes much longer, detailing their findings and justifying their claim.

In a few instances, the reports identified objects as fakes and stated that China did not want them. For the rest, the reports went beyond simply confirming authenticity. They detailed each object's dynasty, its estimated date or date range within that era, its place of origin in China, and its defining stylistic features. The review process concluded on June 13, 2017, when Dayan emailed me China's final claim list, which included 361 objects.

We agreed to the list, and Wen Dayan and I began discussing the logistics of repatriation. I saw an opportunity for a major diplomatic win for both the bureau and the United States as well as the potential for significant media attention in the United States, China, and beyond. With that in mind, I suggested holding the repatriation ceremony in Beijing.

Dayan welcomed the idea, saying that China and its people would fully support such an event. We set a target date for late spring or early summer 2018.

The FBI operates under an international law enforcement charter, but any activity in a foreign country requires the approval and oversight of the State Department. While the bureau has legal attachés (or "legats," as they are called internally) stationed at US embassies and consulates worldwide, these agents work under the authority of the ambassador and the broader diplomatic mission. Any official FBI action abroad must align with US foreign policy and be coordinated through the State Department.

When I informed my counterparts in the State Department's Bureau of Educational and Cultural Affairs about the plan for a repatriation ceremony in Beijing, I expected routine coordination. Instead, I encountered strong resistance from the office of the assistant secretary of state for educational and cultural affairs and the National Security Council.

The senior political appointees at the State Department and the National Security Council viewed the repatriation as a potential bargaining chip for US-China discussions at the G-20 summit in Buenos Aires from November 30 to December 1, 2018. They made it clear that the repatriation should not move forward unless it was tied to those negotiations.

My attempts to persuade the State Department and the NSC otherwise went nowhere. When it became clear they would not budge, I informed Wen that we would have to hold the repatriation in the United States instead. To my surprise, he had no objections. In fact, he seemed to prefer it.

I explained to the office of the assistant secretary, "I understand that we need your approval to take the material to Beijing. But the Miller case is a domestic law enforcement matter, and our legal responsibility is to return stolen property to its rightful owner as soon as possible. We are not going to hold hostage a sovereign nation's cultural heritage to bargain for diplomatic concessions."

I hoped my bosses would agree.

The State Department was not happy. Their opposition was firm, and they made it clear that they saw this as their decision to make. From their perspective, anything involving a foreign country fell under their authority, and they did not seem particularly concerned with my objections.

With little room to maneuver, I had no choice but to escalate the issue through the chain of command at FBI headquarters.

In July 2018, Jay Bartholomew retired from the FBI and took a contractor position in the security division at the bureau's satellite administrative center in Huntsville, Alabama. For a while, his position was filled by a rotating series of acting unit chiefs, leaving no steady leadership in place.

With no clear support at that level, I took the issue up a couple of levels, briefing section chief Max Marker and the assistant director in charge of the Criminal Investigative Division. I was concerned they might give in to State's position, especially since Max had never shown much enthusiasm for the art crime program, the Miller case, or me.

If there is one constant in Washington, DC, however, it is interagency rivalry. FBI executives might have had to accept State's decision against a repatriation in Beijing, but they were not about to let another agency dictate what the bureau could or could not do on US soil. A bit to my surprise, the bosses had my back on this one.

Meanwhile, I quietly reached out to my counterparts in State's Bureau of Educational and Cultural Affairs with a straightforward message: "This is going to happen with or without you. If you keep pushing back, we'll move forward without your involvement—even to the point of not inviting you to the ceremony."

State had the authority to deny Wen Dayan and his colleagues diplomatic entry to the United States for the repatriation, but doing so would have created a diplomatic headache. Even if they took that step, it would not have stopped the process. We could still transfer possession of the artifacts to Chinese officials already in the country with diplomatic status, whether at the embassy in Washington, DC, or at one of China's consulates in a major US city.

In the end, State did not want to be seen as obstructing the return of Chinese cultural patrimony. As the lead US agency on international cultural matters, it understandably wanted to maintain its role in the process—and ensure it had a share of the credit for the repatriation.

By early fall 2018, the resistance faded. Instead of trying to block the event, the State Department shifted gears and insisted on hosting a formal dinner to mark the occasion.

The next big question was where in the United States the repatriation should take place. Leslie Lahr suggested, "Why don't we do it here at the field office in Indianapolis? That way, we won't have to move everything to another city. The Chinese are going to have to ship it home no matter where they take possession."

I couldn't help laughing in disbelief. "There's no way the bureau would allow that," I said. It stood to reason that any delegation from China was bound to include at least one undercover intelligence officer, and I couldn't imagine that the bureau would want them inside an FBI space.

But Leslie had a point about logistics, and there was no harm in asking—if only to rule it out officially. Greg Massa was still serving as an assistant special agent in charge at the Indianapolis field office, and by February 2018, Grant Mendenhall had taken over as the new special agent in charge.

Leslie checked with Massa and Mendenhall, as well as Indy's field intelligence and security personnel. To cover all bases, we also ran it by FBI headquarters, including the Security Division, Counterintelligence Division, and International Operations Division. Surprisingly, none of them raised major concerns. When Leslie reported back, she was grinning. "It's a go!"

Security concerns weren't the only reason the lack of pushback surprised me. Earlier that year, the industrial park where our warehouse was located had been sold to the pharmaceutical giant Roche, which was expanding its Indianapolis operations. That meant we had to find and set up a new warehouse—a process that had taken up far more of my time than I would have liked.

Part of the challenge came from conflicts with the field office's chief security officer. My philosophy for both warehouse spaces was simple. Don't let perfection be the enemy of *good enough*. The second warehouse met all the necessary security requirements, in my view, but the chief security officer kept raising concerns. After a lot of back-and-forth, we agreed to disagree, but the message was clear. The field office was growing weary of the Miller case.

It also surprised me that approvals from headquarters came through without a hitch. One after another, the international operations division, the counterintelligence division, and the security division signed off on holding the repatriation at the field office. A supervisory special agent in the security division told me, "This isn't really unheard of. We've had the Chinese in our facilities quite a few times."

Security remained a priority, of course. There were extensive discussions about ensuring that every member of the Chinese delegation was properly chaperoned at all times while visiting the field office.

The only space on the field office campus large enough to accommodate everyone—including both US and Chinese media—was the mechanics' auto bay in the field office annex. Because of space constraints, the auto bay was where even the FBI director addressed the field office when he visited Indianapolis. So holding the ceremony there wouldn't be treating our Chinese guests any worse than the head of the FBI, but it would also have a security advantage. The Chinese delegation would never be in the field office's main building, which housed our investigative spaces, classified files (analog and digital), computer systems, and secure communications facilities.

I was grateful for the field office's support in hosting the repatriation, but I thought it was poor form to receive a high-level Chinese delegation in the office's auto bay. No matter how many banners, curtains, and finishing touches we added, it was still a garage. I had a pretty clear image of how we would be treated if the situation were reversed, and I was certain we wouldn't be hosted that way in Beijing.

Dayan didn't seem to mind at all. In fact, he expressed enthusiasm for holding the repatriation at the field office. With the location established, we set the date for February 28. The repatriation ceremony would take place late that morning, followed by the formal dinner hosted by the State Department that evening.

We should have been set, but State wasn't done interfering. In late 2018 or early January 2019, they sent me an action plan for a meeting with the Chinese delegation that they wanted to schedule between the repatriation ceremony and the dinner. Ostensibly, the meeting was to discuss the upcoming five-year renewal of a bilateral US-China agreement, one of sixteen such agreements the United States had at the time under the 1970 UNESCO Convention on cultural property.

The core of each agreement was simple. Both countries agreed to impose import controls on designated categories of cultural property to prevent illicit trafficking and ensure that protected artifacts were not smuggled across borders.

These agreements are beneficial—the United States now has more than thirty of them—and it made sense to discuss renewing the one with China alongside the repatriation ceremony. The action plan I received was mostly focused on cultural property, as expected. But much like a rider in a congressional bill, it also included language about combating illicit opioid and human trafficking from China to the United States. As part of the meeting, I was expected to present the FBI's perspective on these issues.

Lumping a discussion of illicit opioid and human trafficking onto a repatriation of Chinese cultural patrimony made no sense to me. The two had nothing to do with each other. What made even less sense was expecting me to speak on these issues. Beyond what I saw on the news, I had no real expertise in either topic.

I told the office of the assistant secretary of state for educational and cultural affairs, "If you want, I can arrange for FBI experts to speak on the illicit opioid trade and human trafficking—at your expense. But I won't say a word about them myself, because I'm not qualified to do so."

The whole thing was an unnecessary distraction, and it nearly derailed the ceremony yet again. In the end, we reached a compromise.

State would hold the meeting, its representatives would address China's cultural heritage officials on illicit opioids and human trafficking, and I would simply sit there and listen.

On January 29, 2019, I sent Wen Dayan the official letter of invitation he and his delegation needed to enter the United States on diplomatic status. The letter outlined all the details—the February 28 repatriation at the Indianapolis field office, the State Department's meeting, and the formal dinner that evening.

Then, less than two weeks before the event, Leslie emailed me with unexpected news. SAC Grant Mendenhall had reversed his support. After further reflection, he had decided he could not allow the repatriation to take place at the field office. Not only that, he was barring all field office personnel except Leslie from assisting with the event.

There was no explanation, and given the authority SACs have over their offices, there was no recourse, other than to curse out loud. Mendenhall's decision was final.

Months of planning were obliterated. Everyone involved at both State and FBI headquarters was furious, and they were looking to me for answers I didn't have. My head was spinning.

The Eiteljorg Museum of American Indians and Western Art saved me—again. Always a great partner, they generously offered to host the repatriation, just as they had welcomed the Native American delegation ahead of the first Miller case repatriation in October 2016. It was asking a lot of them, and I will be ever grateful for their help.

Even with their help, though, getting everything rearranged in time was a frantic scramble. February 28 was a Thursday, and I arrived in Indianapolis at the beginning of the week to make final preparations with Holly and Leslie. Moving the artifacts to the museum, conducting an inventory with the Chinese for their shipping and customs manifest, and deciding what to display for the media was a two-day job.

One exception was a small group of human remains: the arm bone fragment Miller had left inside a heavily encrusted bracelet in his basement display, along with several Tibetan kapalas—ceremonial cups made from human skulls. Out of respect for the Native American artifacts housed at the Eiteljorg and for the Native American community, Dayan and I had arranged for these items to be kept elsewhere. On Wednesday evening, we would move them from the warehouse to a hotel room across the street in downtown Indianapolis. At the last minute, they would be brought to the museum's loading dock and placed on the truck with the rest of the repatriated material, but they would never enter the museum space.

As we began the painstaking process of moving artifacts on Tuesday, *CBS This Morning* aired a segment on the Miller case, tied to the upcoming repatriation of the Chinese artifacts. I had been working with the producer and correspondent on the piece for some time, and both Holly and I had given interviews for it. The timing was perfect, bringing national attention to the case just as we prepared for one of its most significant returns.

As always with the media, *CBS This Morning* was especially interested in the grisliest aspects of Miller's grave robbing. And as always, I made it clear to the producer and correspondent that this material was deeply offensive to Native American communities.

While I allowed them access to some images of seized Native American artifacts, I refused to provide any footage or still photographs that Don and Sue Miller had taken of funerary objects, their excavations of Native American graves, or—most disturbing—themselves posing with skeletal remains.

The producer and correspondent assured me they understood. They promised the segment would respect Native American concerns and would not include images of ancestral remains. I took them at their word, but until the segment aired, I had no idea what they would actually include.

Before the segment even finished airing, my phone started blowing up with calls from the Native American community. *CBS This Morning* had aired the segment nationally and posted it online, and to my shock, it included archival footage that had nothing to do with the Miller case. The footage showed Native American ancestral remains and the desecration of Native American graves—exactly the kind of imagery I had warned them against using.

Folks in the tribal community were justifiably outraged, and many assumed I had been complicit in this aspect of the segment. Explaining that neither the FBI, the art crime team, Holly, nor I had anything to do with the offensive footage wasn't nearly enough. The damage was done, and I was furious.

Through the FBI's public affairs office, I got on the phone with the segment's producer and correspondent. I didn't hold back. I told them in no uncertain terms that what they had done was completely unacceptable and that they needed to take the segment down from the CBS website immediately.

In their defense, CBS had acted out of ignorance, reflecting the cultural indifference of the entire nation. Still, they had ignored my warnings, broken their promises, and shown a blatant disregard for Native American concerns, even if it was unintentional.

Rightly apologetic, they acted quickly. The video was taken down within the hour, and when they reposted it, the offensive footage had been replaced with old National Park Service film showing the excavation of Native American artifacts in the Southwest.

Whether it was changing venues at the last minute or dealing with the CBS debacle, I was largely in problem-solving mode for the entire repatriation. During completion of the inventory the next day, Holly and I saw a grad student unpack an object that had been entered into our database as "possibly Chinese" during the search and seizure operation. Our subject matter experts had later decided that it wasn't Chinese. Wen Dayan's experts agreed with that determination, and China didn't want it. And yet there it was, mixed in with the Chinese material.

I asked Holly, "What's that doing here?"

Her eyes were wide. "It shouldn't be."

Unfortunately, our database had never been corrected and still listed the object as "possibly Chinese." Trusting that information, a graduate student had packed it for transport to the Eiteljorg.

I quietly picked up the object and told a student to take it back to the warehouse. When I explained the mix-up to Dayan, he was gracious, but the problem didn't end there. His team had already logged the object on their customs and shipping manifest, which meant we now had to unravel the error with both US and Chinese customs. Fixing the paperwork turned out to be far more of a hassle than simply removing the object from the shipment.

Although I was on edge all day, worried that something else might go wrong, nothing did. In the end, Grant Mendenhall's last-minute refusal to host the repatriation at the field office had actually worked in our favor.

Instead of a greasy garage on the FBI campus in northeastern Indianapolis, we held the ceremony in the Eiteljorg, surrounded by its world-class collection in a striking, architecturally distinguished building in downtown's White River State Park. The setting was far more fitting for the occasion.

The Chinese delegation, which included the deputy administrator for cultural affairs—a position equivalent to a cabinet-level officer in the United States—and senior officials from the Chinese embassy in Washington, DC, received a private tour of the museum's collection. It was the same courtesy the Eiteljorg had extended to the Native American delegation from the Dakotas during their visit in spring 2016.

Joining us in the US government contingent was our new section chief at headquarters, Kristi Koons Johnson. In late 2018, FBI headquarters had merged Transnational Organized Crime East and West into a single global section under Kristi as section chief. With the merger, TOC East's La Cosa Nostra and major theft unit was dissolved, and art crime was moved under the new section's Africa, Middle East, and Asia unit, which still lacked a permanent unit chief.

Kristi's presence at the repatriation, where she delivered remarks I had written for her, marked her first major involvement in the Miller case and the art crime program. It would not be her last.

Following the ceremony, State's meeting with the Chinese delegation transpired exactly as I thought it would. The Chinese listened politely to State's concerns about the illicit opioid trade and human trafficking, and they said they would convey them to the appropriate officials in China. Otherwise, both sides were in agreement regarding the cultural property bilateral agreement.

The formal dinner that evening, held in a private room at one of Indianapolis's best restaurants, was a fitting end to the day. Say what you will about the State Department—they can be relentless when they want their way—but they know how to put on a first-class event. The setting was elegant, the service impeccable, and the wine flowed freely. For all the battles leading up to the repatriation, everyone was now on the same page, toasting a successful return.

When all was said and done, the Chinese delegation left satisfied, their cultural patrimony returned with the respect and ceremony it deserved. The State Department and FBI headquarters were both pleased, and the US ambassador to China called it our most positive engagement with the Chinese in a decade.

Chinese media ran the story nationwide for days, praising both the FBI and the US government for their roles in the repatriation. For the art crime program, the outcome was a resounding success.

The goodwill on China's side lasted well beyond the ceremony. Due to scheduling conflicts, I was unable to attend the signing of the bilateral agreement in December 2019, so I asked Dave Bass to go in my place. When he arrived in China, he saw just how much the repatriation had resonated. Large photographs of the Indianapolis ceremony were prominently displayed, and Chinese officials constantly asked him to pose for selfies in front of them. The message was clear. They had not forgotten, and they deeply appreciated, the return of their cultural heritage.

The FBI's ability to set things right for the victims of the Miller case relied on a complex framework of American and international law. Unfortunately, US laws regarding Native American cultural property are not as strong or well focused as they need to be.

Before I complete the story of the Miller case, I want to examine the gaps in these laws and explore ways to strengthen them. To do that, I need to tell you about a related case—and two cops drinking beer.

Twelve

Two Cops Drinking Beer and the Case of the Ceremonial Shield

What ARPA, NAGPRA, and the STOP Act Can't Stop

It was a mild night in early June 2018, and we were on our third beers at a bistro in Paris when I decided to take a chance and ask a favor from Marc, a senior officer in the robbery branch of the French national police. We had met the previous June when I led a training session on identifying and grading diamonds and colored gemstones. The session, funded by the Gemological Institute of America, included Marc and his team; officers from the narcotics and financial crimes units of the French police; French customs officers; and FBI agents, including Jake Archer and Ken DiBella, an assistant legal attaché in the FBI's office at the American embassy.

The FBI's gem and jewelry program had become part of my portfolio as art crime manager after Eric Ives retired. Although it would soon fall under the responsibility of the incoming major theft program manager, the gem and jewelry program and the art crime program were a good fit in some ways. The art crime team occasionally handled historic jewelry cases, and the GIA training was valuable for the team's agents.

During the twelve months since that first meeting, I had been to Paris several times for art crime program matters. Each time, Marc and I got together, building a solid rapport both as cops and as people. We naturally traded stories about our cases, and Marc knew I was keeping an eye on an auction house called EVE, short for Estimations et Ventes aux Enchères (Appraisals and Auctions). Over the past few years, EVE had become Europe's leading—or most notorious—auction house specializing in Indigenous cultural goods from around the world, including many Native American items.

At the time, my primary concern was a particular Native American artifact, a sacred ceremonial shield allegedly stolen from the Pueblo of Acoma in the early 1970s. The tribe, along with most of the US government, wanted the shield recovered, and they were counting on the art crime team to get it back.

Due to negative publicity and pressure from the US government on behalf of the tribe, EVE had placed the shield in storage, stalling any sale. However, citing the usual confidentiality provisions in its auction agreements, EVE refused to cooperate with the tribe or the US government by disclosing the consignor's identity. For solid legal reasons, the French government showed little interest in assisting with the shield's recovery and had essentially declined to take unilateral action against EVE. That was a challenge but not an unfamiliar one for the art crime team. We had solved similar cases before, and I believed we could solve this one too—if we were allowed to follow our usual methods.

The odds were that the consignor was based in the United States. If so, and if I could identify them, there was a good chance of persuading them to do the right thing and voluntarily turn the shield over to the FBI for repatriation to Acoma. Over the years, the art crime team had used this approach successfully in many cases. We had gotten quite good at the art of cultural diplomacy.

While there were certainly unscrupulous collectors who didn't care where their holdings came from, most were innocent possessors of stolen or looted cultural items. Once they learned the truth, they were usually willing to surrender them. Just as Don Miller had waived title to the problematic artifacts in his collection, these collectors often did the same, allowing for a swift repatriation of the objects.

That evening in June 2018, I turned to Marc and asked, "How difficult would it be for you to look at EVE's consignment records? In the States, I'd need a search warrant or some other court order."

Marc shook his head. "It's much simpler here. We can just demand to see the records."

"Really?" I was a bit surprised, though I knew that different countries had very different perspectives on property rights and regulatory processes. Sometimes those differences made our work more difficult. Other times, they worked in our favor.

Marc could undoubtedly see the excitement on my face as I said, "EVE has become the bane of my existence, and I really need some help. Could you help a brother out and go to EVE to find out who consigned that shield?"

Marc and I both knew that law enforcement cooperation between our countries was governed by a mutual legal assistance treaty (MLAT), meaning that, technically, I needed an approved MLAT request to obtain the information. But if the French police had the authority to view consignment records on demand, I was hopeful we could handle this a bit more informally.

Marc drained his glass. "Well, if we had an approved MLAT request, the answer would be yes, naturally."

"What about without an MLAT request?"

Marc shrugged and turned to signal the bartender. "I think we need another round, Tim."

The story of the Acoma shield may seem like a detour from the Miller case, which picks up again in the next chapter. However, the obstacles to recovering the shield highlight the gaps in laws protecting Native American cultural property. The shield's story also sheds light on why building probable cause for a search and seizure warrant in the Miller case was so complex—and how that case ultimately reshaped expectations for handling all instances of unlawful possession of Native American cultural property. Taken together, the lessons from both cases point to the need for stronger legal protections for Native American heritage.

EVE first appeared on the radar of both the Native American community and the art crime team two years before it attempted to sell the Acoma shield. In 2013, the auction house ignored tribal protests over the sale of sacred Hopi Kachinas and Navajo masks. Similar sales of sacred Native American objects from the Hopi, Navajo, and other tribes followed in 2014 and 2015. The Acoma shield first appeared in an EVE auction catalog in the spring of 2015, listed with a reserve price of approximately $15,000 and scheduled for auction on June 1 of that year.

In mid-May, while I was on official travel to Florida, Pierre Ciric, a French American lawyer based in New York City, reached out to me. Bonnie Magness-Gardiner had referred him my way because of my experience with Native American cultural property and the law through the Miller case, which had effectively made me the FBI art crime team's de facto expert on the subject.

Representing the tribes, Pierre had already filed a civil lawsuit in France to block EVE's sale of Hopi Kachinas and Navajo masks. However, the French courts had dismissed the case, ruling that only individuals—not tribal entities—had standing to sue over stolen property. Now, he was preparing a similar lawsuit on behalf of the Acoma to stop the sale of the shield.

Pierre sent me information on both the shield and EVE, and we discussed the situation at length in a couple of follow-up calls. Unfortunately, as I explained to him, I thought he had a "nothing burger" in terms of criminal or civil enforcement, for reasons I will explain later in this chapter. That didn't mean, however, that the FBI was powerless to do anything. Instead of pursuing aggressive legal action, which in my experience usually only complicated these matters, I suggested a low-key approach.

"Give the art crime team a chance to see what we can do quietly," I said, although I knew this was not the answer Pierre was hoping for. "We have a good track record of gaining cooperation from auction houses, identifying consignors, and persuading them to work with us. We have learned that combining investigative skill with a little cultural diplomacy can produce real results."

When I returned to Indianapolis a few days later, the auction was two weeks away. In my view, there was still enough time to see what a quiet but well-focused approach could accomplish, while keeping the option of a lawsuit in reserve. However, I also understood that the Acoma might feel time was running out to recover the shield. Like the Hopi and the Navajo, they wanted to prevent future sales of their cultural patrimony, and a court ruling in their favor would be a very public step in that direction.

I wasn't surprised when Pierre Ciric moved forward with a lawsuit on behalf of the Acoma. Unfortunately, the French courts quickly dismissed the suit, just as they had in the Hopi and Navajo case.

Although the shield went to auction as scheduled, EVE had miscalculated its perceived market value. No one bid at or above the reserve price, and it went unsold. Continuing to ignore Acoma Pueblo's concerns, EVE relisted the shield in its spring 2016 catalog, cutting the reserve price in half and setting a fast-approaching auction date of May 30, 2016.

Acoma Pueblo appealed to Congress, the Department of the Interior, the Department of Justice, and the State Department for help in blocking the sale. On May 27, the FBI field office in Albuquerque opened a theft case on the shield. Two days later, on May 29, the Department of Justice's Office of International Affairs sent a stern letter to the French government, demanding that the auction be postponed to allow time to seek a US civil warrant to restrain the sale.

Feeling the pressure, EVE withdrew the shield from the auction scheduled for the next day. However, the auction house remained defensive and refused to cooperate in the face of what was now a looming civil lawsuit from the US government.

On July 20, 2016, the US Attorney's Office for the district of New

Mexico filed a "verified complaint for forfeiture *in rem*" (the Latin phrase means "against the thing") of the Acoma shield. On July 25, the US Attorney's Office filed its "application for warrant of arrest *in rem*" of the shield as a form of "defendant property." And on August 31, 2016, a federal district court judge in New Mexico signed a seizure warrant for, in legal terms, the arrest of the shield. The fact that a federal district court judge—nominated by the president and confirmed by the US Senate—signed the warrant, rather than a federal magistrate judge appointed by the district court, underscored the case's political significance.

High Country News reported in August 2020 that the seizure warrant "allowed France to essentially freeze [the shield] in place; the shield couldn't be [sold], . . . but it was still stuck at EVE." This is misleading. The French government refused to execute the seizure warrant. If they had executed the warrant on behalf of the United States, the shield would quickly have been on its way to Acoma.

The seizure warrant may actually have *indirectly* frozen the shield in place. I believe the consignor, after consulting with EVE, saw the auction house as a safe harbor. With all the negative attention, the shield was unlikely to sell, but sending it to the United States posed even greater risks. US Customs and Border Protection could seize it on a customs hold, which I had already requested through official channels.

The consignor also had to worry that the US government might not stop at seizing the shield but could pursue them for criminal liability as well. Since EVE was protecting their identity, keeping the shield in Paris was likely the safest option—for the time being.

When I took over the art crime program in June 2016, the fate of the shield became a constant headache. The pressure on the FBI to find a way to seize it intensified the next month when Senator Martin Heinrich of New Mexico introduced the first version of the Safeguarding Tribal Objects of Patrimony (STOP) Act.

From that point on, my agenda was flooded with phone calls, emails, and meetings about the shield and how to return it to Acoma. My colleagues in the State Department and the Department of Justice believed there was a legal path forward for seizing it, but I saw no clear basis under US law for either a criminal or civil seizure. In my view, a diplomatic approach was still the best option, but the aggressive legal action taken so far had already shut that door.

Sometime later in 2016, I attended a meeting at the State Department with a group of about twenty officials, including lawyers and administrators from its Bureau of Educational and Cultural Affairs as well as representatives from the Department of the Interior, the Department of Justice's Office of Tribal Affairs, and DOJ Main. A small group of French government officials and lawyers joined via video link.

Everyone on the US side was adamant that the shield be seized and returned. Because of the Miller case and my leadership of the art crime program, I think they all assumed I would be on board with that agenda.

I agreed that the sale of sacred Native American items like the shield was morally offensive and wrong, and I wanted to see it returned to Acoma. No one should be able to traffic in objects with such deep spiritual significance to their rightful owners.

Imagine if one of the holiest relics of the Roman Catholic Church went missing and resurfaced at an auction years later. Even if the consignor had acquired it innocently and the circumstances of its disappearance were unclear, the outcry would be immense. The Acoma shield was no different.

So I told everyone in the meeting the same thing I had been saying since Pierre Ciric first contacted me. The FBI would gladly seize the shield if we had the legal authority to do so. But in my view, there was no basis for seizing it under US law. The seizure warrant affidavit was full of holes, and it was astonishing to me that a federal judge had signed off on it. Though, perhaps, I kept that last part to myself.

To begin with, there was no compelling evidence that the shield had been stolen. It had been one of six shields in the care of a tribal elder, now long deceased, who kept them in his home at Acoma. The only living person who could testify about the shields was his granddaughter, who had grown up in the same house. She recalled that the shield in EVE's catalog, along with five others, had gone missing in the early 1970s when she was about five years old. Any experienced litigator would see an easy path to challenging a seizure warrant based on uncorroborated testimony from someone recalling events in their early childhood, more than forty years in the past.

Although the disappearance had reportedly been mentioned to the tribal sheriff, there were no written records of a burglary—no police report, no crime scene photos, and no other evidence documenting that a theft had occurred. Native American tribes have a long-standing and understandable tendency to keep matters involving sacred objects and spiritual traditions private. The more these items have been exposed, the more vulnerable they have become to appropriation and exploitation by outsiders. But that secrecy, while protective, also complicates law enforcement efforts and legal action. Without a report, how could we effectively allege that a crime had even taken place?

The timing of the alleged theft struck me as the biggest obstacle for law enforcement and legal action. The affidavit for the seizure warrant repeatedly cited the Archaeological Resources Protection Act (ARPA), which did not take effect until October 31, 1979. But the allegation was that the shields had been stolen in the early 1970s, years before ARPA was enacted. Since the US Constitution forbids ex post facto laws, no act committed before ARPA took effect could possibly be a violation of that law.

There is an argument that if someone transferred the shield out of the country after ARPA took effect, they might have violated the statute's anti-trafficking provision. However, that provision defines trafficking as a specific intent crime. For a crime to have occurred, the government would have to prove that the person moving the shield knew it was stolen.

Alongside ARPA, the warrant affidavit also cited the National Stolen Property Act of 1934 (NSPA), relying on the shield's transport across state lines and out of the country. Echoing the NSPA's language, the affidavit stated that the shield had been "stolen, taken, removed from the Pueblo of Acoma . . . and transported in interstate and foreign commerce" and even referred to it as having been "smuggled."

The claim that the shield had been "smuggled . . . [to] its current location in Paris, France" was particularly troubling to me. Smuggling, by definition, involves the secretive or illegal transportation of goods across borders to evade laws or regulations. Yet there was zero evidence to suggest the shield had been transported in such a manner.

Just as the affidavit failed to recognize that trafficking is a specific intent crime under ARPA, it also failed to apply the same standard to potential violations under the NSPA. The NSPA is also a specific intent law, meaning that for a violation to occur, the government must prove that the person transporting stolen property across state lines knew it was stolen. Without that knowledge, there is generally no case.

This is a common challenge for federal law enforcement when investigating interstate transportation of stolen property under the NSPA. Without clear evidence of intent, prosecutions under the statute often fall apart.

The affidavit offered no evidence to explain how the shield left Acoma in the early 1970s, what had happened to it in the decades since, or how it had come to EVE in the first place. It relied entirely on a single, uncorroborated statement claiming the shield had been taken in a burglary.

Even more problematic, the affidavit failed to establish any probable cause that the consignor knew the shield was stolen—or that they were even subject to US federal law. If the shield had been consigned to EVE by someone in, say, Germany, there could be no violation of US law at all under the statutes cited. Without evidence tying the consignor to the United States or proving their knowledge of the shield's origins, I thought the case had no legal footing.

Good faith purchasers and possessors of stolen property generally don't violate the NSPA, unless they move stolen property across state or international lines after being advised of its legal status. That doesn't mean they can keep the stolen goods. With some exceptions under the good faith principle, bad title cannot pass under US law. If John Smith steals your car and sells it to Jane Doe, who has no idea it was stolen, you remain the rightful owner—Jane Doe does not get to keep it. However, criminal liability falls on John Smith, not Jane Doe.

I just couldn't see how the government could build a compelling criminal case with proof beyond a reasonable doubt, or even a civil case with a preponderance of the evidence, when the entire argument rested on the uncorroborated testimony of a single witness who had last seen the shield more than forty years earlier as a very young child. Add the highly questionable application of ARPA and the NSPA, and I was appalled that we were attempting to pursue the case this way.

The Acomas' deep connection to the shield deserved the utmost respect, and we had a duty to do everything possible to help them recover it. But our efforts—and any expectation that a foreign government would intervene—had to be grounded in the law. We could not solve this problem by forcing statutes to apply where they simply did not fit. I still believed that a diplomatic and measured approach was the best path forward, although I was increasingly doubtful that such an approach could be salvaged.

No one on the US side of the meeting openly supported my view, though I had the sense that a few wanted to. Several participants pushed back against my analysis, insisting that we had a legal basis to seize the shield and that France was obligated to assist under its treaty commitments. In their zeal to do the right thing, I believe they were letting passion outweigh both the relevant law and the available facts.

The French government attorneys participating via video, however, did share my viewpoint. They understood US law as well as we did and knew that the seizure warrant did not meet the reasonable belief standard for probable cause. Their position was that the US government had failed to establish a solid basis for suspecting a crime had been committed by the consignor or by EVE. They also appeared unimpressed by the emotional appeals and arguments from our side of the meeting. Polite and professional throughout, they made it clear they had no intention of doing what the US government wanted.

From late 2016 through mid-2018, the pressure on the FBI to seize the shield only intensified. Meetings within the government continued, tribal leaders voiced their concerns directly to me, and even a congressional inquiry was launched. But without cooperation from the French government, we were stuck.

In Washington, no one wanted to hear my repeated concerns about the flaws in the warrant. Nor was there any appetite for stepping back, lowering the temperature, and allowing the art crime team to apply its proven approach of cultural diplomacy.

So in that bistro in June 2018, desperate for a solution, I turned to

TWO COPS DRINKING BEER AND THE CASE OF THE CEREMONIAL SHIELD

Marc for help, cop to cop. It was all I could think of doing to finally put the issue to bed.

Before I left Paris that week, Marc and a few other French officers accompanied me to Hôtel Drouot, the venue where many auction houses rented space for their sales. We attended one of EVE's auctions, which featured a fair number of Native American pieces. As we watched, I quietly pointed out the problematic items and made one last appeal to Marc.

Afterward, he made no promises: "I'll see what I can do, my friend."

A few weeks later, Marc called me at FBI headquarters. His tone was careful but deliberate.

"There's no MLAT request, so I can't tell you anything," he said. "But if there *was* an MLAT, maybe the information you need would be something like this . . ."

He then gave me the name of the consignor and his address in rural New Mexico. I think they heard me whooping on the other side of the Hoover Building. After three years of roadblocks, we finally had the information we needed—information I believed we could have obtained much sooner if we had taken a different approach from the start.

Although the Albuquerque field office had lost its art crime team agent, Kathleen Magnafici, to a new assignment—and the position remained vacant while the Acoma shield case was unfolding—there was now an art crime team agent in place. Susan Garst, who had transferred from the New York office, was stationed at a satellite office in Santa Fe.

Most of the FBI's fifty-six field offices don't have an art crime team agent, but Albuquerque, and particularly Santa Fe, was a priority for the program due to the region's active trade in Southwestern Native American cultural property and other works of art. Despite that, the field office decided to keep the Acoma shield case with the original case agent, a member of the FBI's Indian Country unit.

I asked Susan to monitor the case as closely as possible and be ready to step in if an opportunity arose. At the same time, I instructed the case agent to visit the consignor, reassure him that we had no intention of pursuing charges, and ask if he would consider waiving title to the shield.

The report came back that the consignor was a seventy-six-year-old rancher who had inherited the shield after his mother's death. He had no idea it was allegedly stolen until all of the legal threats started surfacing. Naturally, he was unsure how to proceed.

At that point, he had tried to reach out to the Acoma through an intermediary, offering to negotiate the shield's return. However, the Pueblo government did not take the intermediary seriously, and nothing came of the effort. The consignor had not come forward on his own because the aggressive stance of the US government made him fearful of legal action against him personally—even though he was an innocent possessor of the shield.

As *High Country News* reported in 2020, the consignor's family, like those of many ranchers in the area, had long collected Native American craftwork and sometimes artifacts, buying them at pawnshops and trading posts or from itinerant traders. An avid arrowhead collector as a boy, the consignor had moved on to woven baskets, and he had sometimes bought small collections of tribal craftwork, art, and artifacts for hundreds of dollars.

At his mother's passing in 1984, he had put boxes from her house into storage without opening them. As he told *High Country News*, he did not open the boxes and find the shield in one of them until 2012. The article stated that he "had seen many others like it sold in the past, and . . . it didn't strike him as special." He said, "I didn't have any use for it, and the market in the US was horrible." (I believe the state of the US market was thanks in large part to the Miller case and other art crime team cases involving Native American material.) The consignor had apparently learned of EVE through contacts in the Authentic Tribal Art Dealers Association.

The consignor distrusted the federal government, viewing its approach as "an overreaction on steroids." Before waiving title to the shield and allowing EVE to release it to the FBI, he wanted official acknowledgment that he had been a good faith possessor and a guarantee of qualified immunity from prosecution.

I thought his request was reasonable. It would secure the shield's return to Acoma while still allowing the US government to claim a victory. To my dismay, the Department of Justice refused to grant him any form of immunity.

TWO COPS DRINKING BEER AND THE CASE OF THE CEREMONIAL SHIELD

I understood the government's desire to keep pressure on EVE in hopes of deterring future problematic auctions. What I didn't understand was why they would refuse to grant the consignor immunity regarding the shield, unnecessarily delaying its return to Acoma.

On December 20, 2018, a US Marshal, acting on behalf of the US Attorney's Office in New Mexico, served a summons on the consignor at his ranch. In response, the consignor's attorney in Albuquerque, a commercial litigator whose firm specialized in local real estate and retail development, filed motions in January and February 2019. His filings demonstrated a keen understanding of ARPA and the NSPA, effectively rebutting the government's allegations about the shield and his client's involvement. It was at this point that the identity of the consignor, Jerold L. Collings, became part of the public record and known to the news media, which subsequently mentioned him in a number of stories about the shield.

When I read the filings by Collings's lawyer, I shook my head at all the trouble that might have been avoided if the art crime team had been allowed to quietly investigate the case. Had we approached Collings in a way that respected his rights as a citizen—without heavy-handed threats—and instead appealed to the Acomas' moral right to their sacred cultural property, I believe we could have resolved the issue far more easily. Collings's actions suggested he would have been very open to that approach.

It was July before the Acoma, Collings, and the US Attorney's Office reached an agreement for the shield's return. The deal ensured that all parties, including the government, would hold each other blameless. It took until November to resolve matters with the French government, allowing Ken DiBella to take custody of the shield from EVE and secure it at the US embassy in Paris.

On the evening of November 13, 2019, Jake Archer flew to Paris, arriving early in the morning on November 14. He carefully packed the shield in accordance with guidance from the Acoma, and on November 15 he flew from Paris to Dallas to Albuquerque with the shield sitting in the seat next to him the entire way. In a customs room at the Albuquerque airport, Jake formally transferred custody of the shield to our Bureau of

Indian Affairs colleague, Frank Chavez, a citizen of Acoma Pueblo. The handover took place in the presence of Acoma's then-governor, Brian Vallo, along with members of the local FBI field office and the US Attorney's Office.

At last, the shield was home—not because of the government's legal actions or threats but because the art crime team had quietly found a way to do what it should have been allowed to do three and a half years earlier.

The Acoma shield and Miller cases illustrate two important facts. Our present laws do not adequately protect Native American cultural property, and those laws are widely misunderstood.

Let's start with NAGPRA, which since its November 16, 1990, enactment has become the primary legal framework for protecting Native American cultural property. NAGPRA serves an important and necessary purpose, but its flaws significantly undermine its effectiveness. The problem is that many people focus on NAGPRA's overarching goal while ignoring the law's complexities. This has led to widespread misunderstanding, both inside and outside the tribal community. But once you try to work through the details—what NAGPRA prohibits, what it allows, and the procedural hurdles it creates—you quickly find yourself in a legal quagmire.

The first misconception about NAGPRA is the belief that it has made *all* trade in Native American cultural items illegal. Too many tribal members and US government attorneys assume that NAGPRA protects everything tribal. While NAGPRA is often thought of as a sweeping law that protects all Native American cultural property, its scope is much more limited and specific than many assume.

In reality, NAGPRA protects only four specific categories of material: Native American human remains, associated burial goods, sacred objects, and objects of cultural patrimony (items that belong to a tribe as a whole rather than to an individual tribal member). Anything outside these categories generally falls beyond NAGPRA's reach, despite the common belief that it covers all Native American cultural property.

TWO COPS DRINKING BEER AND THE CASE OF THE CEREMONIAL SHIELD

Like most people, I find the legal trade in historic Native American cultural items offensive, and I believe there should be a law to prohibit it. But NAGPRA is not that law, and neither is ARPA.

As I argued to my counterparts in other agencies during the Acoma shield case, law enforcement does not get to operate in an ethical comfort zone—it has to operate within the law. Acquiring, owning, and trafficking in Native American cultural items remains legal in certain circumstances, and law enforcement cannot simply wish those circumstances away. However, as I will suggest below, Congress has the power to change those circumstances far more effectively than it has so far.

The second misconception about NAGPRA is the belief that it applies to material in these four categories regardless of when it was acquired. But once again, the US Constitution (Article 1, Section 9, Clause 3) explicitly bans ex post facto, or retroactive, laws.

Under NAGPRA, ARPA, or any other state or federal law in the United States, the key question is always when the alleged crime occurred. If an item was obtained before the relevant law took effect, that law cannot be applied retroactively.

The third misconception about NAGPRA is that it applies equally to all owners of material in the four protected categories. In reality, NAGPRA's repatriation requirements apply only to federal agencies; federally funded museums, universities, and other cultural or educational institutions; and state and local government agencies that receive federal funding. These entities must identify, document, and repatriate Native American human remains, funerary objects, sacred objects, and objects of cultural patrimony to federally recognized tribes.

A notable exception among federally funded entities is the Smithsonian Institution. The Smithsonian used its political influence to secure the ability to follow its own repatriation protocols rather than being bound by NAGPRA's processes.

Private individuals and institutions that do not receive federal funding are not subject to NAGPRA's repatriation provisions. However, NAGPRA does contain a criminal anti-trafficking provision that applies to everyone. It is illegal for anyone to knowingly sell, purchase, or transport Native American human remains or protected cultural items if they were acquired in violation of NAGPRA or earlier federal law.

Most of NAGPRA is codified in Title 25 of the US Code, which contains federal statutes related to Native American affairs and cultural materials. Under its formal designation, 25 U.S.C. Chapter 32, Native American Graves Protection and Repatriation, NAGPRA establishes a regulatory framework that dictates what federal agencies and federally funded cultural and educational institutions must do once they determine they possess material in the protected categories.

These institutions are required to prepare a detailed inventory within a year, notify all federally recognized tribes, and consult with the affected tribes to negotiate repatriation. This regulatory framework generally assumes the material in question is part of a known collection, where agencies and institutions can document where, when, and how the items were collected or acquired.

However, NAGPRA was not designed to address the unknown or undocumented materials that law enforcement encounters during investigations. Unlike institutions with cataloged collections, law enforcement often deals with cultural property whose provenance is unclear, making it difficult to apply NAGPRA's repatriation process to seized evidence.

NAGPRA's sole criminal provision is codified in Title 18 of the US Code, which contains federal criminal statutes. This provision, 18 U.S.C. § 1170, Illegal Trafficking in Native American Human Remains and Cultural Items, applies only to the four categories of material protected under NAGPRA: Native American human remains, associated burial goods, sacred objects, and objects of cultural patrimony.

The only category that is completely prohibited from trafficking under all circumstances is Native American human remains. For the other three categories—burial goods, sacred objects, and cultural patrimony—trafficking is illegal only if the items were acquired unlawfully. If obtained legally, their sale and transfer remain permissible under federal law. For example, ceremonial objects such as Hopi katsinam, Pueblo religious items, or Lakota sacred bundles that were removed from tribal communities in the late nineteenth or early twentieth century— long before NAGPRA (1990) or ARPA (1979)—were legally acquired under the laws of the time. While modern statutes now prohibit their removal or sale without tribal consent, their early acquisition places them outside the reach of NAGPRA's criminal provisions unless they are trafficked unlawfully in some other way.

Confused yet? Exactly.

The drafters of NAGPRA clearly did not have law enforcement in mind. The law applies uniformly to all federal agencies, without distinguishing between their different roles and responsibilities. It treats an agency like the Army Corps of Engineers, which might acquire Native American material during an infrastructure project such as building a dam, the same way it treats the FBI or another law enforcement agency that comes into possession of cultural items as evidence in a criminal investigation.

This lack of distinction creates challenges for law enforcement, as NAGPRA's framework was designed for institutions with cataloged collections, not for agencies handling seized or recovered cultural property with evidentiary requirements and uncertain provenance. The FBI is required to abide by NAGPRA, but it must also follow long-standing laws and policies governing the handling of evidence in criminal investigations. In some cases, these evidentiary rules directly contradict NAGPRA's requirements.

Law enforcement often collects sensitive material as part of a sealed criminal investigation, where disclosure is strictly limited. Revealing the existence of certain evidence too soon could compromise an active case. As a result, federal agents may need to hold on to Native American material for years before informing the tribal community, creating a direct conflict with NAGPRA's expectation of prompt notification and repatriation.

On the other hand, once the FBI clears a criminal case, DOJ and FBI policy require that stolen property be returned to its rightful owner as soon as possible. At that point, however, NAGPRA introduces a delay.

Instead of allowing for immediate return, NAGPRA mandates a formal repatriation process overseen by the National NAGPRA program within the Department of the Interior. This process can be lengthy and bureaucratic, slowing down the return of cultural property that would otherwise be promptly restituted under standard FBI and DOJ procedures.

Law enforcement's NAGPRA footprint is small. The Army Corps of Engineers's NAGPRA-related activity represents 75 percent of repatriations. Federally funded cultural and educational institutions represent almost 25 percent. Law enforcement represents less than 1 percent.

The simplest way to strengthen protections for Native American cultural property would be to amend NAGPRA to include a carve-out for law enforcement, much like the exemption granted to the Smithsonian Institution. For years, I argued this very point with the National NAGPRA committee, to no avail.

Frustration with the limited protections provided by ARPA and NAGPRA contributed to the creation of the Safeguarding Tribal Objects of Patrimony (STOP) Act, which aimed to halt the export of Native American cultural patrimony for sale abroad. A major focus of the STOP Act was the trafficking of those cultural items in Paris, France, with EVE Auction House at the center of the controversy. While the Acoma and Hopi were not the bill's only proponents, they were among its strongest advocates, driven by their long-standing efforts to prevent the sale of sacred objects in international markets.

When Senator Martin Heinrich introduced the STOP Act in July 2016, I was part of a federal agency working group on NAGPRA issues, led by the DOJ and including experts from its Office of Tribal Justice, Criminal and Environmental Divisions, and the National NAGPRA program. We were the government's de facto experts on NAGPRA.

I gave the group a law enforcement perspective: "You turn to the FBI to seize things. Here's what we can and cannot do, where the law limits us, and how legislation could improve our ability to enforce NAGPRA and protect Native American cultural property."

Congress routinely sends draft legislation to federal agencies for review and input. As part of that process, the NAGPRA working group reviewed multiple drafts of the STOP Act—going through five or six versions before it finally passed Congress in late 2021 and 2022 and was signed into law by President Biden on December 21, 2022, its effective date.

Everyone in the working group had the opportunity to mark up the bill with their feedback. For five and a half years, my comments remained consistent as I tried—largely in vain—to highlight the bill's shortcomings from a law enforcement perspective.

The STOP Act's main focus is preventing stolen Native American patrimony from being sold abroad, but in that regard, it is largely redundant. Preexisting customs laws and the National Stolen Property Act (NSPA) already provide legal grounds to block the export of stolen cultural property.

It is also redundant in that it invokes NAGPRA and applies only to the four categories of material NAGPRA already protects. Rather than strengthening protections, it repackages existing laws without addressing their core weaknesses.

The STOP Act goes beyond NAGPRA by doubling the maximum penalty for illegal trafficking in the four protected categories, increasing it from five years to ten years. Stiffening this penalty was a good idea, but it would have been simpler and more effective to amend NAGPRA directly—strengthening its penalties while also improving the law in other ways. However, amending an existing law does not make as dramatic a political splash as passing a new law.

Unfortunately, the STOP Act takes an already muddy legal picture and makes it even murkier by requiring the federal government to create an expensive, difficult-to-administer certification process for exports.

In principle, the law makes a noble statement about protecting Native American cultural heritage. But in practice, it adds more bureaucracy than meaningful protection.

Suppose a US-based dealer wants to export an object in one of the four protected categories under NAGPRA and the STOP Act for auction in Paris—except for Native American human remains, which can never be exported legally.

Under the STOP Act, the dealer must apply to the Department of the Interior for an export certificate. Without this certificate, the dealer risks criminal charges for attempting to export the item illegally.

The government then has only thirty days to evaluate the object and determine whether the dealer is lawfully allowed to possess and sell it. This process requires ongoing consultation with all 574 federally recognized tribes to define what falls under NAGPRA's protections—and by extension, what is also restricted under the STOP Act.

I've mentioned gathering a group of middle Missouri River valley tribes in the same room to discuss whether Catlinite pipes should be considered associated burial goods under NAGPRA. Some tribes believed they should be, while one tribe disagreed.

This reflects a broader reality. With 574 federally recognized tribes, each with distinct traditions and beliefs, reaching a universal consensus on what qualifies as protected cultural property is extremely challenging. Expecting complete agreement on such complex matters adds another layer of difficulty to implementing both NAGPRA and the STOP Act effectively.

Let's further suppose that the FBI has been investigating the dealer in question for some time. The Department of Interior doesn't know that, because the FBI doesn't share its investigations with anyone else.

When applying for an export certificate, the dealer attests that the object was lawfully obtained. If, at the end of the STOP Act's thirty-day evaluation period, the Department of the Interior has not found evidence of illegality, it is required by law to issue the export certificate, allowing the object to be legally sent abroad.

Sometime later, the FBI completes its investigation and discovers evidence that the dealer obtained the object illegally. But by then, the dealer can simply point to the export certificate and say, "Here's my proof that the government said it was legal."

At trial, a good defense attorney would have a powerful argument for reasonable doubt: "The FBI claims this was illegal, but the Department of the Interior reviewed the object and certified it for export. My client acted in good faith based on that approval." With conflicting signals from two federal agencies, the case would be dead in the water before it even started.

The STOP Act risks pushing a gray market, where law enforcement has some visibility and can track dealer activity, into a black market, where oversight disappears entirely. Instead of improving enforcement, the law could drive collectors and dealers underground, making it even harder to monitor illicit transactions.

One likely consequence is that collectors and dealers will feel unfairly demonized, which is counterproductive. It would be far more effective to maintain a working relationship between law enforcement and the collecting community rather than alienate them.

While some collectors and dealers are undoubtedly unscrupulous, the vast majority want to do the right thing and take pride in ethical collecting. That fundamental aspect of human nature has often been the key to the art crime team's success in securing the return of stolen and looted cultural property, including Native American artifacts.

For all their good intentions, ARPA, NAGPRA, and the STOP Act still allow a problematic legal trade in Native American cultural items, both in the United States and abroad. However, I believe there are practical and constitutional steps that could limit—or even eliminate—this trade while strengthening protections for Native American heritage.

At the top of my legislative wish list is amending NAGPRA to include a law enforcement exemption, as I previously discussed. Law enforcement needs the ability to apply its established investigative methods and evidentiary protocols first, before being required to comply with NAGPRA's repatriation process. This change would ensure that criminal investigations are not hindered while still respecting the law's intent to return cultural items to their rightful communities.

The second change I would propose is redefining what qualifies as tribal land under NAGPRA and future cultural protection laws. NAGPRA currently defines tribal land as land within the boundaries of Indian reservations, dependent Indian communities, and certain lands administered for Native Hawaiians.

This definition excludes vast areas where tribes historically lived, buried their dead, and conducted sacred traditions before being displaced. Meanwhile, federal environmental laws like the Clean Water Act and the Endangered Species Act impose significant restrictions on private land use to protect natural resources. If federal law can regulate what a private landowner does with wetlands or endangered plants on their property, it seems reasonable that it could also protect culturally significant Native American sites, wherever they might be.

I'm no attorney, but I'd bet that if Congress were serious about protecting tribal heritage, they could find a way.

The third desirable step, in my view, is to stiffen penalties for crimes involving Native American cultural patrimony and property. The maximum punishment should reflect the severity of the harm caused by the most egregious offenses—just as penalties for other serious crimes are designed to deter wrongdoing and signal the gravity of the violation. Simply put, the law should treat the theft and trafficking of irreplaceable cultural heritage with the seriousness they deserve.

In addition, I believe we can and should implement measures that better balance private property rights with the public good, drawing inspiration from laws protecting endangered species. For instance, the Bald and Golden Eagle Protection Act, originally enacted in 1940 and amended in 1962, makes it illegal for non–Native Americans to acquire any part of a bald or golden eagle. Native Americans must obtain a certificate to possess eagle parts, strictly for religious and spiritual purposes, and trafficking in eagle parts is prohibited.

Similarly, the African Elephant Conservation Act of 1988 and the Asian Elephant Conservation Act of 1997, under the umbrella of the Endangered Species Act of 1973, prohibit the acquisition and trafficking of elephant ivory. Individuals who legally acquired eagle parts or elephant ivory before these laws took effect retain the right of possession but cannot legally traffic these items.

A strong step toward protecting Native American cultural property would be to establish a law similar to those protecting eagles and endangered species. Such a law would make it illegal for non–Native Americans to possess these items and prohibit trafficking by anyone, ensuring that sacred and culturally significant objects are no longer treated as commodities.

At the same time, the law would respect the US Constitution's ban on retroactive laws by allowing individuals who legally acquired Native American cultural items before its enactment, as well as their heirs, to retain the right of possession. However, it would ban any future sale, trade, or transfer, effectively closing the market while protecting existing owners from legal repercussions.

Don't misunderstand. I strongly support private property rights. But under eminent domain principles, I believe it would be constitutionally sound to ban trafficking in Native American cultural material not just from public and tribal land but also from private land through a permit and reporting system rather than outright confiscation.

If the federal government can regulate private land use for the public good—such as through the Endangered Species Act or the Bald and Golden Eagle Protection Act—it should also be able to require landowners to report discoveries of Native American cultural material. A permit system could ensure that any significant finds are documented, evaluated, and, when appropriate, repatriated, while still respecting private property rights. This approach would encourage cooperation between landowners, tribes, and the government, helping ensure that important cultural materials are protected rather than trafficked.

There are precedents for this at the state level. Indiana, California, Texas, New Mexico, Mississippi, Oklahoma, and Florida have enacted laws restricting the excavation of Native American artifacts on private land or requiring landowners to report discoveries.

In Indiana, landowners must notify the state if they uncover archaeological resources on their property. California prohibits the possession of Native American artifacts or remains removed from graves after a certain date unless done under an agreement with the state's Native American Heritage Commission. Texas imposes criminal penalties for excavating artifacts without a permit, damaging Native American sites, or trespassing to steal cultural items. New Mexico restricts excavation on private land using heavy equipment and requires archaeological permits for significant site investigations to prevent damage to cultural resources. Mississippi requires landowners' written permission before collecting artifacts. Oklahoma prohibits the defacement of petroglyphs and other archaeological sites, even on private land. Florida imposes penalties for unauthorized excavation of archaeological sites.

These state laws show that requiring landowners to report discoveries and regulating excavation on private land are feasible and enforceable. If states can implement such protections, the federal government should be able to do the same.

Completely banning the trade in Native American cultural items, or at least in sacred objects and objects of cultural patrimony, while still allowing a market for contemporary Native American art and craftsmanship, would have no meaningful economic impact.

There is no compelling economic reason—and certainly no moral justification—for permitting anyone, Native American or not, to traffic in sacred or culturally significant materials. Trade in these objects does not serve any legitimate public interest. Instead, it perpetuates the exploitation of Native heritage.

Thirteen

Getting Stoned in Haiti

PORT-AU-PRINCE, HAITI; THURSDAY, FEBRUARY 13, 2020

Thud! Thud! We'd been hearing gunshots for a while from the political unrest in the Haitian capital's government district. The thuds were new.

"What's that sound, Tim?" Holly asked, her voice a bit concerned but steady.

"Don't worry. They're not bombs. Those are tear gas canisters going off."

Wisps of tear gas drifted into the entrance courtyard of Haiti's National Bureau of Ethnology. The main building was too small to accommodate us; our primary Haitian colleagues, General Director Erol Josué and contract scholar Joseph Sony Jean, along with a few other bureau employees; and 479 museum-quality Taino stone and pottery artifacts. Instead, we worked at folding tables in the courtyard, checking the artifacts against our inventory.

"If the tear gas gets bad, we can pull our shirts up over our mouths," I said.

Holly nodded and kept on working. She was stoic and focused, like a war correspondent. The largest international repatriation of the Miller case was set for the next morning, with Haitian prime minister Jean-Michel Lapin, US ambassador Michele Sison, and FBI section chief Mike Nordwall scheduled to speak. We had to finish the inventory before then, no matter what was happening beyond the courtyard's concrete walls and wrought iron fencing. Protesters were rioting outside, and our security team was tense, but for now, there was no cause for serious alarm.

As the STOP Act moved from draft legislation to law, I was focused on bringing the Miller case to a successful conclusion while positioning the art crime program for the future. By mid-2019, both internal and external obstacles were already complicating these efforts—and soon, they would make things even more difficult.

The repatriation of ancestral remains and artifacts to tribes along the Arizona–New Mexico border remained stalled. The Gila River Indian Community (GRIC) and Salt River Pima-Maricopa Indian Community (SRPMIC) opposed the plan for the Hopi to receive and rebury unaffiliated ancestral remains on behalf of all the tribes. Because of this divide, we were consulting with GRIC and SRPMIC separately. Under NAGPRA regulations, we couldn't move forward with the other tribes without their acquiescence, leaving us stuck in a bureaucratic deadlock.

Meanwhile, the Indianapolis field office was further scaling back its support for the Miller case. As Leslie Lahr's FBI retirement date approached, Indianapolis SAC Grant Mendenhall, who had previously revoked approval for the Chinese repatriation to take place at the field office, was now refusing to assign a new case agent to replace her. Instead, he was pressuring TOC Section Chief Kristi Koons Johnson to transfer the case back to headquarters and reinstate me as the case agent.

By FBI policy and precedent, the Miller case remained the responsibility of the Indianapolis field office until it was officially closed. Transferring it to headquarters and assigning me, a supervisory special agent, as the case agent violated that policy. The Office of the Inspector General (OIG) had criticized this very issue in its review of Crossfire Hurricane, the FBI's investigation into potential ties between the Trump campaign and Russia. The OIG found that FBI headquarters' direct management of investigative case files undermined proper field office oversight. Yet here we were, repeating the same mistake.

The artifacts and human remains were still housed in our warehouse in Indianapolis, where Holly continued working with her graduate students and collaborating with me on tribal consultations and repatriations. As a contractor, she couldn't manage critical tasks like paying warehouse bills or approving her own travel for consultations and repatriations. We needed an agent in the field office to handle these basic but essential responsibilities. I was already facing challenges advancing the case from six hundred miles away at headquarters. Making me the case agent would only make that problem worse.

I understood why some in the FBI, both at headquarters and in the field, were eager to put an end to the complications and costs of the Miller case. I wanted to wrap things up too and had hoped to do so by 2020. But from the start, I had been clear that the case would likely take ten years or more.

We had a duty not just under NAGPRA but also under other statutory authority and long-standing DOJ and FBI policy to make every reasonable effort to culturally affiliate the human remains and objects seized from Miller's collection. Frustrating delays, like the disagreement between the tribes in the Southwest, were an unavoidable part of the process. But given our commitment to noninvasive analysis of Native American human remains and the need for careful consultation with tribal communities, the affiliation process was never going to be quick or easy.

Kristi Koons Johnson listened as I made my case to her more than once, but in the end, she sided with Grant Mendenhall. They reassigned me as the Miller case agent and transferred the case to headquarters, an unusual departure from standard FBI procedure. It was just bureaucratic politics and a reflection of the power SACs held. I had no choice but to make the best of it, at least for the time being.

One thing was crystal clear, however. I simply didn't have the time to run the entire art crime program and manage 100 percent of the Miller case on my own. I needed a new plan.

Holly was doing an excellent job managing the collection and leading our tribal consultation efforts, but she lacked the authority and internal FBI experience to handle the administrative and case management tasks that would normally fall to an agent. After Leslie retired from the FBI on November 30, 2019, I hired her as a contractor on the case. That provided continuity and ensured someone familiar with FBI systems and protocols remained on the scene with Holly. And it took some of the administrative burden off of me.

Despite some of our domestic challenges, we made somewhat better progress on international repatriations in 2019. On April 9, through the US embassy in Mexico City, we transferred two small Mesoamerican clay figurines to Mexico's Ministry of Culture and National Institute of Anthropology. Miller had looted the figurines from Teotihuacan, an ancient city on the central Mexican plateau that flourished from 200 to 700 CE. Teotihuacan is famous for its Avenue of the Dead (a name later given by the Aztecs) and for the two largest pyramids in Mesoamerica, the Pyramid of the Sun and the Pyramid of the Moon.

That summer, we held two ceremonies, one in Washington, DC, and the other in Rome, for the repatriation of a small ancient Roman mosaic fragment, roughly twenty-one inches square. The mosaic featured a full-face depiction of a Roman faun, or perhaps a Greek satyr—both deities of nature and the wilderness—with laurel leaves in his hair. We had seized it based on Miller's account that he obtained it from fellow GIs in Italy at the end of World War II, after they had looted it from a Roman bathhouse.

Italy's il Comando Carabinieri per la Tutela del Patrimonio Culturale ("the Carabinieri Command for the Protection of Cultural Heritage," TPC for short) had its experts examine photographs of the mosaic. In their judgment, it was not from ancient Italy but from the broader Roman Empire. However, Miller's account was all we had to go on, and we had no reason to doubt it. After the Allies defeated Nazi Germany, an enormous volume of cultural material circulated through the black market in Italy and across Europe.

I told my main contact in the TPC, Angelo Ragusa, "This mosaic has to go somewhere, and you're it."

"We're not it," Angelo replied.

"You're it. Miller said he got it in Italy. From the FBI's perspective, Italy is the victim. You guys can research it all you want and then send it wherever you think it belongs."

"We don't want it."

Angelo and I had this conversation many times whenever he asked the art crime team to seize something in the United States for Italy. Highly professional and well funded, the TPC is much larger than the FBI art crime program, with around three hundred officers dedicated to Italian cultural heritage cases. Angelo often called me to ask, "Can you seize X, Y, and Z for us?" During my time as art crime program manager, the FBI and its other federal partners recovered hundreds of cultural items for the TPC.

Finally, I had to strong-arm Angelo a bit. When he called with his latest request, I told him, "We're not seizing anything else for you until you take this mosaic off our hands."

Luckily for me, Liz Rivas, our art crime team agent in Los Angeles, had recently recovered an autograph letter written by the late nineteenth-century Italian saint Giovanni Bosco, known in English as St. John Bosco. He founded schools for the poor, and many Catholic schools in the United States and other countries bear his name.

I said, "If you want the letter, it comes with the mosaic. It's a package deal."

All Angelo could say was, "Okay. Fine."

The Italian TPC frequently traveled to the United States, usually to New York or Washington, DC, to recover artifacts secured by the FBI or Homeland Security Investigations. One such planned trip to DC in late June was the perfect chance to return both the Bosco letter and the mosaic.

Rather than a low-profile handoff, Angelo and I aimed to maximize the press impact. We intended a two-step approach. First, we would transfer legal custody in Washington, DC, so the TPC could transport the pieces back to Rome. A few weeks later, I would join them there for an official repatriation ceremony at the US embassy.

With the plan in place, Liz packaged the letter and shipped it to me at headquarters for the upcoming return to the TPC. This was standard practice. Since I often visited embassies around Washington, DC, art crime team agents routinely sent me objects for return to foreign partners. I sometimes hand-delivered smaller returns to embassy staff without any ceremony, dealing with the necessary paperwork in their offices. Larger returns or more culturally and politically significant items were transferred in ceremonies before invited guests, with the participation of higher-level embassy officials.

A day or two before the TPC's planned visit in late June, I learned that they would be bringing a high-level executive to FBI headquarters to meet with Deputy Director Dave Bowdich. While the visit wasn't related to art crime, I suspected the return of the letter might come up, so I prepared a few talking points for the deputy director just in case. That turned out to be a smart move.

Though I had anticipated the request for talking points, the morning of June 25, the day of the planned meeting, brought an unexpected call to my desk. It was from the deputy director's personal assistant, with an urgent request—or perhaps more of a directive.

The seventh floor recognized the diplomatic value of returning the letter and wasn't about to miss a good photo opportunity. The request—or demand, depending on how you looked at it? I was to bring the letter up to the deputy director's office and leave it with them for the photo op.

A long silence followed on my end of the call as I processed what I had just heard.

"You want me to do what?" I finally blurted out.

Were they serious? The letter was 142 years old, carefully packaged in storage-safe materials. Until the Italians signed for it, the letter was still classified as evidence—extremely valuable evidence that I was now responsible for.

"Bring the letter up to me," the deputy's assistant repeated. "They want the deputy to hold it for a photo op with the Italians later."

My reply wouldn't have surprised anyone on the art crime team, but it definitely caught the deputy's assistant off guard.

"Um, yeah . . . no."

I wasn't trying to be insubordinate. I fully recognized that this was a directive from the second-highest official in the FBI, but it was also a grossly uninformed one. I couldn't just roll over and comply.

So I patiently explained the issues to the assistant, outlining the letter's age, its market value, and its status as valuable evidence. By the FBI's own policy, I couldn't simply drop it off upstairs and hope for the best. It just wasn't going to happen.

After a curt but professional back-and-forth, I finally agreed to pull the letter and personally bring it up to the seventh floor. However, under no circumstances would I leave it behind, nor would I allow anyone but me to handle it. The assistant wasn't happy but conceded—likely assuming the deputy would handle me himself.

I set aside everything else, carefully removed the letter from its packaging, and carried it to the director's conference room. Inside, Deputy Director Bowdich and his entire staff were waiting. Several were old colleagues from the field, now watching with quiet smiles, clearly amused that I hadn't just gone along with the request.

Bowdich took it in stride. Having spent years as a case agent in the field, he was well liked by those who had served with him. He was the boss, no doubt, but he was also an agent who knew the rules. My memory of the meeting is that he just chuckled and asked what needed to be done. At least he didn't seem like he was about to fire me.

The photo op went smoothly. The Italians arrived, had their meeting, and afterward, Deputy Director Bowdich graciously presented the Bosco letter to the Carabinieri on behalf of the FBI. I made them wear cotton gloves, carefully placed the letter in their hands just long enough for a few photos, then immediately took it back and repackaged it. Everyone was happy.

The next day, I officially transferred the letter and the mosaic to Lieutenant Colonel Luigi Bramati, the Carabinieri's attaché to the Italian embassy in Washington, DC. Bramati secured the pieces, crated them under a diplomatic seal, and sent them off to Rome to await our official repatriation ceremony at the US embassy.

On July 11, 2019, I stood at the podium in the US embassy in Rome, delivering remarks on the return of the Bosco letter and the mosaic while highlighting our ever-growing and reliable partnership with the TPC. Representing the FBI alongside me were Legal Attaché David Orozco and Assistant Legal Attaché Elizabeth Rosato. Several high-ranking

TPC officials attended, including General Claudio Vincelli and Brigadier General Fabrizio Parrulli, the overall commander of the TPC and a valued partner to the FBI's art crime team. US ambassador to Italy Lewis Eisenberg opened the ceremony with his remarks.

Standing at the podium with the mosaic displayed front and center on an easel, I said, "We're giving Italy back an ancient Roman mosaic that may not be Italian." It was an inside joke with Angelo.

I was traveling to Europe frequently, often with a stop in Italy. I spent so much time there during those years that I jokingly told the legat he should set aside an office for me. An embassy-funded apartment would have been nice too, but he always just smiled and walked away.

During another visit in November, I attended an exhibition in Rome dedicated entirely to artifacts the FBI and Customs and Border Protection had recovered for Italy. General Parrulli and my TPC colleagues gave me a red-carpet tour of the display, which was part of a traveling exhibition scheduled to appear across Italy.

It was a stark reminder of how differently our agencies—and our countries—viewed cultural property crime. It made me wonder, if the FBI put together an exhibit showcasing stolen or looted American cultural heritage that had been recovered and returned, would anyone go see it? Probably not many.

Late fall 2019 was the *before* moment in one of the world's most significant recent before-and-after turning points. Many of the TPC officers I worked with that November were either coming down with or recovering from flu-like symptoms. Across Europe, news reports highlighted the severity and early onset of that year's flu season.

I flew home the day before Thanksgiving feeling fine. Nine days later I became really sick with flu-like symptoms and was in bed for three days. Afterward I had a dry, hacking cough but no other symptoms. So I went back to work and immediately infected the whole office.

Through December and January, the world slowly realized that the flu-like illness spreading around had a novel cause—the COVID virus. I can't say with absolute certainty that I caught COVID in Italy in mid-November and brought it back to the United States, but I'd bet dollars to donuts that I did. I might not have been patient zero for the entire country, but I suspect I was patient zero at FBI headquarters.

The cough lingered for weeks, hitting me with fits every fifteen or twenty minutes. But since I was past the contagious stage, I ignored it and kept working.

In 2019 we also repatriated two Māori toki (stone adzes) to Te Papa Tongarewa ("The Precious Treasure Chest," the Museum of New Zealand in English), located in the country's capital, Wellington. But the international repatriation that required the most effort that year was one planned for February 2020 in Haiti's capital, Port-au-Prince. Since late 2018, I'd been working on the repatriation with an impressive young Haitian archaeologist, Joseph Sony Jean.

A postdoctoral researcher in archaeology and heritage studies at Leiden University in the Netherlands, Joseph was a contract consultant to Erol Josué, the general director of Haiti's National Bureau of Ethnology. Because he was not as comfortable in English as in his native French, Erol really communicated with me through Joseph. Thanks to Joseph's smarts and dedication, that never became a cause for confusion, and the three of us always stayed in sync.

Joseph and I began by identifying the 479 Taino artifacts that Don Miller had looted during his church and school-building missions in Haiti. Miller had also taken a smaller number of Taino artifacts from the Dominican Republic, which shares the island of Hispaniola with Haiti.

Once we determined exactly what the repatriation would include, Joseph and I turned our focus to planning the ceremony. By fall 2019, most of the details were in place. The repatriation was scheduled for February 14, 2020, at the National Bureau of Ethnology in Port-au-Prince. Haiti's prime minister, Jean-Michel Lapin—the country's second-highest official, appointed by the president and confirmed by the national legislature—was set to attend and speak. US ambassador Michele Sison was also slated to give remarks.

Diplomatic parity was always a concern in international repatriations. The receiving countries tended to treat the return of their cultural patrimony with great importance. The US State Department reciprocated by sending the US ambassador or their proxy, the US chargé d'affaires.

Too often, though, the only person the FBI sent to join them on the dais was GS-14 supervisory special agent and art crime program manager Timothy S. Carpenter.

The State Department strongly opposed this breach of diplomatic protocol. They insisted that the FBI should send the director, the bureau's only cabinet-level officer, appointed by the president and confirmed by the Senate, or at least the deputy director. I made the same argument inside the FBI, though I knew neither the director nor the deputy director would prioritize a cultural property repatriation anytime soon.

Instead, I pushed for a compromise, stressing the importance of diplomatic parity and urging the bureau to at least send the assistant director in charge of the Criminal Division.

Most of the time, I was still the only FBI representative at the podium. However, Kristi Koons Johnson, the TOC section chief, had attended and spoken at the Chinese repatriation in Indianapolis. Given the scale of the Haiti repatriation, the exceptional quality of the artifacts—experts said Miller's Taino collection rivaled or even surpassed that of the Metropolitan Museum of Art in New York City—and the participation of Prime Minister Lapin and Ambassador Sison, I hoped the FBI might send the assistant director.

I knew that securing an assistant director's presence would start with making a compelling case to my direct supervisor—the chief of the unit overseeing the art crime program. The unit chief would then have to brief the matter up the chain to the section chief, the assistant director, and ultimately the assistant director's bosses.

In fall 2019, both the unit chief and section chief roles were transitioning to new leadership. After Jay Bartholomew's retirement as La Cosa Nostra and major theft unit chief, headquarters had disbanded the unit as part of a broader reorganization, merging TOC East and TOC West into a global TOC section. The art crime program was then reassigned to the newly formed Africa/Asia/Middle East (AAME) unit inside TOC.

During the transition, a series of acting unit chiefs filled the role, but now the AAME unit was finally getting a permanent chief—a man I'll call "Tom." I had never met Tom, but I had heard troubling things about him. Those who had worked with him during his previous headquarters stint as a supervisory special agent despised him—there is no other way to put it. Agents and support professionals alike were stunned that he had been promoted to unit chief over a highly respected and well-liked female candidate.

The support staff who had previously worked under him were particularly upset, feeling that the hiring process had ignored his history with them. No one had a kind or even neutral word to say about him. They described him as toxic, abusive, and counterproductive as a leader.

In the only instance of its kind I ever witnessed at FBI headquarters or in the field, they formally protested his hiring, saying they couldn't work for him. When told the decision was final and asked to give him a second chance, both agents and support staff scrambled to transfer out of the unit to avoid working with him.

I was determined to keep an open mind and judge Tom based on my own interactions with him. However, given my colleagues' unanimously negative view, I put extra effort into preparing a solid briefing package for the Haiti repatriation ceremony. I wanted to make the case as clear and compelling as possible, anticipating any potential pushback.

One of the surprising things about Tom's appointment as unit chief was that he didn't follow the customary ninety-day reporting period. Instead of transitioning to headquarters full-time, he spent only a brief period there in the fall before returning to his previous post at a legal attaché office overseas for a couple of months—an unusual departure from standard procedure.

When I introduced myself during his short visit to headquarters, he responded loftily, "Oh, you run the art crime program. Senior management thinks that's 'the lost and found department'"—making air quotes with his fingers—"of the cultural property world."

Not all leaders in the FBI saw it that way, but I knew many did. Some had yet to grasp the sheer dollar volume and variety of art crime as well as its ties to money laundering, tax and sanctions evasion, and terrorism financing. Even fewer recognized that the Miller case was at the forefront of a global shift in attitudes toward the return of cultural patrimony.

Both law enforcement and political realities were making it clear that the FBI would need to do more, not less, on cultural property issues in the future. At that moment—on the eve of the COVID pandemic—the art crime program was outperforming other specialty programs on a per-agent basis. The team had grown to around twenty agents, managing approximately 240 active cases spanning the full spectrum of art crime, from theft and forgery to illicit antiquities trafficking and money laundering.

Tom didn't stop with his snide "lost and found" remark. He immediately added that we should offload the case to another agency and then started criticizing the Miller case budget, which continued to run around $300,000 a year for the maintenance of the warehouse, consultation and repatriation-related travel and other costs, and the consulting contracts for Holly and Leslie. The Miller case was expensive and lengthy, but it had been approved all the way up to the director's office. In my view, the importance of the case and the ongoing results justified the money and time we were spending on it.

This first conversation was a discouraging start to my interactions with Tom as my new direct supervisor. It gave me a clear sense of why no one in the unit who had worked with him before had anything positive to say. Worse, it planted the suspicion that he had come in with a deliberate objective—to shut down the Miller case and undermine the art crime program.

By contrast, the candidate the unit staff had hoped would become unit chief was a strong supporter of the art crime program and well respected by her colleagues. Many saw her as the right choice for the role, given her leadership style and experience.

Despite my misgivings, I kept things positive and professional, continuing to brief Tom in person and via email on the Haiti repatriation. He assured me he would escalate the request up the management chain and let me know if the assistant director would be unable to attend.

After Tom returned to his prior posting for those couple of months, I tried to follow up on the repatriation. He never responded. But it wasn't just me he was ignoring—he wasn't answering anyone's emails or approving routine budgetary and procedural requests.

The entire unit's work began to grind to a halt. Only the unit chief could sign off on the documentation required for FBI administrative and investigative processes, and without his approvals, nothing was moving forward.

Tom was still not back at headquarters in late February. The day before my flight to Haiti, the new TOC section chief, Mike Nordwall, stopped me in the hall, visibly frustrated.

He angrily demanded to know why I hadn't briefed the Haiti repatriation up the chain of command. The assistant director in charge of the Criminal Division had just found out that the State Department expected him to attend the ceremony that Friday—something he hadn't been told in advance. With another major commitment already on his calendar, he tapped Mike to go in his place. Understandably, Mike wasn't happy.

All I could do was explain to Mike that I had fully briefed Tom and that he had assured me he would escalate the matter. Fortunately, I had email exchanges and documentation to back me up.

Mike was a good leader and a thorough professional. He quickly recognized that the situation wasn't my fault. I handed him the white paper I had prepared on the repatriation back in the fall, along with a set of remarks I had drafted for the assistant director. With a few necessary adjustments, he would be ready to step in.

On Wednesday, February 12, 2020, Holly and I landed at the international airport in Port-au-Prince, Haiti, where we were met by embassy staff to help move us through customs and security. The artifacts had been shipped via a fine art shipping firm and were already at the embassy awaiting our arrival.

COVID-related travel procedures were still being rolled out in many places, and I was a little concerned that my occasional coughing spells might cause issues entering Haiti. Because of our official status, and because we had embassy expeditors to move us around the usual lines, I felt reasonably confident we'd get through without issue. As we were ushered quickly through customs, someone held a thermometer to my forehead. The reading was normal, and we were waved through without trouble.

I had been to Haiti twice before, but for Holly, the drive from the airport to the US embassy was her first exposure to the country's extreme poverty. The damage from the devastating 2010 earthquake was still visible, with many buildings and structures largely unrepaired.

Because of chronic civil and political unrest and the presence of violent gangs in the capital, the embassy had arranged an armed security detail of four local Haitian officers who were on contract with the US government. Over the course of the next two days they would transport us in hard cars—SUVs with bulletproof glass and armor plating—to the National Bureau of Ethnology in downtown Port-au-Prince, in the heart of the government district.

After a night's rest in one of only two lodging facilities deemed safe by the embassy, we woke early the next morning, Thursday, February 13, to prepare for our trip to the museum. Navigating the difficult Port-au-Prince traffic, we arrived at the museum around 9 a.m., where we met Erol Josué and Joseph Sony Jean to begin preparations.

Erol, a slightly built man of medium height, carried an air of mystery and flamboyance while still being warm and approachable. Joseph, with his burly frame and long dreadlocks, was just as kind, competent, and easygoing in person as he had been in our calls and emails over the past year.

They gave us a quick tour of the National Bureau of Ethnology, a small compound consisting of a single-story main building with a high ceiling and a smaller two-story structure behind it, both partially enclosed by a curving concrete wall and slatted wrought iron fencing. The buildings and courtyard all looked worse for wear.

Both the main building, which also served as Haiti's national museum of antiquities, and the smaller building lacked a room big enough for us to work in. To accommodate the repatriation process, the bureau staff had set up folding tables in the entrance courtyard, giving us space to inventory the artifacts before officially transferring them to Haiti.

For the next morning's ceremony, the podium would be placed in front of the main building's massive double doors, which were flanked by gold-painted plaster reliefs of two giant snakes winding up the facade between blue-painted concrete columns. Leading up to the entrance were six decorative tiled steps, but five workmen had stripped off the tiles and were busy repairing the concrete and cement underlayment beneath them.

Much of what we were returning to Haiti had been chiseled and carved from stone, with a total shipping weight of over two and a half tons. Everything was carefully packed and cushioned inside three wooden crates. Two of the crates were four-foot cubes, each weighing about a ton. The third was half their height and weighed half a ton.

When a truck arrived carrying all three crates, the unloading was done entirely by hand. Holly was worried that someone—or the artifacts—might be seriously injured in the process. Having spent a fair amount of time deployed in the third world, I was confident they would manage. But even I was surprised to see it all done without a forklift, block and tackle, moving dollies, or even a simple hand truck.

Erol grew visibly emotional as we unpacked the artifacts. He wept over some, while kissing and embracing others. But I could only guess at how powerful his reaction would be regarding the only human remains included in the repatriation.

Among the skulls that we found in Miller's bomb shelter, stuffed inside a black plastic garbage bag—the one with the raccoon nesting in it—was one that Miller had written on with a black Sharpie.

On the left temporal bone, just above the opening for the left ear, he had hand-printed in bold letters, from top to bottom,

HAITI
1980
VOODOO ALTAR

During our later review of the general evidence, we found color snapshots that Miller had taken of three skulls arranged on an altar inside a small Vodou temple somewhere in Haiti. (Vodou is the correct name for the Haitian spiritual tradition that blends West and Central African beliefs with Roman Catholicism.)

The photos showed the skulls arranged in a triangular pattern—one in front, two behind—on a table covered with a pink cloth. The front skull partially rested on a blue banner with a white cross, which draped down in front of the table. To the left of the skull stood a crucifix, and to the right, a lit candle.

Miller had looted many skulls from many locations, but the shape and features of the skull he had labeled with a Sharpie as coming from a "voodoo altar" perfectly matched the front skull in the photographs. The handwritten inscription on the skull and the evidence in the photos gave us high confidence that it belonged in the repatriation to Haiti.

However, at the time of the repatriation, I didn't fully appreciate the skull's deeper significance for Erol. Only recently did I learn that, in addition to being the general director of Haiti's National Bureau of Ethnology, he is also an ordained Vodou priest. In hindsight, it was another lesson in how cultural property carries layered meanings, holding immense value not only for its culture of origin but for all of human heritage.

We hadn't been working very long before the sounds of approaching protesters reached us. The tumult in the streets soon included gunshots and tear gas grenades. Holly stopped what she was doing only long enough to ask me what the thuds of the tear gas grenades were.

Protests like this were so common in Port-au-Prince that our hosts didn't seem too concerned at first. I had worked in worse situations, and Holly stayed focused, unfazed by the chaos outside. Determined to keep going, we pressed on with the inventory.

By midday, however, the protest had escalated into a full-blown riot, and our security detail insisted we take cover. We moved inside to a second-floor room in the small building at the rear of the compound, where a few employees were having lunch. It was February, so the heat wasn't unbearable, but without air conditioning, we were sweltering.

At one point we heard sustained volleys of gunshots. "I guess the police are using rubber bullets on the protesters now," I said.

"Oh no," the head of the security detail said. "It's live ammo."

That shocked me. But the way it was said—so matter-of-fact—left no room for doubt.

After about an hour, things calmed slightly, and I insisted we get back to work. The security detail wasn't happy, but they reluctantly allowed us to return to the courtyard. We worked through the afternoon and into the evening, stopping only when we saw that we could wrap up early in the morning before the ceremony.

Midmorning the next day, our inventory work completed, about two dozen of the finest artifacts were carefully arranged on display tables in the courtyard and gleaming in the bright sun. The decorative tiling was back on the front steps to the ethnology bureau, and the reliefs of the snakes and the rest of the facade had been freshly painted. A few attendants in traditional Taino costume added to the event's distinctive Haitian flair.

The complex reality of present-day Haiti meant that protesters were again in the streets surrounding the ethnology bureau compound. One way or another all the speakers at the ceremony acknowledged that reality, demonstrating how objects of cultural patrimony like the extraordinary Taino artifacts in the repatriation never lose their importance and relevance to the present and the future.

Ambassador Sison had just finished her remarks, following Erol Josué, Prime Minister Lapin, and Mike Nordwall, as I stepped to the podium to take questions from the press. Suddenly, protesters began hurling bricks and rocks into the courtyard from nearby rooftops.

The dignitaries' security details reacted instantly, rushing them into hard cars and speeding them away. Our security detail tried to do the same with Holly and me, urging us to leave immediately.

"No effing way," I told them, while Holly stood with her fists on her hips, vehemently shaking her head no. She wasn't going to stand by and watch the artifacts be destroyed either.

Time felt distorted, stretching out in those tense moments. I watched a brick sail past a priceless pot, missing it by mere inches, as if in slow motion. Then, without hesitation, Holly, Erol, Joseph, and I sprang into action, rushing to save the artifacts from destruction. For my thanks, I took a brick to the ear.

Only when the last piece was safely inside the building, and we had gathered our equipment and personal belongings, did we finally allow the security detail to put us in hard cars and get us out of there.

What stays with me most vividly is not the tumult in the streets but the effort to spruce up Haiti's National Bureau of Ethnology for the repatriation ceremony. Amid severe economic hardship and unrest, it was deeply moving to see Haiti spend resources—however meager—to welcome its cultural patrimony home with dignity, respect, and joy.

These moments of resolution in the Miller case underscored just how important the repatriations were. My unit chief—and whoever ensured he got the job—might not have seen their value, but Section Chief Mike Nordwall did. He was one of the senior FBI executives who understood that the Miller case was something the bureau could be proud of and that the art crime program had an increasingly vital role to play.

Of course, Mike still kids me about getting him stoned in Haiti.

Fourteen

Good Resting Places

In March 2020, following the Haiti repatriation, my nagging cough started to go downhill. In the middle of the month, it got so bad that I could barely breathe and had to go to the emergency room. The doctor who saw me agreed that it was impossible to be sure that I had contracted COVID in November. Four months later, pandemic protocols were very much in flux. COVID tests were in short supply and being used only when a fever was present.

The doctor also agreed that we should assume that I had contracted COVID in the fall and that the cough, my only persistent issue, was a lingering symptom. He put me on a nebulizer with albuterol, and fifteen minutes of that switched off the cough for good.

COVID complicated everything that year, of course. All repatriations to the tribes went on hold, and we had to keep consultations moving forward remotely.

In March 2020, Tom finally completed his transfer to headquarters and assumed his unit chief duties full-time. After ghosting emails for weeks, he shifted gears, subjecting the unit to micromanagement and power plays, such as calling unnecessary meetings and making people wait in a conference room for fifteen minutes before he arrived.

As the longest-serving supervisor in the unit, I tried to bridge the gap. I took Tom to lunch a couple of times and, as diplomatically as possible, attempted to explain what we needed from him as a leader.

At headquarters, a unit chief's role is to provide leadership, oversight, and support while ensuring the unit's work stays on track. A core part of the job is signing off on approvals and facilitating the day-to-day operations of their team. They need to know when to step in to resolve issues but also when to step back, allowing program managers to run their programs effectively while giving them the resources and backing they need.

Micromanagement is counterproductive in any organization, and the FBI is no exception. Tom's pattern of micromanaging combined with his openly condescending attitude quickly began to alienate both his peers and subordinates.

One of the other unit chiefs confided in me that several of them had taken Tom to a "welcome aboard" lunch. During the conversation, he casually remarked that he wanted to look out over his coffee cup at his subordinates working at their desks.

Major groan. But beyond the eye-roll factor, his mindset raised serious concerns. The other unit chiefs feared that Tom's leadership style would negatively impact the entire section.

Unfortunately, Tom resented my attempt to offer constructive suggestions, insisting that he was no "rubber stamp." He continued to take shots at the art crime program in general and the Miller case in particular. Some people don't understand the difference between leading and managing—or have the ability to do either effectively. It quickly became clear that my efforts to build and protect the art crime program, including advancing the Miller case, were going to put me in serious conflict with Tom.

Before Jay Bartholomew retired as unit chief, he had approved my initiative to write a policy guide for the art crime program, establishing it as a stand-alone specialty program. Every specialty program must develop standard requirements and protocols that conform with FBI policies and ensure continuity through a succession of program managers. The art crime program policy guide needed to cover everything from the selection of art crime team agents to training, the responsibilities of both team members and the program manager, and even a fair mechanism for removing an agent from the program if necessary.

Writing a policy guide takes time, and I followed the FBI's established procedures throughout the process. After Jay's retirement, I continued working on the art crime program policy guide under the various acting unit chiefs who replaced him, keeping everyone in the section chain of command informed of my progress.

When Tom took over, I fully briefed him on the policy guide during our first meetings in fall 2019. On his return to headquarters in spring 2020, the policy guide was in its final draft with the bureau's Internal Policy Office (IPO). Following FBI procedure, all fifty-six field offices, every FBI legat at US embassies worldwide, and all headquarters divisions had been given the opportunity to review the guide, offer suggestions, or challenge any of its provisions. The guide had received a few comments—all reflected in the final draft—but not a single objection. It was time for final approvals.

As my direct supervisor, Tom had to sign off on the final draft first. He sat on it for weeks, changing *which* to *that*, *big* to *large*, and so on, and challenging guidelines that had been vetted and approved by the bureau's lawyers and IPO. Tom's objections were nothing but petty power plays and micromanagement, and he was applying the same tactics throughout the unit. He was always looking for ways to put his direct reports on the defensive and cross-examine them rather than help them do their jobs.

I was one of many—not just program managers under Tom but also unit chiefs working alongside him—who urged Assistant Section Chief Joe Rothrock to rein him in. Joe made the effort and managed to curb Tom's behavior in some instances, but the impact was limited.

During Tom's first six months at headquarters, there were multiple attempts to intervene, but none gained much traction. As long as he remained unit chief, it was clear Tom was going to be a serious problem. Over a couple of beers, one of the section executives let his guard down and admitted what we all knew—Tom was a counterproductive control freak who made everyone's life miserable for no good reason.

But as I've said before, every senior executive at headquarters was there on a TDY assignment, focused on checking a box for their next promotion. To do that, they had to walk the halls without brushing against the walls and getting wet paint on their shoulders.

Tom was a bucket of paint.

The only real solution—removing him as unit chief—would have required escalating the issue to the deputy assistant director (DAD) and assistant director (AD). That, in turn, would have raised uncomfortable questions about why those at a lower level hadn't handled the problem and whether they were fit for promotion themselves. For ambitious executives, the safest move was to contain the damage Tom caused but leave him in place for someone else to deal with later.

Eventually, Tom released the policy guide, allowing it to move forward in the IPO approval process. A few weeks later, when I checked on its progress, I was stunned to learn that he had quietly pulled the draft back for yet another review—without informing anyone in the unit. IPO was just as perplexed as I was.

Tom said nothing about the draft for weeks, needlessly delaying the process. And then once again, he began picking it apart, plucking at minor details like loose threads on a sweater.

He repeatedly summoned me to meetings, challenging sections that were entirely standard and aligned with FBI policy. His objections were petty and arbitrary—like demanding, "Why do you want to canvass for new art crime team agents every year instead of every two years?"

Before I could fully answer, he would cut me off, firing off follow-up questions in rapid succession, clearly trying to throw me off balance. His objections were so pointless, and his manner so passive-aggressively hostile, that it became hard to ignore the possibility that he was deliberately provoking me, hoping I'd react in a way he could use against me.

One day in early summer, the art crime program's new MAPA, Colleen Childers, texted me that Tom had called her into his office for a one-on-one discussion of the policy guide. Colleen had come to work in the program at headquarters in April, only a couple of weeks after Tom himself had reported full-time. Before then she had been a support professional in the Louisville field office. She was following in the footsteps of her father, who'd been a senior support professional when I went to Louisville on my first field office assignment in 2004.

When I canvassed for a new MAPA, the job description and requirements emphasized an interest in art, strong interpersonal skills, a willingness to learn and work hard, and dedication to the mission of the program and the FBI. Colleen stood out in her interview, excelling in every category. She had a background in graphic arts, a genuine passion for the program's mission, and the drive to make an impact.

Once on the job, she exceeded even my high expectations. Within weeks, she was functioning as a highly capable executive officer, and her contributions to the art crime program grew by leaps and bounds. Hiring her was one of the best decisions of my FBI career.

The fact that Colleen discreetly texted me about the meeting spoke volumes. She might have been early in her career and new to headquarters, but she immediately recognized that Tom's calling her in to discuss the policy guide without informing me was inappropriate. She understood that it put her in an untenable position—one she should never have been placed in.

It didn't sit well with me—not one bit. I went straight to Tom's office, where poor Colleen was still sitting, clearly uncomfortable. Standing in the doorway, I let him have it: "What are you doing meeting with Colleen about the policy guide without including me? She's my direct report, and you're trying to use her like a pawn in some kind of sick chess game. The policy guide is my work. If you have a problem with it or with me, deal with me directly."

The whole TOC section heard me that day.

No surprise—things between Tom and me went even more steeply downhill after that. But thanks in part to Joe Rothrock's efforts to intercede on behalf of both me and the art crime program, Tom eventually released the policy guide back to IPO. From there, everyone up the chain of command signed off, and IPO officially published the guide on the bureau's internal website.

Tom's behavior had accomplished nothing positive. When all was said and done, he made trivial edits but no substantive changes to the policy guide, making it crystal clear that his actions were nothing but a power play. He had simply added months to the approval process, eating up time I would otherwise have been able to devote to advancing the Miller case and other art crime program work. But maybe that was accomplishment enough for Tom.

After the Haiti repatriation in February, the only other Miller case repatriation in 2020 was the return of 133 artifacts to Papua New Guinea in September. Like much of the world, Papua New Guinea was in COVID lockdown. Although we could have returned the artifacts to their embassy in Washington, DC, many were too large for that to be a practical option. We also knew that Papua New Guinea had limited financial resources for transporting the artifacts home, and we felt it was the FBI's responsibility to manage the transfer, as we had done in other international repatriations.

However, there was no FBI agent stationed at the US embassy in Port Moresby, the country's capital. The closest FBI agent, based in Canberra, Australia, was unable to enter Papua New Guinea due to the lockdown restrictions.

We had to get creative and find a cost-effective way to ship the collection to Papua New Guinea in the middle of a global pandemic. Although there was no FBI agent in the country, the Diplomatic Security Service—the law enforcement and security arm of the US Department of State—had a regional security officer stationed at the US embassy in Port Moresby.

My plan was to leverage that resource by transferring custody of the artifacts, which were still classified as evidence, to the regional security officer, who could then legally transfer them to Papua New Guinea. The regional security officer and the entire US embassy staff went above and beyond to make it happen.

Shipping everything to Port Moresby for the repatriation ceremony with US ambassador Erin McKee was expensive, but we had always known that some countries would not have the means to recover their looted artifacts on their own. Absorbing the cost to safeguard and return cultural heritage was not just a practical necessity, it was the right thing for the FBI to do.

The repatriation to Papua New Guinea was a resounding success, drawing significant media attention across the region and beyond.

As 2021 began, the core members of the art crime team, my family, and I were all worried about the strain that dealing with Tom was putting on me.

A program manager's success in the FBI depends heavily on the support of their direct supervisor. Under Jay Bartholomew, I had that support. He kept the chain of command informed with positive, accurate briefings on both the art crime program and the Miller case, ensuring they recognized the program's value.

With Tom, the situation was completely different. Instead of advocating for the program, he was undermining it—and me.

As senior executives cycled in and out on TDY assignments, fewer and fewer of them had any real understanding of the art crime program or the Miller case, both of which predated Tom and his negative attitude. Most program managers at headquarters were also on TDY assignments, using their time there to advance their careers. But I had no higher ambitions in the FBI. My plan was to retire in early 2024 after twenty years of service, then transition into a consulting career focused on art crime and cultural property issues.

Instead, I found myself facing a future of constant conflict with Tom, whose relentless efforts to undermine the art crime program and attack the Miller case made my job increasingly difficult. I worried that one day his behavior would push me too far, and if I lost my temper, it could put my FBI retirement and my family's financial security at risk.

Ironically, in early 2021, the team running the FBI Museum at headquarters approached me about a new social space they were helping to develop. A couple of years earlier, Starbucks had opened a storefront off the main courtyard, and its never-ending line made it clear that headquarters needed more seating. To address this, they planned to set up an adjoining area with tables and seating for casual conversations and informal meetings.

The FBI Museum staff thought art crime would make a great theme for the space, providing engaging visual material. They asked Colleen and me to help select fake artworks that the art crime team had seized over the years to be curated in the display. It was a cool project, and I was honored to take part.

Not everyone shared that enthusiasm. Some of the other specialty programs were put off that the space would feature the art crime program's work. And rather than being proud that it was part of his unit, Tom joined the ranks of its critics.

For the sake of my mental health and my family, and at this point the good of the art crime program and the Miller case, I had to leave headquarters and transfer to a job in the field. Again, FBI policy is that someone can be a GS-14 supervisory agent for seven years before promoting up to a GS-15 executive job or stepping back down to being a GS-13 case agent. Approaching the end of my fifth year at headquarters, I could either apply for supervisory desks at field offices or become a case agent again.

Risa and I wanted to move to the Atlanta area. But instead of applying for a supervisory position at the Atlanta field office, I decided it would be better to return as a case agent on the TOC squad. I had a great working relationship with Dominique Evans, the squad supervisor, and knew she could put my skills to good use. We had previously tried without success to get an art crime team agent in Atlanta, which left a significant geographical gap in the art crime program. I was still determined to fix that.

At the time, the TOC squad was down an agent, and Dominique was open to my idea. She agreed to post a specialty transfer for an art crime agent to fill the empty slot, which would allow me to step into the role.

The Atlanta SAC approved the plan, and Dominique and I thought it was a done deal. I was looking forward to returning to investigative work, which I enjoyed most, handling a range of TOC cases, along with the Miller case and other art crime investigations. It was also a great opportunity to establish Atlanta as an art crime team hub.

At the last minute, headquarters shut it down. Specialty transfers were commonplace for other specialty programs, but for some reason, there was reluctance to extend that to art crime. It was yet another reminder that, despite all the progress the art crime program had made, some decision-makers in the bureau still weren't convinced of its value. With Atlanta no longer an option, I had to start applying for supervisory jobs.

Nothing was working out in my favor until I heard about a supervisory desk opening at the Little Rock field office. Little Rock was forming a new squad to handle administrative, noninvestigative functions like community outreach, surveillance, and polygraphy. On making some inquiries, I learned that I would likely be a highly competitive candidate. After discussing it with my family, I applied for the job and was selected.

One of the main reasons I took the position was that it was noninvestigative. The slower pace was a drastic shift from the high-intensity work I had been doing since I started with the FBI, but after a year and a half of dealing with Tom, I needed the breather. Slowing down also gave me more time to focus on finishing the Miller case.

Leaving my role as head of the art crime team was not easy. I had spent years building and fighting for the team, and in many ways, it had become my baby, as they say. The team itself felt like family to me. But I also knew I had accomplished nearly everything I had set out to do and was leaving the art crime program in a far stronger position than when I took it over—which is all any leader can hope for.

The program had Colleen, who had already proven to be a huge asset as MAPA, the peanut butter that held the sandwich together. More important, it had a team of talented and dedicated agents who had worked tirelessly to build the program's reputation and ensure its continued success. I was confident that with strong leadership, a committed team, and a solid foundation, the art crime program would continue to thrive and move forward.

As the world began to emerge from its COVID cocoon, activity in the Miller case surged. In early March 2021, I traveled to Indianapolis to reassess the case inventory. About 55 percent of the items seized from Miller were still in storage. Three key factors had slowed repatriation efforts to Native American communities: the challenge of affiliating human remains noninvasively, the difficulty of linking artifacts to specific tribes (especially when multiple groups shared similar cultural and artistic traditions), and the bureaucratic hurdles of the NAGPRA process, all compounded by the disruptions of the pandemic.

The tribes were comfortable with NAGPRA and wanted us to use it as much as possible. Holly's prior experience with repatriations came from working with museum and university collections—the very institutions NAGPRA was designed to regulate. I initially expected we would operate mostly within its framework as well. But as we dug deeper, it became clear that many of the artifacts Miller had looted didn't fit into the four categories protected by NAGPRA.

National NAGPRA's program manager, Melanie O'Brien, played a key role in resolving this issue. When she objected to the inclusion of utilitarian pottery in an inventory, it forced a shift in approach. From then on, we sent Melanie a summary of these types of items and prepared them for return to the tribes simply as stolen property, bypassing the cumbersome NAGPRA process altogether.

There was an inevitable, mostly productive tension between Holly's academic perspective and my law enforcement approach. While we often found common ground, the differences became more pronounced when it came to ancestral remains rather than artifacts.

At the conclusion of the search and seizure at Miller's farm, I expected that noninvasive analysis would leave most of the remains unaffiliated. The available evidence supported that assumption. In only a handful of cases did the Millers' itineraries, travel journals, scrapbooks, photographs, or home movies provide clear indications of where specific remains had been unearthed.

We also knew from Miller himself, his extended family, and the original tipsters that he had moved remains multiple times across different buildings on his farm, often unpacking and repacking them in the process. That meant the container a set of remains was found in told us little about its original context. An old cardboard box, for example, didn't necessarily hold what Miller had originally placed inside it.

But Holly saw it differently. If a page from an old South Dakota newspaper was wedged into the corner of a box, she felt it strongly suggested that any human remains inside came from South Dakota. As an investigator, I found that reasoning too tenuous. Without additional evidence, I believed it was more appropriate to classify those remains as unaffiliated and include them in the larger group that the Pokagon Band of the Potawatomi had agreed to rebury on behalf of the broader Native American community.

Every decision I made required compromise from both Holly and me, grounded in mutual respect for each other's dedication and expertise. Despite our differing perspectives, we were always aligned on the fundamental guiding principle of the Miller case: ensuring that Native American ancestral remains were laid to rest in appropriate places within their tribal communities. Our approach was guided not just by material evidence but also by the voices and wishes of those communities, ensuring the remains were returned with the dignity they deserved.

Four years after our initial consultation in Albuquerque, that guiding principle had led us to a consensus with the tribes along the Arizona–New Mexico border regarding the repatriation of sixteen sets of human remains and numerous artifacts. The Gila River Indian Community (GRIC) and the Salt River Pima-Maricopa Indian Community (SRPMIC) agreed that the evidence supported the Hopi receiving all the human remains on behalf of the collective tribes. With that understanding in place, we finally scheduled a series of repatriations to the tribes in the second week of May.

On Thursday, May 6, 2021, just before Holly, Leslie, and I set out on the repatriation trip with Sean Dudley, a new art crime team agent from the Minneapolis field office, a delegation from the Pokagon Band of Potawatomi and the Oglala Sioux visited the warehouse in Indianapolis. The Oglala Sioux had made the trip from South Dakota not just on their own behalf, but also representing their fellow Siouan tribes from the middle and upper Missouri River valley. At the warehouse, Oglala elders conducted a ceremony to reverently prepare both ancestral remains and artifacts for their eventual journey to South Dakota in 2022.

In consultation with us, the Pokagon Band of Potawatomi and the Oglala Sioux agreed that we should send seventy-six sets of human remains to the University of Indianapolis's Human Identification Center. This would serve as a final effort to determine whether noninvasive analysis could provide any insight into their place of origin.

After the consultation, Holly, Leslie, Sean, and I set out for the Southwest in a two-vehicle convoy. We loaded around 220 artifacts, including large pottery pieces and about a dozen Navajo items recovered in a separate case, into a rented twenty-six-foot-long box truck. The ancestral remains were transported in a rented Chevrolet Suburban.

Taking turns driving both vehicles, we covered the 1,300-mile journey from Indianapolis to Acoma Pueblo, New Mexico, in two and a half days. At night, we secured the vehicles inside FBI field offices along the route to ensure their safety.

First thing on the morning of Monday, May 10, 2021, we met with art crime team agent Susan Garst at the FBI field office in Albuquerque. Since this was her region, Susan would accompany us to Acoma Pueblo and assist with the transfer.

Later that morning, we arrived at Acoma Pueblo, which was still under COVID restrictions. By prior arrangement, members of the pueblo met us at the border, where we transferred 111 artifacts from our truck to theirs.

Our next stop was one hundred miles west on I-40 in Gallup, New Mexico, where we returned the Navajo Nation's artifacts. With that transfer complete, we split up. Leslie continued with the truck to Flagstaff, Arizona, while the rest of us left the highway to deliver the ancestral remains to the Hopi.

Late the next morning, Holly, Sean, and I joined a small caravan of vehicles, following a rocky, rutted road to the top of a mesa sacred to the Hopi. The site was deep in the remote stretches of Sitgreaves National Forest in east-central Arizona, accessible to the Hopi through a special arrangement with the US Forest Service. Under a brilliant blue sky, the 360-degree views from the mesa made it feel as though we could see forever. The Hopi explained that they had chosen this location so the ancestors could rest with a clear view of a sacred mountain across the valley.

The reburial ceremony was solemn and deeply moving, with smudging and prayers offered in tribute to those being laid to rest. We were honored to take part, helping to carry the ancestral remains from the SUV and place them in a shared grave. Then one of the Hopi medicine men carefully adjusted the positions of the remains before the grave was filled in.

When the ceremony concluded, we gathered with our Hopi hosts for group photos—treasured reminders of that morning and the significance of what had been done.

By midday, we met up with Leslie in Flagstaff at Northern Arizona University. Professor of anthropology Kelley Hays-Gilpin, who had played a key role in affiliating the Southwestern Native American artifacts, was also the curator of NAU's Museum of Northern Arizona. At the request of the tribes, she had agreed to temporarily house seventy-three artifacts for the Hopi and fifteen artifacts for the Hopi and Zuni jointly. The museum would safeguard the artifacts until the tribes were ready to take custody and care for them themselves.

Whenever tribes requested, we helped arrange temporary housing for artifacts with nearby universities and museums. Unlike past collections, which were taken without tribal consent, these agreements put control in the hands of the tribes. They decided how researchers could study the artifacts, which items could be displayed, and how they should be handled. The artifacts remained theirs, held in safekeeping until they were ready to care for them on their own.

Responsible research on the artifacts had the potential to benefit the tribes by helping recover pieces of knowledge lost because of the upheaval of European conquest and settlement. This loss was something I came to understand more deeply when the art crime team recovered stolen sacred objects from an unscrupulous dealer in the northeastern United States and the affected tribe was reluctant to receive them. Nearly two years into repatriation discussions, a tribal elder finally explained their hesitation.

Over generations, the tribe had suffered repeated disruptions to its cultural traditions. Children had been taken from their families and sent to boarding schools where they were forbidden to speak their language or practice their faith. Because of these experiences, the elders feared that the tribe no longer had full knowledge of the ceremonies required to properly receive and care for objects imbued with spiritual power—power that, if mishandled, could bring great harm as well as good.

Imagine a history where the government had worked so hard to erase your culture that the return of your own sacred objects felt like a risk rather than a blessing. In the end, the tribal elders chose to receive the objects with hope and humility, trusting that the right path would reveal itself when the time came. Later, it was reassuring to hear that they felt at peace with their decision and grateful for the outcome.

After transferring the Hopi and Zuni artifacts to Professor Hays-Gilpin at the Museum of Northern Arizona, we had one final repatriation to complete at the GRIC reservation just south of Phoenix. With plenty of time before our scheduled meeting with elders from both the GRIC and SRPMIC, Holly, Leslie, and Sean suggested stopping for a late lunch in Sedona. They had all been there before and raved about its beauty and the great food we could find.

I had never been to Sedona myself, and after days of highway fast food, a good meal in a scenic town sounded great. The question wasn't whether we should stop for lunch—that was a given. We were all ready for a proper meal. The real question was how to get there with our giant box truck.

We had two options: take the scenic but winding thirty-mile route down Arizona's two-lane Highway 89A or the longer but easier sixty-mile drive south on I-17, then back north on the straighter, less scenic Highway 179. Holly and Sean jumped into the SUV and took 89A without hesitation. I suggested to Leslie that we take the longer, safer route in the truck, but she waved it off, saying 89A wouldn't be a big deal.

I was busy working on the phone to coordinate our next repatriations, and since Leslie was driving, I let it go. But in a large box truck, those tight switchbacks on 89A turned out to be no joke. It was white-knuckle driving the whole way. We nearly made it through without incident—until one particularly sharp curve. Trying to navigate the turn, Leslie clipped the edge of a guardrail, catching it under the truck's frame.

We ripped about twenty feet of guardrail off its support posts. I thought for sure we'd ripped a gash in the truck's side panel, possibly damaging the remaining artifacts. But the truck was unmarked, the artifacts were okay, and the Sedona police were not very concerned when we reported what we'd done.

What could have been a disaster ended up as nothing more than a good story to tell Holly and Sean over lunch. And they were right—Sedona was just as beautiful as they had promised, and the meal was well worth the detour.

The 116-mile drive from Sedona to Phoenix, mostly along I-17 and I-10, was smooth and uneventful. When we arrived, the GRIC and SRPMIC welcomed us warmly. They expressed their joy in receiving twenty artifacts jointly, and, as always in these moments, we did our best to humbly share our gratitude for being part of the process. It was a fitting and deeply satisfying conclusion to our journey through the Southwest.

We dropped off our rented vehicles at the Phoenix airport before heading to our separate flights. I had booked the earliest possible direct flight to Indianapolis, where I was met by Randy Deaton, who was soon to replace me as the art crime program manager. From there, Randy and I loaded about fifty international artifacts into a vehicle and began the 650-mile drive to Washington, DC. Over the next nineteen months, Randy, Colleen Childers, and other art crime team agents returned these artifacts to various foreign governments through their embassies in Washington.

Meanwhile, Sean Dudley was making his own journey. After driving from Phoenix to Indianapolis, he was heading home to Minneapolis, transporting a female cranium for repatriation to the Three Affiliated Tribes in North Dakota.

Taken together, our efforts in May resulted in another 15 percent of the seized Miller material either back with or on its way to its rightful owners. With these major repatriations complete, I was finally ready to leave headquarters and step into a new role.

On July 13, 2021, I started my new post in Little Rock. The transition to leading a noninvestigative squad was a shock to the system after the twelve-to-fourteen-hour days at headquarters. I regretted not being able to oversee the art crime program as long as I had hoped, but the change was exactly what I needed.

Not long after, Little Rock SAC Jim Dawson asked me to take over the public corruption, white-collar crime, and civil rights violations squad, and later to serve as acting ASAC during the field office's five-year inspection by headquarters. Even so, my posting in Little Rock gave me the reset I needed, recharging my batteries for the final push to complete the repatriation process and close the Miller case.

I've mentioned how tribes in the middle and upper Missouri River valley disagreed on the status of Catlinite pipes. Among those who considered all Catlinite pipes to be burial goods requiring special care were the Three Affiliated Tribes. On December 7, 2021, in Rapid City, South Dakota, Sean Dudley transferred thirteen of these pipes to Mary Baker, who had succeeded Pete Coffey-One Feather as the tribe's THPO.

However, it wasn't until May 17, 2022, that Sean was able to repatriate the female cranium to Mary Baker for reburial by the Three Affiliated Tribes. The delay was due to COVID, which had affected one of the tribal members involved in the ceremony.

With Tom still unit chief for part of 2022, maintaining the Miller case's $300,000 annual budget for the warehouse and consulting contracts became impossible. To be fair, even with a more supportive unit chief, I knew the budget would be cut sooner rather than later. At best, we might have bought another year or two, but the reality was unavoidable.

I often reminded Holly that we had to keep up the momentum on repatriations because, in the FBI's eyes, the Miller case was never a priority. We had been fortunate to receive as much support as we had, but we had to be ready for the funding to disappear at any moment. Now, with over 60 percent of the seized material repatriated and the case winding down, that moment had arrived.

With the Miller case budget reduced for fiscal year 2023, we had to complete repatriations or secure temporary custodial arrangements for the remaining seized material before the warehouse lease expired on April 30, 2023. The cuts also meant we couldn't renew Holly's consulting contract when the new fiscal year began on October 1, 2022.

But that didn't stop her. As committed at the end as she had been at the beginning, Holly chose to continue her work as a volunteer and see the case through.

From July 18 to 29, 2022, nine art crime team agents rotated through the warehouse to package and transport a small amount of unrepatriated foreign material to headquarters and plan the next steps for the remaining Native American artifacts. As part of this effort, art crime team agent Brian Brusokas traveled from Chicago to Indianapolis to return general evidence—such as travel journals, photographs, and home movies—to Don Miller's widow, Sandra. He also returned several Shipibo pots from Peru after confirming that Peruvian patrimony laws allowed for the legal trade of Shipibo pottery from the Amazon River basin. Along with it, he returned eight objects identified as modern reproductions rather than authentic artifacts. This return of materials to Sandra Miller fulfilled the terms of the relinquishment agreement the Millers had signed in February 2015.

As efforts to complete the Miller case shifted into high gear, Colleen Childers found herself increasingly responsible for helping to finalize an investigation that had begun long before she even joined the FBI. On November 3, 2022, she was in Indianapolis to oversee the packaging and shipping of 138 Caddoan and Mississippian culture artifacts to me in Little Rock.

The tribes of the Caddo Confederacy once occupied lands stretching from what is now northeast Texas to southwest Arkansas. The present-day Caddo Nation of Oklahoma, like many other tribes—including the Cherokee, Chickasaw, Choctaw, and Seminole—traces its heritage to the Mississippian culture, which thrived between 800 and 1600 CE. The Mississippian culture tribes of the lower Mississippi River valley and southeastern United States built extensive mound complexes surrounded by dense settlements and satellite villages. Through our investigation, we had linked Miller to the looting of these sites, often carried out by groups of pothunters in southern Indiana, Arkansas, and other regions.

As one of the 574 federally recognized tribes, the Caddo Nation had received emails about the Miller case and the website with photos of seized artifacts back in 2014. Over the years, I had also given numerous presentations about the case at conferences attended by the Native American community. While the Caddo had not actively engaged with the case or requested access to the website, we understood that many tribes faced complex priorities and challenges when it came to repatriation efforts.

Meanwhile, we had been steadily working through the seized collection, prioritizing artifacts affiliated with tribes that had reached out to us.

After Colleen shipped the Caddoan and Mississippian culture material to me in Little Rock, I called Jonathan Rohrer, the Caddo Nation's tribal historic preservation officer, to discuss the next steps for the Caddoan artifacts.

Once we were able to connect, Jonathan explained that the Caddo were not yet in a position, financially or otherwise, to receive the Caddoan artifacts. He added that they planned to seek a grant from National NAGPRA to help fund the care of the artifacts during an extended transition period.

"It's too late for that now, Jonathan, at least as far as the FBI is concerned," I had to tell him. "The grant application process will take at least a year. Assuming your application is successful, it will likely be several months or more before any funds reach the Caddo Nation. We've got to find a solution for the tribe's material before I retire from the FBI, or those artifacts could be in limbo for another decade. If we can find a good custodian for the artifacts, then you will have time to pursue a National NAGPRA grant and take charge of the artifacts on the tribe's own schedule."

Jonathan agreed with that and said, "The Arkansas Archeological Survey at the University of Arkansas in Fayetteville is probably our best bet." He called his contacts there and soon put me in touch with Sarah Shepard, the survey's registrar and NAGPRA coordinator. Sarah and her colleagues were very receptive to caring for the Caddoan material on behalf of the Caddo Nation. At my request, they also generously agreed to take charge of the Mississippian culture material and to consult with the appropriate tribes about its ultimate disposition.

Meanwhile, on November 10, 2022, in Indianapolis, Brian Brusokas and Holly repatriated sixty-eight unaffiliated sets of Native American ancestral remains to the Pokagon Band of the Potawatomi and 162 sets to the Oglala Sioux of South Dakota. Among the remains transferred to the Oglala Sioux were the seventy-six sets examined by the University of Indianapolis's Human Identification Center in the summer of 2021. The results of the analysis were, at best, inconclusive. However, given the Oglala Sioux's willingness to receive them, Holly and I agreed that they should take custody. The Potawatomi had no objections, and no other tribe submitted a competing claim when our intent to repatriate the remains to the Oglala Sioux was published in the Federal Register.

On December 14, 2022, the FBI repatriated twenty-one Taino artifacts to the Dominican Republic in a ceremony held in Santo Domingo, the nation's capital. Representing the government of the Dominican Republic was Carlos Andújar, general director of museums for the Ministry of Culture. The American contingent included Chargé d'Affaires Robert W. Thomas from the US embassy and Raymond P. Duda, the assistant director in charge of the FBI's International Operations Division. As the Miller case was closing, the FBI was at least marking its importance by sending an assistant director to this repatriation.

In early 2023, a final group of Native American ancestral remains stayed in the Indianapolis warehouse. This group, representing at least twenty-four individuals, had been linked to the Arizona–New Mexico border region through soil matrix analysis.

On March 13, 2023, these remains, along with twenty-nine artifacts, were transferred to Susan Garst at the FBI's satellite office in Santa Fe. There, they would remain pending an agreement for repatriation to one or more tribes in Arizona or New Mexico.

On October 5, 2023, I delivered 138 Caddoan and Mississippian culture artifacts to the Arkansas Archeological Survey in Fayetteville. As survey archaeologists and their graduate student assistants unpacked the collection, a small piece from the lip of one pot came loose along a glue line—a common occurrence when old adhesive dries out on pottery that has been reassembled from fragments. It was no big deal, and the survey was happy to handle the repair.

What was remarkable, however, was that this minor, easily repairable break was the only instance of damage in the entire Miller case, despite the seizure and repatriation of nearly seven thousand pieces. It was a record of care and handling that any museum in the world would be proud of.

As I prepared to retire from the FBI on February 9, 2024, the art crime team had successfully repatriated 92 percent of the artifacts seized from Don Miller's collection. In fiscal years 2022 and 2023 alone, we had repatriated more than 30 percent of the seized material while simultaneously shutting down the warehouse. Once Susan Garst is able to complete the repatriation of the material now secured at the FBI's Santa Fe office, that total will rise to over 96 percent.

Eighteen objects from Miller's collection remain unidentified or unclaimed. The FBI will likely hold these items indefinitely, either because geopolitical conditions make repatriation impossible or because no rightful claimant has come forward. This was an eventuality we always knew was possible, and, truthfully, I'm a bit surprised that the number is so low.

Think about it this way. We seized nearly seven thousand individual artifacts and human remains, most with little to no provenience or provenance documentation. Miller's records were sparse, to say the least, leaving us to piece together their origins through painstaking analysis of his photographs and videos—some dating back decades.

Expert analysis was crucial, but it was no easy task given the vast scope of the collection. Despite the countless challenges we faced over ten long years, we managed to identify and culturally affiliate all but eighteen items. Considering where we started, that's a number I can live with.

Without the right people in the right place at the right time, the Miller case would never have gotten off the ground in November 2013. Over the next decade, it was those same kinds of people—inside and outside the FBI, within the Native American tribal community, and across foreign law enforcement and cultural heritage departments—who kept the case moving forward despite countless challenges.

The FBI has plenty of what law enforcement calls "dog cases"— cases that either follow investigators throughout their careers or linger for decades. Long-term cases in the FBI can stretch ten, twenty, even thirty years or more, passing from one case agent to the next as investigators promote, transfer, or retire.

Most of these cases eventually fade into obscurity, even if they technically remain open. A lack of interest and dedication, institutional fatigue, and bureaucratic obstacles such as petty animosities and personal agendas often prevent them from ever reaching a meaningful resolution.

From experience, I can attest that taking over a long-running investigation is no easy task. It takes time and dedication to sort through what may be thousands of documents, build relationships with those involved, and get up to speed on what has been done, where the gaps are, and what might move the case forward. All too often, "dog cases" fade away when the assigned agent has no personal investment in seeing them through.

The Miller case was an exception to the rule. I was privileged to be involved from start to finish in some capacity, and I will always be grateful to the many dedicated people who committed themselves to doing the right thing. Without their effort and determination, there would have been little to no chance of securing good resting places for the ancestral remains and artifacts that Don Miller looted.

Throughout this book, I have tried to highlight and honor these individuals. For a fuller list, I encourage readers to see the Acknowledgments section. However, because space in any book is limited, even that section will likely fall short of recognizing everyone who made this case possible and, ultimately, a success.

That said, I must single out Holly Cusack-McVeigh, Jake Archer, Leslie Lahr, Drew Northern, and Colleen Childers for their extraordinary efforts. I hope I have done justice to them and to all who played a role in this case. They embody a lesson I first learned as a young US Air Force recruit in explosive ordnance disposal school: improvise, adapt, and overcome. Again and again, no matter the setbacks or opposition, that is exactly what they did.

Together, we worked to find meaningful ways to engage with the victims of Don Miller's crimes, both in the United States and abroad, with a special focus on the Native American tribal community. First, last, and always, we sought to listen carefully to tribal members and collaborate with them as true partners.

In doing so, I hope we have helped the FBI take a step forward in its historically troubled relationship with Native American communities and provided a model for strengthening that relationship in the future. I also hope, and humbly believe, that we have set a new standard for the repatriation of cultural patrimony worldwide.

That legacy inspires me as I continue to work on cultural heritage and related art crime issues as a private consultant. May it also inspire others to join in treating every culture's traditions and patrimony with the respect and care they deserve.

Acknowledgments

Resolving a complex case and publishing a book both require the wholehearted work of many people.

First and foremost, I want to thank my colleagues on the FBI Art Crime Team. To Jake Archer, Elizabeth Rivas, Dave Bass, Ronnie Walker, Susan Garst, Colleen Childers, Randy Deaton, Chris (Sean) Dudley, Brian Brusokas, Dave White, Bonnie Magness-Gardiner, Tim DeMann, and the rest of the team, your expertise, dedication, and unwavering commitment to this mission embody the very best of public service. What we accomplished together in the Miller case was not just investigative work. It was the painstaking restoration of stolen history.

To the agents, analysts, and professional staff in the Indianapolis Field Office and across the FBI, especially Leslie Lahr, Drew Northern, Jeff Croake, Greg Massa, Kevin Lyons, Bob Jones, Jay Bartholomew, Ken Dibella, Kristi Johnson, Eric Ives, Bob Wittman, Mike Nordwall, Joe Rothrock, Danny Barkley, Diana Ryll, Noel Gil, Joe Carpenter, Jim Dawson, Scott Reinhardt, Jason Vangoor, and countless others, your hard work, skill, and determination made this unprecedented recovery possible.

I am especially indebted to Dr. Holly Cusack-McVeigh. Holly's contributions to the Miller case went far beyond what anyone could have asked or expected, offering tireless hours, boundless compassion, and

ACKNOWLEDGMENTS

exceptional expertise, often without recognition or credit. Though we came from the very different professional worlds of law enforcement and academia, Holly navigated those differences with grace, professionalism, and a shared sense of mission. Her knowledge, integrity, and devotion to the communities most affected by Don Miller's crimes elevated every aspect of the investigation. Without her, the case would have been infinitely more difficult. She will always have my deepest respect and my enduring thanks.

To the tribal communities whose patience and guidance made this work possible, I owe you a debt I can never fully repay. Yours are the voices too long unheard, the communities most victimized by Miller and those like him who have operated under the self-serving fiction that it was their manifest destiny to plunder Indigenous cultures as they pleased. That you allowed me, an outsider, to stand beside you in the effort to return ancestral remains and belongings home was a profound act of trust. Your wisdom and resilience shaped every step of the investigation. I hope this book helps to give voice to the truths you have carried for generations.

To the many museum professionals, archaeologists, and cultural heritage experts who gave their time and knowledge, including Larry Zimmerman, Charli Champion-Shaw, Allison Davis, Catherine Foster and the rest of the team at the State Department's Cultural Heritage Center, Kelley Hays-Gilpin, Mary Cook, Patty Gerstenblith, and so many more, your expertise and wisdom were essential to our success.

To my family, friends, and mentors—Risa, Ailyn, Marleah, and Macauley Carpenter, Roger and Pamela Sawyer, Terry and Carol Carpenter, Rob Carpenter, Sage Carpenter, Harriet Russo, Peter, Ryan and Nolan Russo, Hertsel, Ruth, Orit, Elinor and Adi Corech, William Barkley, Jimmy and Rachelle Gleaton—thank you for your constant patience, love, and encouragement throughout this long journey. You have kept me grounded, even when the work pulled me far away.

To Mark Mitten and Lindsay Newton, who helped me find the start of this long road, your wisdom and insight were crucial in getting this project off the ground. Thank you.

I am also deeply grateful to my literary agent, Leslie Meredith of Dystel, Goderich & Bourret, LLC, whose steady guidance and belief in

ACKNOWLEDGMENTS

this project made publication possible, and to Hilary Hinzmann, whose patient counsel, editorial insight, and dedication to helping me shape and tell this story cannot be repaid. Their partnership made this book stronger in every way.

To Austin Ross, my editor at Harper Horizon, thank you for seeing the importance of the Miller case and its potential as a book subject, your sage advice and stewardship throughout the publishing process, and all of your and your colleagues' efforts on the book's behalf.

And to the many others who contributed to the Miller case (far more than I could ever list here, including foreign law enforcement and cultural heritage officials), please know this. Even if your name is not printed on these pages, your contributions live in these pages. Thank you.

To readers, whether you come from law enforcement, academia, the museum world, or simply share a passion for history, thank you for taking the time to engage with this story. The fight to protect cultural heritage is not over. Awareness is only the beginning.

About the Author

TIM CARPENTER is formerly the FBI's Art Crime Team Senior Special Advisor. Carpenter also led the Art Crime Team for nearly six years. He has been featured in *Vanity Fair* and the *Washington Post Magazine*, and on NPR, CBS, and more. He has also served as a speaker, lecturer, and panelist at a variety of prestigious venues, including Congress, the Smithsonian, and George Washington University Law School. For his efforts in the repatriation process of ancestral remains and historic objects, Carpenter received the Public Service Award from the Society for American Archeology. He is also the recipient of the FBI Director's Award—the highest honor in the FBI.